Critical Humanism and

Critical Humanism and the Politics of Difference

JEFF NOONAN

McGill-Queen's University Press
Montreal & Kingston · London · Ithaca

© McGill-Queen's University Press 2003
ISBN 0-7735-2578-5 (cloth)
ISBN 0-7735-2579-3 (paper)

Legal deposit third quarter 2003
Bibliothèque nationale du Québec

Printed in Canada on acid-free paper.

This book has been published with the help of a grant from the Humanities and Social Sciences Federation of Canada, using funds provided by the Social Sciences and Humanities Research Council of Canada.

McGill-Queen's University Press acknowledges the support of the Canada Council for the Arts for our publishing program. We also acknowledge the financial support of the Government of Canada through the Book Publishing Industry Development Program (BPIDP) for our publishing activities.

National Library of Canada Cataloguing in Publication

Noonan, Jeff
    Critical humanism and the politics of difference / Jeff Noonan

Includes bibliographical references and index.
ISBN 0-7735-2578-5 (bnd)
ISBN 0-7735-2579-3 (pbk)

    1. Difference (Philosophy)—Political aspects.
2. Humanism.   I. Title.

B809.9.N65 2003   191   C2003-901479-7

Typeset in 10/12 Palatino by True to Type

*To the memory of my father
Who should have lived to see this day*

Contents

Acknowledgments ix

Introduction: The Fear of Difference 3

PART ONE   THE POSTMODERN CRITIQUE

1 The Emergence of Difference 11
2 The Dynamics of Difference 24
3 The Twilight of Subjecthood 41
4 Postmodern Freedom 57

PART TWO   THE CONTRADICTIONS OF THE POSTMODERN POLITICS OF DIFFERENCE

5 Realizing Postmodern Politics 81
6 Is Radical Pluralism a Coherent Idea? 92
7 The Universal Voice of the Other 106
8 The Return of the Repressed 125

Conclusion 159

Notes 163

Bibliography 177

Index 185

Acknowledgments

The work of conceiving of a book and bringing it to completion is labyrinthine and brings one into contact with so many people, depends upon so many insights gleaned from so many sources, and incurs so many debts, intellectual and otherwise, that it really is a collective work. The author who signs his or her name remains responsible for the claims asserted, of course, but is the final link in a chain of inquiry and argument without which no project could come to fruition.

In my case this chain is long, and the debts that I have incurred demand at least that I acknowledge them. The text that you have before you began life as my doctoral dissertation, and for his expert guidance during that process, as well as his unflagging support as my supervisor and now as my philosophical colleague and friend, I must thank John McMurtry of the University of Guelph. Marina Vitkin and Evan Simpson, both of McMaster University at the time this project was first coming to light, also merit recognition. After graduating with my PHD I set the dissertation aside for a time to pursue other ideas and came back to this text only two years ago. I fundamentally revised the work but kept intact its central claim, that contrary to prevailing orthodoxy, an essentialist understanding of human being remains a necessity for coherent critical political philosophy.

For taking a keen interest and for all his help shepherding this book through the various committees and stages of the review process, I am indebted to Philip Cercone at McGill-Queen's University Press. For their very illuminating criticisms, which have made this a better book, I must also recognize the reviewers who freely gave of their time to referee the work. Joan McGilvray, also of McGill-Queen's, deserves thanks for her assistance in helping me reformat and edit the book.

Of course, intellectual endeavours require other forms of support. My road to philosophy was inspired by my uncle and life-long friend, John Brown. My parents, even when they did not quite understand why I wanted to study philosophy, never doubted my choices and remained by my side. Whatever I have achieved I owe to that support. The many evenings spent discussing politics and philosophy as a young student in Toronto with Joe Kispal Kovacs, Debbie Simmons, and David McNally greatly shaped my subsequent thinking. The encouragement given me and the confidence shown in me by my colleagues at the University of Windsor were also a great help.

Although the finished book might be a collective effort, the actual writing of it was an often private and sometimes selfish act that required both tolerance and emotional support from the people with whom I share my life. In that regard I have two debts to acknowledge: first to Simone and now to Josie, whose strength and *joie de vivre* in the face of difficulty and love while I was reworking this project were invaluable. Finally my friend Jim, who knows what it is to struggle, must be acknowledged.

Critical Humanism and the Politics of Difference

He therefore took man as a creature of indeterminate nature and, assigning him a place in the middle of the world, addressed him thus: "Neither a fixed abode nor a form that is thine alone nor any function peculiar to thyself have we given thee, Adam, to the end that according to thy longing and according to thy judgement thou mayest have and possess what abode, what form, and what functions thou thyself shalt desire. The nature of all other beings is limited and constrained within the bounds of laws prescribed by Us. Thus, constrained by no limits, in accordance with thine own free will, in whose hand We have placed thee, shalt ordain for thyself the limits of thy nature.
  Giovanni Pico della Mirandola, *Oration of the Dignity of Man*

Introduction:
The Fear of Difference

In a recent column, noted Toronto playwright Sky Gilbert laments the failure of political correctness to check the spread of racist, sexist, and homophobic ideas. In fact, Gilbert contends that the superficial focus of political correctness on the diction of public utterance has made matters worse. Although public discourse may be free of sexist, racist, and homophobic terms, the social practices that structure sexism, racism, and homophobia have been left untouched. The fact that people are more hesitant to utter racial epithets in public, for example, encourages the belief that racism has been defeated, when in fact it has merely been driven out of the speech of respectable society. The deep structures of oppressive practices remain. The deepest structure of oppression, Gilbert contends, is a pervasive "resentment against anyone who dares step out and challenge the norm." This resentment is "a signal of our ingrained, overpowering fear of difference."[1]

Gilbert's argument eloquently states the fundamental principle of the radical postmodern politics of difference that this book will examine. That principle maintains that the system of thinking dominant in the Western world, a system that lies at the root of both the existing structures of political society and traditional socialist criticism of it, is rooted in a concept of human nature and freedom built upon the exclusion of marginalised voices (women, Africans, Asians, aboriginals, gays and lesbians). Western philosophy and its most cherished concept – human freedom – are rooted in the conceit that they have tapped into the very core of human being. According to postmodern criticism, that core, the essence or nature of human being, is the product of an abiding fear of difference. Human nature, therefore, is not natural, but the product of systematic exclusions of other traditions, cultures, beliefs, and practices. The belief in an essence of humanity is, according to postmodern radicalism, merely a projection of the ideal nature of the wielders of power, dependent for its coherence upon the subordination of "the Other," the subordination of all people and cultures who, for whatever reason, fail to conform to the norm.

To be sure weighty evidence could be marshalled in support of this position. Aristotle, the ancient world's greatest metaphysician, legitimated slavery by appeal to his metaphysical doctrines, arguing that the rule of free man over slave follows from the rule of the rational over the irrational in nature.[2] John Stuart Mill, the most important liberal philosopher of the nineteenth century and a man whose ethical philosophy continues to resound in contemporary defences of the value of individuality, believed that England was entitled to rule over India for the same reason that a father is entitled to rule over his children.[3] And we are still witnessing the terrifying outcome in Canada of the century-long policy of residential schools in which children of the people of the First Nations were imprisoned and force-fed the lessons of Christian "civilization."

Similar examples could be adduced almost without limit. The point to be gleaned from them is that in each case there is an alliance between universal principles and social and political power. The postmodern contention is that the model of human nature that is said to be universal and that is invoked as justification for the subordination or destruction of an opposed culture is in reality a particular interpretation of human nature raised to universality by the ruling authority. Those invested with the power to speak conflate their idea of what human nature ought to be with what human nature is and set to work remaking the world according to their oppressive ideal. The model of human nature that Aristotle, for example, employed to justify the slavery of non-Greeks is therefore not a true and universal model of human nature; it is the model of Athenian citizenship raised to universality. The same holds true for the other instances of oppression.

If universal definitions of human nature are always the products of the exercise of power, if every universal definition is made possible by the forcible exclusion and subordination of nonconforming differences, then it follows, postmodern political theory argues, that a radical politics must somehow do away with the idea of human nature. There simply is no underlying identity shared by all human beings. That identity, postmodern philosophers argue, is an illusion whose real function is to justify the remaking of the world according to the definition of human nature that suits the ruling power. Only by breaking with the belief that all human beings share an essence can differences speak in their own voice, and only when differences speak in their own voice can they be said to be free.

If postmodern philosophy rested content with just this argument, then it would indeed be a profound contribution to the struggle for human freedom. However, as the present text will argue, radical postmodern theory does not limit itself to simply arguing that definitions of human nature have been tendentious and that they have been used to justify the given political authorities. It is a much more radical critique than that. Central to the most influential philosophical theories of human nature is the idea that human beings are essentially subjects. The meaning of this term is quite complex, taking on many different inflections throughout the history of philosophy, but at root it means that human beings are an active force in the order of things. The definition of human beings as subjects means that at root human beings are in control of the environments in which they live. In other words, human beings are not essentially determined by factors external to themselves but are self-determining. The drive of human subjecthood is towards social conditions in which that essence is fully realized, towards a world in which we comprehend ourselves as its creators, to paraphrase Marx. Subjecthood as the essence of human being focusses attention on our world-making activity. Freedom means the release of this world-making activity from social dynamics that obstruct it.

This critical inquiry into the fundamental principles and problems of postmodern political philosophy will take as its guiding focus the deconstruction of this idea of the human essence as subjecthood. While postmodern theory is famously multifaceted, touching as it does on every subject from architecture to the philosophy of science, understanding its nuances and diverse pathways demands that a through-line of argument be followed. While it is true that the very meaning of the term "postmodern" is contested, there is nonetheless a clear through-line connecting the major thinkers commonly called postmodern. Tying together the various themes that postmodern philosophy touches upon is a consistent argument that human beings are not defined by any essence or nature. Not only does this theme unite the disparate researches of postmodern philosophy, it is also the argument that has enabled it to have practical effects on the social and political landscape of North American society. Philosophy must always be studied at the point where it touches the nonphilosophical world. Unless it is studied from the perspective of its effects on social reality, philosophy degenerates into the merely private disputes of scholars segregated and isolated from the world and thus fails in its historical mission of trying not only to understand the world but also to contribute to its improvement.

Thus, my analysis of the three most influential postmodern philosophers will argue that in breaking with all universal conceptions of human nature, radical postmodern thought is essentially breaking with the idea of the human being as subject, as (at least potentially) the free creator of its own world. No doubt this postmodern argument is thoroughly radical. However, as we will see, if its radicalism is taken seriously, the very values (difference and pluralism) that are the guiding aims of its critical strategies are undermined. If human beings are not subjects, if they are not the potentially free creators of their world, then they are, I will demonstrate, the products of that world. If subjects are always functions of social, cultural, linguistic, and political dynamics, then freedom for such beings is an impossibility. And yet, as we will see, Derrida, Foucault, and Lyotard all see behind the idea of the human subject and the universalist philosophy it grounds the spectre of mastery, control, and domination. Hence its oppressive effects on nonconforming minorities. What is unlike the self must be mastered, made into the self. By breaking with this understanding of freedom, they hope to let those oppressed differences roam free.

But what can freedom mean in a philosophy that deconstructs the necessary presupposition of any concept of human freedom, i.e., the principle that humans are defined by a self-determining or self-making capacity? If human beings are not essentially self-determining then no sense can be made of the terms oppression and freedom. To be oppressed means to be determined by dynamics and structures that are imposed from without and enforced by a ruling group opposed to the freedom of the group that is called oppressed. But postmodern criticism contends that everyone is always determined by external forces and consequently never self-determining, and if human beings are not in essence self-determining, then the ground of contrast necessary for a coherent understanding of oppression is lost. A woman confined to the house, prevented from working in the public sphere, could say she was oppressed only if she was conscious of being essentially capable of more. If subjects were functions of cultural systems, as the postmodern critique contends, then a function of a sexist culture could never become conscious of being oppressed by the sexist culture. She would simply do what she is programmed to do by the forces that situate and determine her horizons.

7 The Fear of Difference

In short, if differences are the functions of cultural dynamics and cultural dynamics are not the expression of the human self-determining capacity but autonomous systems, then no coherent conception of freedom is possible. If critical political philosophy does not root itself in an essential understanding of human freedom, then it cannot coherently criticize a social world for being unfree. Nevertheless, postmodern political philosophy is essentially critical. Because it is essentially critical both of the world and of the idea of subjecthood that is necessary for coherent criticism of this world, the philosophy that undergirds the postmodern politics of difference is, I will argue, essentially self-contradictory. This argument will be substantiated in numerous ways, but the most solid evidence in its favour comes from the postmodern critics of essentialism themselves. As we will see, the three thinkers whose work best exemplifies the radical deconstruction of subjecthood each presuppose that very idea of human subjecthood insofar as their deconstruction is a political project. Not only will I argue that this idea of subjecthood as self-determination is presupposed by their deconstruction, I will demonstrate that the most important features of the essentialist understanding of human being reenter their work in its later developments. The coherence of its values – diversity, tolerance, unimpeded manifestation of differences – makes sense only if those values are grounded in an understanding of human being as essentially self-determining. In order to advance those values, then, critical political philosophy must reject the deconstruction of subjecthood and set about its tasks on the basis of a renewed understanding of a shared, universal human essence.

My argument against radical postmodern criticism and in defence of a critical-humanist alternative is divided into two parts. The four chapters of part 1 demonstrate, through a close reading of the works of Derrida, Foucault, and Lyotard, that they share a common critique of the idea of the human essence as subjecthood. Chapter 1 explains the critique of the logic of identity thinking that is basic to postmodern philosophy, and chapter 2 then proceeds to show how this critique of identity thinking leads to the conclusion that social differences are the product of linguistic and power dynamics rather than human agency. Chapter 3 shows how this conclusion about the origin and nature of social differences grounds the deconstruction of the idea of human subjecthood that is definitive of postmodern criticism. The radical political inferences that Lyotard, Foucault, and Derrida draw from their criticism of the idea of subjecthood are the focus of chapter 4. In part 2 the postmodern politics of difference is put to the test of practice. Chapter 5, which is transitional, examines two influential attempts to translate the philosophical deconstruction of subjecthood into a practical-political agenda for a free society whose defining value is radical pluralism, and chapter 6 reveals the self-contradictions of this radical form of pluralism. Chapter 7 discloses the contradiction between the self-understanding manifested by the oppressed in struggle and the understanding of those same struggles by the postmodern politics of difference. My critique of the politics of difference culminates in chapter 8, which reveals that postmodern radical criticism can be consistent with its values only if it in fact presupposes the very idea of subjecthood that it deconstructs. The existence of these contradictions will be brought to light by applying the principles gleaned from part 1 to actual struggles of oppressed minorities. By focussing on the history of struggles of the Québécois, the people of the First Nations, and Canada's immigrant communities, all struggles that the politics of difference would embrace, I will argue that the struggles for difference all follow from the universal capacity for self-determination that postmodernism deconstructs. Against postmodernism I will assert that struggles for particularity have a universal ground and that only if that ground is consciously affirmed by philosophical supporters of the struggles of the oppressed and by the oppressed themselves can a free world be won. The text will close with a defence of a critical humanist notion of self-determination as the necessary philosophical framework for the understanding of the value of cultural differences and the practical resolution of oppression and intergroup conflict.

PART ONE
The Postmodern Critique

1 The Emergence of Difference

Before we can understand the self-confuting logic of the radical politics of difference, we must understand the critique of metaphysical philosophy from which it proceeds. That task demands that we first come to an understanding of the meaning of the key terms "identity" and "difference" in the significations that they are given by postmodern criticism. To do so, we must ask ourselves why identity and difference became a problem when they did, how postmodern criticism understands the relationship between the metaphysical problem of identity and difference and the writing of history and social theory, and what the general political implications are of the postmodern contention that traditional philosophy and social theory have suppressed differences in favour of identity. I will address these questions through a close reading of some key texts of Derrida, Foucault, and Lyotard.

DERRIDA: THE TYRANNY OF IDENTITY THINKING

Since Derrida's work provides the deepest critical engagement with the metaphysical ideas of identity and difference, it is best for my argument to begin with his work. For Derrida, Western philosophy is the product of what we can call identity thinking. By identity thinking Derrida means that the metaphysical tradition in philosophy, from Plato to Hegel, has understood truth as the identity of concept and essence. A knowing human subject knows a truth when the concept according to which he or she thinks an object is identical to the essence of that object. In this way truth is, to use Derrida's term, "presence." Truth is the presence to mind of the essence of the object of thought, where essence means "that which makes the thing that which it is." To know what an orange is, for example, is more than simply recognizing its observable properties, it is to have "in mind" the specific difference or essence of that type of fruit.

It seems very difficult to see what possible relevance such an abstruse understanding of truth could have. Yet as distant from everyday concerns as it may seem, the logic of identity thinking is decisively important for understanding what Derrida and postmodern criticism generally take to be the grounds of oppression. If we pay close attention to the definition of truth given above, we can see that it depends upon a certainty fixity both in our concepts and in the essences of the things that our concepts are supposed to grasp. If it is possible to grasp in mind the essence of things, then that essence must be something quite different from the thing that we observe, and our concept must be something quite different from the words we use to express it. Derrida explains this point with reference to Aristotle: "If, for Aristotle, for example, 'spoken words' ... are the symbols of mental experiences ... and written words are the symbols of spoken words ... it is because the voice, producer of *the first symbols*, has a relationship of essential and immediate proximity with the mind. It signifies 'mental experiences' which themselves reflect or mirror things by natural resemblance."[1] The appearances of things and the words we use in everyday language are not fixed or stable and do not name the essence of things. Things appear differently from different perspectives; words mean something new in different contexts. In short, the logic of identity thinking can operate only in abstraction or separation from real-world contexts, because those real world contexts are always characterised by differences – different appearances, different meanings, different interpretations.

In order therefore to make the truth of things present to mind, metaphysical philosophy must put itself in tension with the ordinary world of changing experience. It therefore has cast out, in various ways in various periods, for a "world behind the world," an order of truth behind the mutable, contradictory world of experience – what Derrida calls the "transcendental signified." That search in itself does not sound pernicious. In order to understand why Derrida thinks that it is, we must consider the difference between reason and the world reason tries to know. In the sense in which the term is used in speculative philosophy, reason refers to a certain type of logical order. Reason cannot tolerate contradictions or multiple meanings

13 The Emergence of Difference

attaching to the same concept. If an item of fruit is an orange, it cannot simultaneously be not-an-orange. If a concept knows the essence of an orange, it cannot simultaneously mean the essence of not-orange. This is the metaphysical ground of the principle of noncontradiction, the bedrock of logic. Failing to find adequate satisfaction of this principle in the world of words and things, reason claims for itself the right and capacity to go beyond the world of appearances to a purportedly rational, nonapparent region of pure identities or essences.

Traditional metaphysical philosophy thus insists on a certain hierarchical division of things into appearances and essences. Since it is the essence that determines the appearance, it follows that the essence is more important than the appearance (there would be no appearance without the essence), but the essence is not reciprocally dependent on the appearance. The one who knows essences, the philosopher, knows something other and more important than ordinary people; s/he knows what really is the case about things. It is for this reason that Plato, for example, insists that social problems will not be solved until philosophers become kings. Since the philosopher alone knows the truth about justice, freedom, the proper modes of human activity, and the Good, only the philosopher can put humanity's house in order.

We are now able to see in general a danger attaching to identity thinking. Philosophical thought claims a certain privilege for itself. This privilege is not simply to name the essence of things but, more importantly, to reorganize the everyday world on the basis of this form of knowledge. Moreover, the concrete world of everyday experience and ordinary competence has now been demoted to secondary importance. Metaphysical thinking is, Derrida contends, by its very nature hierarchical. If something is essential, it follows that something else is inessential. What is essential to philosophy is stability, unitary meaning, and identity. What is inessential is change, polysemy (multiple meaning), and difference. The problem is that the world as it appears to us in our ordinary lives is changing, our words (especially written words) are polysemic, and everything appears differently depending upon context and perspective. From the metaphysical standpoint, then, the world as it is must be subordinated to and transformed in accordance with the world as it essentially is. Those who are "in the know" are the only ones who are up to this job.

From a seemingly benign search after truth, metaphysics thus becomes, from Derrida's perspective, a practice of exclusion. Metaphysics is defined as much by what it excludes (inessential modes of knowing and being) as by what it includes. Plato's exclusion of poetry that does not conform to the laws of his ideal state is a classic example of the exclusive logic that identity thinking brings in its wake. Hence, Derrida's attempt to "deconstruct" philosophy is not an abstract critique of the definition of truth as understood by metaphysics but is rather a critique of the way metaphysical definitions of truth establish hierarchies and thereby exclude other possibilities for being and thinking. He argues that "to 'deconstruct' philosophy, thus, would be to think – in the most faithful, interior way – the structured genealogy of philosophy's concepts, but at the same time to determine – from a certain exterior that is unqualifiable or unnameable by philosophy – what this history has been able to dissimulate or forbid, making itself into a history by reason of this somewhere motivated repression. By means of this simultaneously faithful and violent circulation between the inside and the outside of philosophy – that is *of the West* – there is produced a certain textual work that gives great pleasure ... which also enables us to read philosophemes – and consequently *all the texts of our culture* as kinds of symptoms ... of something that could not be presented in the history of philosophy" [emphasis added].² This passage is crucial not only for understanding Derrida but also for understanding the philosophical and political stakes of the deconstruction of identity thinking.

First, it is essential to note that philosophy is for Derrida a type of fundamental grid or framework that defines normality for our entire Western culture. Identity thinking permeates not just philosophy, not just science, but the whole moral and political apparatus of Western history. The practical effect of identity thinking in the political and institutional apparatus of the West is to mark a series of differences that determine who is entitled to speak and what they are entitled to say, what is to be taken as valuable and what is to be ignored, and what is to count as a valid way of acting and what is to be denounced or repressed. Deconstruction operates both within and outside of philosophy, and its aim is to bring to light the insidious nature of the hierarchies according to which philosophy and the institutions that it implicitly organizes operate. It attempts to reveal that the inside (identity) is dependent on the exclusion of the outside (difference). The philosophical aim of deconstruction is thus essentially tied to a politics of difference, or otherness.

Deconstruction is not, as it is often criticised for being, simply a criticism of texts. Its true goal is to create a breach in the philosophical edifice so that the excluded outside both comes to light and is able to speak. As Derrida argues, "the rapport of self-identity is itself always a rapport of violence with the other; so that the notions of property, appropriation, and self-presence, so central to logocentric metaphysics, are essentially dependent on an oppositional relationship with otherness. In this sense, identity *presupposes* otherness."[3] Derrida's point is that a self can constitute itself as self-identical only by excluding that which is not itself or by remaking the not-self in its own image. If the appearances of the world are not like the categories according to which a rational self thinks, then appearances must be excluded from knowing. If another person who confronts the self appears unlike the self (because s/he is of a different gender or race or speaks a different language), then that other person too must be remade in the image of the self. The "normal" self thus seeks out beneath the differences some underlying humanity and in this way obliterates the differences that really define the other. However, as Derrida points out, the identity of the self depends crucially upon the existence and the alterity (difference) of the other. Identity thinking can only become dominant through the violent exclusion and subordination of this other.

However, it is not always necessary to physically liquidate the differences that confront and threaten identity. It is also possible to check the danger posed by differences by assimilating them into a structure of normality that manages them. Plato does not banish poets from his city, he only insists that the poets not say anything which the laws forbid. Non-European cultures are not any longer forbidden from entering Canada, but they are expected to ensure that their cultural practices conform to the limits assigned by official multiculturalism programs. Identity thinking, whether in philosophy or social science or public policy, always revolves around a centre, an organizing principle whose function is to assign different elements to their "proper" place. As Derrida argues, "the function of this centre was not only to orient, balance, and organize the structure ... but above all to make sure that the organizing principle would limit what we might call the *play* of the structure. By orienting and organizing the coherence of the system, the centre of a structure permits the play of its elements inside the total form ... Nevertheless, the centre also closes off the play which it opens up."[4] In this way differences can be maintained and yet also controlled. The "other" is thus reduced in its otherness and yet not completely destroyed.

If, however, identity thinking spans more than two millennia of human thought and practice, if Western thinking has always constituted itself by excluding or defining others, why has it taken until now for philosophers within the West to turn their critical gaze upon their own history? The short answer, which I will elaborate upon as the text unfolds, is that philosophy had to be confronted with its outside: the margins, or the other, had to begin to speak in their own voice before the deconstruction of philosophy could begin. As Derrida says, "deconstruction is, in itself, a positive response to an alterity which necessarily calls, summons or motivates it. Deconstruction is therefore a vocation ... The other, as other than self, the other that opposes self-identity, is not something that can be detected and disclosed within a philosophical space."[5] Derrida means "other" in two senses. The first and fundamental meaning draws attention to that which is not thought or not reducible to the categories of identity thinking. In this sense, Derrida is drawing attention to the complexity and irreducibility of the world and of meaning. More concretely, as we will see below, Derrida understands by "other" the other person, the irreducible singularity of human existence, and the violence that attends the attempt to name or define the other. Deconstruction as a response to the call of the other is thus an openness to the complexity of the world and the undefinable being of the other person. I will explore in more detail the political implications of this sense of otherness in the remaining chapters. At this point, however, I will explore through an examination of the work of Michel Foucault the effects that the deconstruction of identity thinking has on our understanding of human history.

FOUCAULT: FRAGMENTING HISTORY

It is not my intention to suggest that there are no important differences between Derrida, Foucault, and Lyotard. Each has his own interests, strategies, and aims. To draw attention to an underlying thematic unity is not to suggest that there are no differences. Nevertheless, whatever important differences separate these three figures, there are shared concerns relating to the insidious dangers of identity thinking, the conception of subjecthood that underlies identity thinking, and the pernicious political effects of that idea of subjecthood. My interpretation will concentrate on these points of convergence.

While Foucault and Derrida had their disagreements, they also both focus their criticism on the metaphysical understanding of identity.[6] While Derrida concentrates his fire on the meaning of identity in the metaphysical tradition, Foucault is more interested in understanding its specific effects in given institutional domains and practices. Nevertheless, Foucault too is interested in general questions about the implications of identity thinking, especially as it affects the writing of history. The metaphysical understanding of identity has, Foucault contends, privileged a certain speculative philosophy of history (paradigmatically expressed in Hegel) that sees history as an inexorable human drive for self-understanding and freedom. Just as identity thinking in general seeks to exclude, or at least manage, difference, identity thinking in the form of the philosophy of history seeks to reduce all social, cultural, political, and moral differences to elements in a universal narrative of human self-realization. Foucault's critique aims to reveal the strategy of exclusion at the heart of this speculative approach to history, to confront it with what it excludes, to release from the margins the voices that speculation necessarily silences. Politically, he intends "to break with all themes that claim to be global and radical."[7] He thus rejects all-encompassing political projects purportedly authorized by historical laws or tendencies.

Foucault draws his methodological and political conclusions from his observation of the changing nature of political struggles. The struggles of "women, prisoners, conscripted soldiers" insofar as they were directed against "the particularized power, the constraints and controls, that are exerted over them," disclosed to Foucault the inadequacy of universal interpretations of history.[8] These struggles could not be understood if they were reduced to secondary manifestations of some more fundamental human drive to know oneself, or to make all humans equal, or to establish the material conditions for freedom. On the contrary, these local conflicts signify a historical change for Foucault, one that makes old forms of theorizing obsolete. Analysing his contemporary political reality, he argues that "what has emerged in the course of the last fifteen years is a sense of the increasing vulnerability to criticism of things, institutions, practices, discourses ... But together with this sense of instability and this amazing efficacy of discontinuous, particular, and local criticism one in fact also discovers something that perhaps was not initially foreseen, something one might describe as precisely the inhibiting effect of global, *totalitarian* theories ... In each case, the attempt to think in terms of totality has in fact proved a hindrance to research."[9] In order to grasp the specificities of local struggles and criticisms one has to study the specifics of the operation of power in each case. In other words, one has to study struggles as different from one another rather than simply as different manifestations of the same human struggle. Instead of seeking out beneath the specific demands of local struggles some universal demand, one must stick with the appearances, so to speak, and deal with given struggles on their own terms.

While Foucault avoids for the most part a direct engagement with the classical sources of identity thinking, it is clear that, like Derrida, he is concerned with the pervasive failure of identity thinking to comprehend social contradictions in their specificity and difference. If one desires to understand the fault-lines of contemporary society, one must, according to Foucault, reject the idea that history and society form totalities. The category of totality structures all contradictions and struggles according to the assumption that "humanity ... progresses from combat to combat until it arrives at universal reciprocity." The truth is, however, that "humanity installs each of its violences in a system of rules and thus proceeds from domination to domination."[10] By transforming all contradictions into the off-shoots of one fundamental contradiction, the proponents of the philosophy of history hide the ongoing play of domination, in order to ensure that they remain dominant. Foucault sees in the category of totality central to the philosophy of history the same Western abhorrence for difference, noncommensurability, and otherness that Derrida saw operative in the category of "centre."

Foucault explains the drive to reduce all differences to offshoots of a fundamental governing dynamic as the effect of the privilege accorded human consciousness in the philosophy of history from the nineteenth century to the 1960s. Reflecting on the practice of French historians in the postwar period, he argues that they "felt a particular repugnance to conceiving of difference, to describing separations and dispersions, to dissociating the reassuring form of the identical ... As if we were afraid to conceive of the *Other* in the time of our own thought. There is a reason for this. If the history of thought could remain the locus of uninterrupted continuities, if it could endlessly forge connections that no analysis could undo without abstraction ... it would provide a privileged shelter for the sovereignty of consciousness. Continuous history is the indispensable correlative for the founding function of the subject."[11] Foucault, like Derrida, is concerned with confronting the seamless unities of identity thinking with their other, with what they excluded as a condition of their own unity.

Initially in Foucault's early archaeological work, this effort took a methodological form with little direct political content. Archaeology was empirically oriented and sought to unravel the grand unities of Hegelian-inspired philosophies of history by focussing on the structures of inclusion and exclusion that determined different discursive formations in any given period. The rules that define discursive formations form "a principle of determination that permits or excludes, within a given discourse, a certain number of statements: these are ... groups and organizations of objects that might have been possible ... but which are excluded by a discursive constellation at a higher level and in a broader space."[12] For example, once scientific psychiatry has developed as a distinct discourse, it rules out folk psychology as a possible explanation of human behaviour, even though there is nothing in the nature of folk psychology that makes it intrinsically incapable of explanation. Discursive formations define what counts as a valid object of scientific research, knowledge claim, or research project. They vary from period to period, but empirical analysis does not reveal any progressive dynamic governing the change. Human reason does not approach ever more closely to the truth but rather defines and redefines different scientific problems in response to changing epistemic rules not obeisant to anyone's conscious control. Changes in these underlying rules for the formation of statements determining the formation of the objects of science are not governed by any overall end grounded in the nature of human reason. If this is the case, then it is a tendentious falsehood to claim that historical change is consciously directed by a collective historical subject that manifests the irresistible development of reason. At root, historical transformations are motivated by changes at the unconscious level. Such changes then redefine the structural conditions for scientific statements and research.

As this empirical work progressed, however, Foucault began to notice that the rules that determined what counted as knowledge for any period were always bound up with or invested with power. Even when his concern was simply with the structure of discursive formations, he emphasized how they excluded different possible objects that, considered in themselves, were no more or less fit as objects of scientific research. However, the idea of power was absent in his archaeological works. The recognition that power and knowledge were always intertwined led Foucault to make a key self-criticism. In 1977, reflecting on works such as *The Order of Things* and *The Birth of the Clinic*, he lamented that "what was lacking here was the problem of the discursive regime, of the effects of power peculiar to the play of statements." These he had "confused too much with systematicity, theoretical form, or something like a paradigm."[13] That is, Foucault believed that he had abstracted from the sociopolitical interests operative in the constitution of knowledge within various institutions. He had attributed this constitutive function to the unconscious rules operative across disciplines and had thus committed an error similar to totalizing theory. In other words, he had allowed the coercive nature of institutional knowledge to disappear behind neutral rules governing the production of knowledge.[14] However, alerted to the operations of power within institutions by the eruption of the struggles he identified, Foucault developed his celebrated analysis of the various constellations of power/knowledge characteristic of contemporary social formations. This analysis of power will be treated in detail in the following two chapters. At this point, however, I must examine how the philosophical and historical criticisms developed by Foucault and Derrida come together in Jean Francois Lyotard's idea of postmodernity.

LYOTARD: DEVELOPMENT, COMPLEXITY, AND POSTMODERNITY

Both Foucault and Derrida are suspicious of the term postmodernity, and they were reluctant, if not outright hostile, to it being applied to their work. Here I am not concerned with revisiting sociological debates of the 1980s as to whether Western society has entered into a new postmodern phase, or with trying to impose upon Foucault and Derrida a term that they repudiated.[15] The idea of postmodernity is interesting to us only insofar as it is commonly used to denote the deconstructive philosophical strategies I am investigating, and in that sense it is no injustice to use it in reference to Foucault and Derrida. The work of Jean Francois Lyotard was instrumental in the popularisation of the concept. As we will see, his definition of postmodernity centres on the critique of identity thinking.

Lyotard rose to prominence in North America following the publication of a study commissioned by the government of Quebec in 1979. In *The Postmodern Condition* he defined postmodernity, as "incredulity towards metanarratives," that is, towards any general explanation of events by reference to some general principle, whether it be "the dialectics of Spirit, the hermeneutics of meaning, the emancipation of the rational or working subject, or the creation of wealth."[16] Postmodern thinking thus breaks fundamentally with the unities forged by the modern philosophy of history that Foucault criticized and, by extension, with the identity thinking that, according to Derrida, is their deep ground of possibility.

The roots of Lyotard's critical engagement with the grand unities of Western philosophy go back long before he popularised the term "postmodern." The guiding impulse of postmodern thought, the impulse towards disunity, fragmentation, and difference, is announced clearly in Lyotard's idea of libidinal history. He argues that, "A libidinal history refuses itself that finality which is that of knowledge and princely power. It must at least apply to its 'corpus' ... the principle of generalized relativity that nuclear physicists know well, and that implies that there are no privileged posts for the decoding of organizations of energy."[17] Lyotard announces here a theme that runs throughout his work, an ongoing attempt to link universal philosophy and centralized forms of political control.

Lyotard roots his critique of metanarrative within a historical analysis of the post-Second World War globe. This world is characterized by growing scientific specialization and increasingly fragmented sites of political struggle. The relationship between these two forces is the central focus of his ground-breaking work, *The Postmodern Condition*. Lyotard contends that the very development of rationality in the West is responsible for the dissolution of the link between reason and freedom. Ever more numerous branches of knowledge have developed, and each has generated an ever growing collection of data. This fragmentation, driven forward by the principle of performativity (efficiency), extends out from the sciences and works its shattering effects throughout society. Politics becomes management, work is reduced to meaningless detail labour, and consumer society develops to fill the void left by the destruction of meaningful vocations. In short, people find themselves situated within ever more numerous social practices over which they have no control and between which no necessary connections are to be found. The consequences of this development are profound: "We may form a pessimistic impression of this splintering: nobody speaks all of those languages, they have no universal metalanguage, the project of a system subject is a failure, the goal of emancipation has nothing to do with science, we are all stuck in the positivism of this or that discipline of learning, the learned scholars have turned into scientists, the diminished tasks of research have become compartmentalized and no one can master them all. Speculative or humanist philosophy is forced to relinquish its legitimation duties, which explains why philosophy is facing a crisis wherever it persists in arrogating such functions."[18] At root, Lyotard contends that social complexity has exceeded the capacity of philosophical thought to forge meaningful connections between different regions of reality, research, and activity. The very success of scientific research has spelt doom for disciplines like philosophy whose function it was to interpret the normative meaning of the conclusions of science and to synthesise humanity's disparate practices into meaningful wholes. It no longer makes sense to talk of the progress of reason or the struggle against superstition. Science produces technology and technology produces wealth. Universal meaning is completely absent from the equation.

It is certainly true that the accelerating specialization of social roles raises questions about the continued viability of humanist philosophy. If it is perhaps no longer the case that one can think of society as unified by an essential dynamic, it may also be necessary to question the correlative attempt to provide a unified account of history. Lyotard raises this problem in the assertion cited above to the effect that humanistic philosophy is facing a crisis. Its hero, the "system-subject," that is, humanity, has disappeared. Science is not unambiguously harnessed to human freedom. The unbridled development of technology has meant ecological destruction and the subjugation of nontechnological cultures just as much as it has meant increased control over the environment. This failure entails the failure for Lyotard of each modern metanarrative. Neither the growth of wealth nor the growth of scientific knowledge has in fact resulted in a positively free society. The radical alternative to capitalism, Marxism, has also failed miserably. Thus, postmodern thought must reconsider the basic structures of the social in the absence of universal principles: "The narrative function is losing its functors, its great hero ... its great goal. It is being dispersed in clouds of narrative language elements – narrative, but also denotative, prescriptive, descriptive, and so on. Conveyed within each cloud are pragmatic valencies specific to its kind. Each of us lives at the intersection of many of these."[19] Postmodern analysis, therefore, will focus upon tracing out the logic specific to discrete social practices, while postmodern politics will focus upon diversifying the practices operative in society by trying to "invent new moves [or] even better, to invent new games."[20] The specifics of this analysis and this politics will be considered in the subsequent chapters of part 1. For the moment this inquiry must sum up the conclusions this overview permits.

There are three key points to keep in mind as we proceed to the more difficult task of understanding the deconstruction of subjecthood and its political implications:

1 Postmodern criticism holds that Western philosophy is rooted in identity thinking that is based upon a strict separation between the subject and the object of knowledge. The object of knowledge is other than the subject. The task of thinking is to make the object identical to the subject, to reduce difference to identity. The goal of identity thinking is, from the postmodern perspective, to master and manage differences.
2 There are therefore decisive political stakes involved in the form of philosophising and theorising rooted in identity thinking. Philosophy and theory are not abstract practices, they inform the history and politics of the West and have conditioned the response of Western powers to the concrete others encountered in the course of historical development. The real goal of identity thinking and the

politics that follows from it is to eliminate differences, either absolutely or by reducing differences to inessential moments of an underlying essential identity.
3 The postmodern criticism of identity thinking aims to break with this tyrannical form of knowing and acting by letting the other speak for itself. This means accepting difference and contradiction as, in a sense, basic to the world. More concretely, it means exposing the metanarratives of Western culture as discourses that work only by reserving the right to name relevant differences and thereby exclude and silence them. Identity is always the product of the exclusion of difference.

With these points in mind we are ready to begin the more detailed analysis of the postmodern deconstruction of identity thinking. The task of the next chapter is two-fold. First, it will uncover the postmodern explanation of the origin and nature of the differences it takes to be constitutive of human societies. Second, it will link this account of the origin and nature of differences to the deconstruction of the modern understanding of human subjecthood.

2 The Dynamics of Difference

The previous chapter introduced us to the critique of identity thinking that is central to postmodern criticism. This critique, however, is only preparatory to the elaboration of new modes of criticism and practice central to the positive project of the politics of difference. The goal of that politics is not simply to expose the exclusionary logic of identity thinking but to create a space in which new modes of thinking and acting, modes rooted in the logic of difference, may unfold. This new mode of thinking centres on a different way of relating to what the exclusionary hierarchies of metaphysical thinking relate to as "the Other." The positive or affirmative values that orient postmodern criticism are the values of difference, singularity, nonconformity, transgression, and experimentation.

In order to understand the postmodern sense of these values, it is crucial to investigate how postmodern theory accounts for the existence of the differences that it takes to be definitive of sociocultural worlds. As I mentioned in the previous chapter, postmodern criticism believes that social differences are not rooted in an underlying human capacity for self-determination. Instead, postmodern theory contends that social differences are in a sense basic and not products of a more fundamental identity. The problem for postmodern criticism is not so much how differences arise but, rather, why those differences are continually subordinated to an underlying human essence in the history of philosophical thought. The world is awash with differences, but philosophy and social theory have generally ignored their existence. Philosophy and social theory therefore must

25   The Dynamics of Difference

concretize and particularize their focus in order to be adequate to the plural character of social dynamics. The key postmodern tenet that emerges from the three positions to be examined is that these dynamics do not follow from the essential needs, desires, and capacities of human beings. On the contrary, the social and cultural dynamics of difference determine the needs, desires, and capacities of human being. As Lyotard's account is perhaps the most concrete, let us begin with him.

NARRATION AND THE SOCIAL

A long tradition of social philosophy attempted to account for sociocultural differences in terms of the creative response of natural human capacities to different sets of material (geographic, climatic, topographical) conditions. This argument asserted that human beings are defined by a basic set of needs and capacities but that these capacities give rise to different political and cultural dynamics in response to the different demands placed upon human beings in different material contexts. The initial differentiation of capacities gives rise to different traditions, and around different traditions different languages, class structures, political forms, and artistic practices develop. At root, however, it is the same human nature articulating itself in different forms in response to different natural contexts.[1] Lyotard takes issue with this tradition.

The essential problem of the notion of a natural basis to society according to Lyotard is that it can never be isolated from its concrete sociocultural instantiations. That is, the purportedly natural basis is never found in a natural state but always in this or that society, under such and such conditions. Theory never comes upon "human nature" in a natural, immediate state. Instead, it comes upon social differences and argues, without evidence, that a common nature must somehow underlie these differences. In other words, human nature is the product of a theory that responds to particular sociohistorical exigencies. Wherever one encounters a purported natural need, one encounters a theory of natural needs. Wherever one encounters theory, one encounters language. Wherever one encounters language, one encounters particular rules governing particular linguistic constructions. These particular sites of linguistic production define the social field. Society is thus characterized as a dispersed plurality of language-games that are defined by incommensurable rules. Lyotard argues that "there is no need to resort to some fiction of social origins to establish that language-games are the minimum relation required for society to exist: even before he is born, if only by virtue of the name he is given, the human child is already positioned as the referent in the story recounted by those around him, in relation to which he will *inevitably* chart his course. Or more simply still, the question of the social bond, in so far as it is a question, is itself a language game, the game of inquiry. It immediately positions the person who asks, as well as the addressee and the referent asked about: it is already the social bond" (emphasis added).[2] There is no universal translator that could reduce the meanings of these different games to some underlying narrative of human origins and social development. The strategies implicit in different language games, the rules they obey and the ends they seek, do not stem from human needs or interests at all. As Lyotard argues, "the rules regulating language-games are unknown to the players," and therefore these games are "in no sense played by people using specific languages as instruments."[3]

By focussing on the irreducible linguistic element in social practices, Lyotard attempts to deconstruct the idea of a common human nature as the origin of social and cultural differences. Human beings, as his example of the child shows, are also referents in various stories. What counts as human nature, too, is always a product of specific language games in definite contexts. While people may also tell stories, they do so only by following rules in definite contexts that they did not and could not determine. Thus, society is conceived pluralistically as a dispersed constellation of language-games, and the human being as a sender, an addressee, or a referent of discourse with no depth proper to itself. In fact, Lyotard writes, "A self does not amount to much, but no self is an island; each exists in a fabric of relations that is more complex and mobile than ever before ... a person is always located at "nodal points" of specific communication circuits, however tiny these may be. Or better, one is always located at a post through which various kinds of messages pass."[4] The dynamic, creative, and productive element of the social is thus language and not any natural capacity of human beings. Commenting on this central claim, John Keane observes that for Lyotard the social bond "resembles a complex labyrinth of different, sometimes hostile, slippery and sliding language-games" that "obey rules of an indeterminate variety" and that, consequently, "cannot be apprehended or synthesized under the authority of a single metadiscourse."[5]

As a consequence of the dispersed nature of social practices and institutions, Lyotard opts for what he terms a pragmatic approach to understanding social differences. His social pragmatics rejects the modern belief that there are grounds to be found in human nature for a social philosophy that would unite science (understanding the world), politics (how we should organize ourselves in this world), and ethics (how we ought to act in the world). There is also no reason to believe that any consensus could "embrace the totality of metaprescriptives regulating the totality of statements circulating in the social collectivity."[6] More simply, what Lyotard means is that philosophy cannot gather together the different fields of human practice under a universal idea of humanity's mission to understand and free itself. According to Lyotard, importing the rules of one language-game into a different language-game is both illegitimate and terroristic.

The very heart of authoritarian forms of discourse is, Lyotard contends, the effort to subsume complex and differential social realities under a single theory. What he resists above all is a politics that aims to teach people their "interests" and ground "scientific" strategies for social renewal. Under the influence of the desire to resist theoretical totalization, his work after *The Postmodern Condition* is increasingly insistent on the nontranslatability of discrete discourses and the need to keep some social or individual space free of discursive determination altogether. This preoccupation is best exemplified in the text *The Differend*. Gone is the notion of the language-game, which he abandoned because "it seemed to me that 'language games' implied players that made use of language like a toolbox, thus repeating the constant arrogance of Western anthropocentrism."[7] Language-games are replaced by the phrase, the basic unit of discourse according to Lyotard. Phrases organize themselves into different genres that in turn constitute different universes. What is crucial is the manner in which phrases are linked together. Such linkage is always a unique and unreproducible event rather than a moment in a process defined by universal rules. There are no rules specifiable in advance governing the linkage of phrases to one another, and there is therefore no way to subsume phrases and genres under any grand narrative.

The idea of the "differend" signifies the absence of any common principle to which disputants could appeal in order to resolve conflicts over the meaning, interpretation, and implications of different discourses. "As distinguished from a litigation," Lyotard writes, "a differend would be a case of conflict between (at least) two parties that cannot be equitably resolved for lack of a rule of judgement applicable to both arguments. One side's legitimacy does not imply the other's lack of legitimacy."[8] This notion is the culminating point of Lyotard's celebration of the particular. The fragmentation of the world by these differends must be respected. One may think here of the need to respect different cultural practices, of the need to refrain from judging one culture by the norms of another. To that extent

Lyotard is touching here on something like the ethnocentric fallacy, which cautions against drawing universal conclusions from the norms of one's own culture. Valued advice, to be sure. But can we also not detect a danger? If it is the case that differences are in a sense self-organizing, if they determine human beings and not the other way around, then it seems to follow that what human beings "really" are at any given moment they owe not to their own activity but to the play of language, the rules that determine it, rules that can never be brought under any collective logic of control. But if humans are just nodes in discursive networks, then it is difficult to discover any grounds according to which one could discriminate between different networks. Since the human being has been emptied of all content proper to himself or herself, how could a human even become conscious that there is a problem in the way s/he is being "situated" by language? That problem, as we will see, afflicts the thought of Foucault and Derrida, as well, and is the ultimate source of the political incoherence of postmodern criticism.

POWER, OBJECTIVITY, AND NORMALIZATION

While Foucault would agree with Lyotard that social structures cannot be explained by reference to a set of underlying human needs and capacities, he does not account for social differences solely by reference to the nature of language. Like his attitude towards historical periodization, Foucault's views on the relative weight of language in the constitution of human differences changed throughout his career. In his early archaeological work, language does play the determining role. But when he later shifts attention to the operations of power, a more interesting and complex account of the constitution of differences emerges. While it would be incorrect to attribute Lyotard's claim that the social bond is essentially linguistic to Foucault, it is the case that his celebrated analysis of power concludes on a similar point, namely, that the dynamics characteristic of different social practices and constitutive of different identities and subjects are not reducible to some underlying universal purpose that follows from a core human nature. The differences definitive of actual social formations are not the conscious work of a self-determining human capacity. Instead, that capacity itself is the product of networks of power not under the conscious control of any human individual or group. In order to understand Foucault's analysis of power, we must first examine his evolution from archaeologist to genealogist in more detail.

The basic principle of Foucault's archaeology is that what counts as an object of knowledge in a given historical period is a function of deep, unconscious rules for the formation of scientific statements. These statements are variously reconfigured through history, but they do not manifest any teleological development towards ultimate truth. Foucault does not maintain, of course, that objects understood as material things are products of discourse. There are rocks and trees. But whether those rocks or trees are understood as the expression of a dynamic form in passive matter or atomic compounds is a function of the rules defining science in the age in question. Science and theory are "discursive practices" and "are characterized by the delimitation of a field of objects, the definition of a legitimate perspective for the agent of knowledge, and the fixing of norms for the elaboration of concepts and theories. Thus, each discursive practice implies a play of prescriptions that designate its exclusions and choices."[9] The basic rules structuring the play of the various discursive practices vary from period to period, recall, and thus so do the objects of discourse. There are no transhistorical criteria to which one could appeal to define a real object as opposed to one that was merely posited by a "bad" theory. What archaeology reveals is that in a given period different sciences all obey "the same rules to define the objects proper to their own study, to form their concepts, to build their theories."[10] The same applies to human being. Humanity is not a subject independent of the systems of knowledge that aim to know it. The "human" in Greece is a different object of knowledge from the "human" of Hegel's philosophy. As Peter Wilkins correctly says of Foucault's archaeology, it assumes that "each historical period can be marked by the range of discourses that construct the beliefs we have about the social and natural world. It is the rules of understanding established by these discourses that construct and set the parameters to what we take to be true about the world."[11] There is no common substance uniting the various constructions and reconstructions of these belief sets. Just as science does not progress from failure to rational triumph, so too humanity does not progress from servitude to freedom.

While Foucault rejects the defining modern belief that historical change is progressive, he does not deny that changes occur. But the deep structural analysis characteristic of his archaeologies leaves the question of why *epistemes* (systems of knowledge defined by the unconscious rules for the production of statements) change. He answers the lingering question of how and why discursive practices change with a decisive shift of theoretical strategy. While archaeology aimed simply to bring to light the rules definitive of a given *episteme,* genealogy aimed to highlight the struggle between different systems of knowledge that alone could account for why one system rather than another became dominant. Most interesting for our purposes is the notion of power that Foucault developed as he shifted theoretical strategies.

Foucault rejects the traditional notion of power, according to which it is a force that is possessed or controlled by a definite group and whose proper use is to repress. He contends that power is not rooted in large-scale social forces, in a ruling class that controls the means of production and has a monopoly on the means of violence, for example. Like gravity, which operates between any two bodies with mass in relative proximity to one another, so too power exists between any two people or groups who are connected to one another and structures their reciprocal relations. Its origins are inscrutable to his analysis, but its effects are everywhere manifest. It is not a whole waiting to be seized, it is relational, circulating, "capillary," like the microscopic blood vessels that bring oxygen to our cells.[12] As he writes, "power comes from below, that is, there is no binary and all-encompassing opposition between ruler and ruled at the root of power relations ... One must suppose, rather, that the manifold relations of force that take shape and come into play in the machinery of production, in families, in limited groups, and institutions are the basis for wide-ranging effects of cleavage that run through the social body as a whole."[13] This power does not repress but rather produces discourses, identities, and truths. Power does not mask or distort but is rather constitutive of what becomes manifest at any given time. It "induces pleasure, forms knowledge, produces discourse" and thus must be considered, "a productive network ... much more than as a negative instance."[14] It is power that determines the identity of individuals and groups and the interests, needs, and capacities that define them. There is thus no question of any relationship of correspondence between the "true" interest of humanity and a set of social practices adequate to those needs. What is important for Foucault is not truth but what he calls "truth effects." "I believe," he states, "that the problem does not consist in drawing a line between that in a discourse which falls under the category of scientificity or truth, and that which falls under some other category." The analysis of discursive practices shaped by power relations consists rather "in seeing historically how effects of truth are produced within discourses which are themselves neither true not false."[15] That is, true statements do not mirror the natural world or correctly model a material object or process. Truth is what gains acceptance at any given time insofar as the statements that pass for true structure the activity of those who accept them.

That is the meaning of "truth-effect." There is no nonrelative criterion of truth to which one could appeal in an effort to construct a transhistorical account of the growth of knowledge or human freedom. Moreover, these truth-effects are produced within different institutions that do not obey any over-arching principle of social coordination. Each institution must be understood in its own right, according to its specific regime of truth. There is no master key that one could turn to unlock a universal language of power uniting its effects across all institutions.

In general, history is now conceived by Foucault as an ongoing struggle between discourses, each seeking to establish itself as dominant. No one discourse is in itself better than another. What becomes socially predominant is the result of force and exclusion, not rationality or moral value. History is intelligible only "in accordance with the intelligibility of struggles, strategy, and tactics."[16] Beatrice Hansen, tracing the Nietzschean origins of Foucault's genealogy, explains that it is "an analysis of the use of force which invariably attended the imparting of meaning." Success is measured by "how well [adversaries] managed to bend existing interpretations to their wills."[17] From the perspective of genealogy, what is valuable in history is what is said to be valuable by a discourse that manages to exclude other possibilities. Most important for our purposes is the manner in which genealogy understands the formation of individuals, their identity, needs, and capacities. We can best understand this moment of the theory by developing an example.

The example comes from *Discipline and Punish*, perhaps Foucault's most powerful and fascinating text. The example of how prison constitutes the criminal and the delinquent brings together the general epistemological strategy discussed above with Foucault's later analysis of the operations of power specific to the play of discourse within different institutions. What is at issue in this text is neither the truism that crime is relative to a criminal code nor the sociological inference that prisons do not reform criminals so much as make first-time criminals lifelong offenders. Foucault's argument, if it has any distinctiveness, must operate at a deeper level. His essential claim is that through the discourse of criminology, within the context of a total institution whose function is to control every aspect of behaviour, a new entity is produced. It is not only (as a humanistic critique might maintain) that criminology flattens out and objectifies a person, it is moreover productive of a whole history and identity for that person. The criminal is not an empirical individual who has broken a law. The criminal is the product of a knowledge invested with disciplinary power: "At the point that marked the disappearance of the branded, dismembered, burnt, annihilated body of the tortured criminal, there appeared the body of the prisoner, duplicated by the individuality of the 'delinquent,' by the little soul of the criminal, which the very apparatus of punishment *fabricated as a point of application of the power to punish* and as the object of what is still today called penitentiary science" (emphasis added).[18] Thus, Foucault argues that the rules governing discursive practices are at the same time the rules for the constitution of the objects of those discourses. These rules define institutions within whose walls power coalesces with knowledge in order to produce individuals of various types.

In general, "the individual is not a pre-given entity, the individual with his identity and characteristics, is the product of a relation of power exercised over bodies, multiplicities, movements, desires, forces."[19] The various institutions of society – schools, factories, hospitals, courts, and so on, each contribute their share to the final product. Human individuals are not the product of their own labour or the particular outcome of a universal creative capacity. In modern society it is power, articulated into the various institutions definitive of that society, that produces human beings. What human beings take themselves to be – rational self-maximisers, transgressive outsiders, revolutionary workers – is not a product of any self-determining capacity, it is the result of the work of power on their bodies. Social differences, in all their permutations, follow from disciplinary institutions whose goal is to produce normalized beings, people who keep themselves in line. Foucault argues that "in its function the power to punish is not essentially different from that of curing or that of educating. It receives from them... a sanction from below... the sanction of technique and rationality ... [by] circulating the same calculated, mechanical and discreet methods from one to the other, the carceral makes it possible to carry out that great 'economy' of power whose formula the eighteenth century had sought, when the problem of the accumulation and administration of men first appeared."[20] This claim is the heart of Foucault's decentring of the subject. As Peter Dews observes, "indeed, the supposed expressive unity between an individual and her/his 'personality' – the human 'soul' – is itself constituted by relations of power in which the formation of knowledge plays a central role. It is through the internalization of such knowledge that the individual is first produced as a 'subject' on which the strategies of power can operate. Subjectification, in this sense, is the necessary preliminary to subjection."[21] Thus, there is no underlying basis in human nature from which human beings could create a society in which they would be free in the positive sense. All human beings are the product of power. However, one can see the problem that threatens Lyotard recurring with Foucault. It is clear that Foucault is opposed to the normalizing practices of disciplinary society. But the only coherent basis of resistance to this disciplinary society must involve a notion of human being with some capacities that are not simply the products of power. If everything about us is the product of disciplinary power, including the belief that we are or could become free beings, then there is no ground from which resistance to the effects of power could be marshalled. As Habermas asks in a very telling criticism of Foucault's genealogy, if everything about human being is the product of power, even the forms of resistance human beings manifest, "Why fight at all?"[22] Foucault's radical genealogy cannot come to grips with the desire to escape the tentacles of power. Foucault, as we will see, does attempt to address the self-undermining nature of his genealogy of power but succeeds only at the cost of undermining its specific radicality. I will return to this crucial issue in the final two chapters. For the moment, I must turn to examine Derrida's approach to the question of the origin of social difference.

THE SURPLUS OF THE WORD

We have seen that Derrida's work has much to say about the relationship between philosophy and the structure of history and society. Yet if one is to fully grasp the implications of deconstruction vis-à-vis the question of the relationship between identity and difference a detour is necessary. The road leads us away from concrete social analysis into Derrida's deconstructive reading of classical metaphysics, which, as we have seen, he takes to be at the heart of our world's fear of difference. The analysis must begin by examining Derrida's arguments concerning the "other" of metaphysics, the unbounded meaning-generating capacity of writing. While Derrida operates from a different perspective than Foucault and Lyotard, we will see that at the end of the day his deconstruction too rejects the argument that social differences are grounded in a core human nature.

The deconstruction of the opposition between the natural (as foundation and limit) and the social (the artificial, mutable) is at the core of deconstruction. As John Caputo notes, "the very meaning of deconstruction is to show that things – texts, institutions, traditions, societies – do not have determinable meanings or missions."[23] To understand why they do not have ultimately definable meanings, however, we have to examine the way in which metaphysics structures its content according to certain binary oppositions. One of the key oppositions is, according to Derrida, the pair natural/social. Whether by deriving the structure of society from first principles of the universe or the material nature of human being, metaphysical thinking, driven by the anxiety to master unmanageable elements, always aims at limiting the play of the social differences by deducing them from some natural cause. The opposition "between *physis/nomos* [nature/law], *physis/techne* [nature/art]" has served a dual purpose throughout Western history. This opposition is used both to "derive historicity; and, paradoxically, not to recognize the rights of history."[24] The rights of history amount to the right to difference. That is, human society viewed outside of metaphysical schemas presents us with an astounding diversity or peoples, practices, and values. By deriving those differences from a theory of underlying human nature, the metaphysical approach provides us with an explanation of those differences (derives historicity), but at the cost of negating their being as differences (denies the rights of history).

Derrida, however, does not deconstruct the unity of metaphysical history by counterposing it to the empirical diversity of histories (as, in some sense, Lyotard and Foucault both do). Instead, Derrida works at a deeper level, counterposing the logic of signification to the logic of metaphysics. Derrida believes that language at once makes metaphysics possible and impossible. There is no metaphysics without concepts, and there are no concepts without language. However, there are no concepts in the metaphysical sense of the term (universal ideas whose meaning is singular and invariant), precisely because they have meaning only within chains of signification. Since every concept must be named by a word and since words derive their meaning from their position in a signifying chain and not by relation to the essence of an object, meaning is always variable. If that is true, then the binary oppositions upon which metaphysics depends for its coherence and upon which, by extension, its understanding of society and history depend are impossible. Those oppositions, like nature/society, are meaningful only if both terms have a discrete and fixed meaning. But what they mean can change, depending on the context in which they are used. The production of meaning thus always depends upon what Derrida calls *différance*. We must understand the meaning of this neologism if we are to fully appreciate the meaning of his deconstruction of metaphysics.

To begin, we must understand the relationship between human consciousness and linguistic signs. As we have seen, classical metaphysics understands signs as copies of mental acts or contents whose meaning depends upon the concept that they name. This explanation of meaning, however, ignores the dependence of signs on an underlying system of repetition. As Derrida explains, "when in fact I effectively use words, and whether or not I do it for communicative ends ... I must from the outset operate (within) a structure of repetition whose basic element can only be representative. A sign is never an event, if by event we mean an irreplaceable and irreversible empirical particular ... a purely idiomatic sign would not be a sign."[25] If a sign were the "name" of unique mental content, it would have no meaning, because no one else would be able to recognize the sign as a unit of meaning. A sign has meaning only because it can be exchanged for other signs, and it can be exchanged for other signs only because the users of signs, human beings, recognize the signs employed to disseminate meaning. A unique sign would be unrecognizable and hence would not be a sign.

The iterability of signs has two consequences. First of all, it shifts primacy from the human consciousness that uses signs to the structure or system according to which signs circulate. That is, signs do not have meaning because some human intelligence "intends" them to mean something but because they have an assigned value within a system of meaning. If truth can be made present only through signifying and if signification depends upon the system of signs, then truth does not depend upon either human consciousness or the structure of the world but on the dynamics of the sign system according to which signs circulate.

If this were the case, however, then the metaphysics of presence, dependent as it is upon a conception of truth in which the essence will be *immediately* present to subjective rationality, would be impossible. Signs, as will become clear, have as their "essence" the function of pointing beyond themselves to another sign. Thus, the metaphysical adventure has played itself out through ongoing attempts to eliminate signs. The philosophy of presence "eliminates signs by making them derivative; it annuls reproduction and representation by making signs a modification of a simple presence. But because it is just such a philosophy – which is in fact the philosophy and history of the West – which has so constituted and established the very concept of signs, the sign is from the very origin marked by this will to derivation or effacement. Thus, to restore the original and non-derivative character of signs is ... to eliminate a concept of signs whose whole history and meaning belong to the adventure of the metaphysics of presence."[26] It is just such a restoration that Derrida aims to carry out. If, as he indicates above, the philosophy and the history of the West may be considered as an ongoing effort to efface the nonderivative nature of signs, then the deconstruction of metaphysics will have far-reaching consequences for all forms of theorizing and action. To grasp these effects, it is essential to examine the second consequence of the iterability of signs, which is that it disrupts the metaphysical quest for unchanging meanings. Signs do not just repeat themselves; they repeat themselves differently, endlessly differing in meaning each time they come into play. This mutability of meaning is what Derrida tries to convey with his neologism *différance*.

The "essence" of a sign is to point beyond itself to the object or substance that will fulfil the meaning of the sign. However, when one follows this journey, one arrives not at an unmediated object, not at a clear intuition of substance but simply at another sign. For Derrida, "from the very moment there is meaning there is nothing but signs. We think only in signs. Which amounts to ruining the notion of sign at the very moment when, as in Nietzsche, its exigency is recognized in the absoluteness of its right. One could call play the absence of the transcendental signified as the limitlessness of play, that is, the destruction of onto-theology and the metaphysics of presence."[27] The metaphysics of presence, recall, demanded that meaning ultimately be anchored in a stable, unchanging reality. If play is limitless, then this foundation is lacking, and the metaphysics of presence is destroyed. Because totalizing social theory depended upon a centre that limited play, to negate the metaphysics of presence by bringing the limitless play of signs to the forefront is to undermine all the centres that managed play within totalized social theory. Any basis that one may assign to the social may be undone through a deconstruction that illuminates that the basis is, in fact, a signifier, one that therefore is not immediately natural but, rather, semiotic and therefore capable of unbounded variation.

The deconstructive movement of signification is conveyed through Derrida's neologism *différance*. The word combines the two senses of the Latin verb *differer* – to differ and to defer in time.[28] *Différance* is not a concept, according to Derrida, not a universal mental representation of the process it illuminates, but rather an attempt to express the differing/deferring movement of signs themselves. Thus, when one signifies, one puts in play the signs that one believes will express one's meaning. There is thus a two-fold temporal element involved in signification. One strand leads back in time towards one's intention, and the other leads forward to the object that, as the referent of the intention, will fulfil one's intention if it is successfully pointed out. If one examines these termini, however, one finds that each is also a sign that points beyond itself. Each sign differs from the sign that is supposed to express the meaning of the first, and the whole process is marked by ongoing temporal deferral in which "the signified concept is never present in and of itself, in a sufficient presence that would refer only to itself. Essentially and lawfully, every concept is inscribed in a chain or in a system within which it refers to the other, to other concepts by means of the systematic play of differences.

Such a play, *différance,* is thus no longer simply a concept but rather the possibility of conceptuality, of a conceptual process or system in general.[29] It is the possibility of conceptuality in general because *différance* is the gap, the absence of presence that compels one to signify in the first place. One signifies when one does not have the truth of the matter in hand. This applies equally to metaphysical speculation and scientific inquiry. One desires to know the foundation of things and how they work; thus one begins to produce signs. One begins this production, however, upon a basis established by other signs, and the signs one produces enter into play and acquire unintended meanings because it is of the character of signs to always differ from their intended meaning. The signs one requires to fulfil one's desire would need to be transcendental, beyond the reach of play. This no sign can be, because all signs express an absence, not a presence: "The sign is usually said to be put in the place of the thing itself, the present thing, 'thing' here standing equally for meaning or referent. The sign represents the present in its absence. It takes the place of the present. When we cannot grasp or show the thing ... we signify, we go through the detour of the sign ... The sign ... is deferred presence."[30] This deferral is essentially unbounded because all signs are iterable, but in ever different contexts and therefore always different in meaning and devoid of the essential identity required of a universal concept.

This movement of *différance* is intimately connected with Derrida's central aim – the overturning of unified accounts of history and society. It may easily be perceived, by entailment, what will happen to all purportedly "natural" grounds of social practice. For any such ground must be signified. The signs thus employed must point back towards the prior signs that motivated them, and these in turn will flow from a definite, particular, and variable context. Any "natural" basis is thus always already "cultural" insofar as the natural basis must be constituted through signs and proceed from the meanings those signs have at a given time. This is the fundamental implication of Derrida's oft-quoted remark that "There is nothing outside of the text."[31] This does not mean that everything should be considered like a book or that society is composed of mere words, quite the contrary. The book is a metaphor for fixed, enclosed meaning. The *text*, on the other hand, points towards a complex interweaving of "texts" – lives, practices, institutions and forces – of which society is composed.[32]

In order to emphasize this complexity and to obviate the charges of a crude linguistic determinism, Derrida later supplanted "text" with "context." Statements acquire their meaning only within a fabric of relations that include the speaker, the addressee, the place, the time, the institutional setting, and the general social and political environment. However, while meaning must always be taken in context, the limits of context are always open. There is no essential, appropriate context that would distinguish proper from parasitical or metaphorical meaning. He argues that "a context is never absolutely determinable ... its determination is never certain or saturated."[33] New contexts can always arise, new meanings can always be generated, and there are no noncontextual criteria that would permit the determination of the true context in which to interpret a statement, a practice, or a program.

The critical upshot of this is that social theory cannot be founded upon an ontology with universal pretensions, since the contextuality of existent things rules out any final reading of their underlying nature. Derrida's critique of metaphysics is just as much a critique of social theory, and especially radical social theory, because it has traditionally attempted to ground its political prescriptions in a theory of the nature of things (ontology). Derrida thus says of Marxism that its key problem is that "Marx continues to ground his critique ... on an ontology."[34] While Marxism was a valuable criticism, it remains "pre-deconstructive," since it does not question at a radical level presence and objectivity. Derrida, however, believes he has opened up a more radical level of critique insofar as he goes beyond the naive naturalism inherent in previous attempts to criticize society. The overriding aim of deconstruction is thus not mere interpretation but social change. He writes that "if there is nothing beyond the text, in this new sense, then that leaves room for the most open type of political... practices and pragmatics."[35] These implications will be considered in the final chapter of part 1, but already there is a certain tension evident that should be noted.

The tension is this. Deconstructive critique gains its critical orientation from an appreciation of the open-ended manner in which meanings are generated. It deconstructs the metaphysics of presence or logocentrism in order to release the subjugated meanings that logocentrism tries to suppress. There are political stakes here, because these meanings are not disembodied words but rather the thoughts, beliefs, and actions of people marginalised and suppressed by the ruling powers of Western society. However, if these differences of belief, thought, and action are the product of signifying chains and *différance* positioning people in different ways, then the suppression of these differences cannot be any crime against the people themselves, since what is suppressed is not essentially related to them or their capacities. Hence, Derrida faces the same double bind as Lyotard and Foucault. His work both brings to light the oppressive and exclusionary systems of the modern world and deconstructs the very grounds necessary for coherently criticising them.

Let us stop here and spell out the underlying identity between the three positions under consideration. In each case the critique of totalized social theory entails the elimination of binding universal criteria in the evaluation of political systems. Whether one begins from language-games, discursively constituted regimes of power/knowledge, or the endless variety of contexts, the conclusion is the same – fixed norms are not deducible from a shared human nature, because there is no human nature. What modern theory identifies as human nature is in reality but a nodal point in theories subject to the contextual variability of meaning and power. The idea of human nature is not therefore the undeconstructible, solid foundation it is supposed to be. As a result of the lack of stable foundations for theory, one is left to judge political systems from definite perspectives that are not themselves reducible to an overweening, authoritative perspective. Before examining the concrete political implications of this position, it is important to tie the conclusions of chapters 1 and 2 together.

In chapter 1 I sketched out the basic arguments made against the logic of identity thinking. The present section has concentrated on the positive side of the deconstruction of identity thinking, the postmodern explanation of the origin and nature of social differences. Two essential points of convergence on the subject of the "nature" of the social have emerged in this chapter. The first is that human society and the differences that characterise it are not grounded in a shared set of defining needs, interests, and capacities. Nor is there is any essential governing dynamic to society that, if known, would permit a complete grasp of each specific element of society. The second point claims that the various institutions, practices, and discourses constitutive of society produce needs, interests, and capacities and that these vary across historical time and social space. Thus, human being has no underlying nature; it does not create itself at ever higher levels of organization and unity but is, rather, created by language, power, and the institutional apparatus of society. At this point postmodern criticism faces the double bind we have noted. It charges modern theory with the crime of attempting to understand society and coordinate political action on the basis of a theory of *human* nature and with thereby illegitimately excluding different systems of thought, belief, and action. However, by deconstructing the idea of human nature as self-determination, postmodern critique deconstructs the normative basis that must be presupposed by any coherent criticism of exclusion, marginalization, and oppression.

In the next chapter I will examine in detail the deconstruction of the idea of human nature as subjecthood and deepen our understanding of the structure of, as well as the decisive problem faced by, postmodern radical criticism.

3 The Twilight of Subjecthood

The following chapter will be concerned with the most radical element of the philosophy, or critique of philosophy, practised by Lyotard, Foucault, and Derrida. The radicality of this postmodern critique lies not in its identification of different logics inherent in different social practices, nor in its supposition that history cannot be understood according to an essential dynamic, nor even in the claim that needs and capacities are thoroughly cultural and mutable. The radicality proper to its critique lies in its open rejection of the idea that humanity may be defined as essentially subject, as distinguished by its capacity to determine its future in line with universal interests. Postmodern criticism contends that rather than establishing the conditions for a positively free society, struggles rooted in that idea of human nature have led necessarily to the exclusion and oppression of minority differences. This chapter will concentrate focus upon this asserted link between essentialist ideas of subjecthood and exclusionary, even totalitarian politics.

THE SPOKEN SELF

As was noted in chapter 1, Lyotard claims that modern thought is defined by its metanarrative structure. That is, modern theory legitimates itself by claiming to be the intellectual expression of the universal historical mission of humanity. Linking together all the different metadiscourses characteristic of modernity is the idea of emancipation. He argues that "the thought and action of the nineteenth and twentieth centuries are governed by an Idea (I am using Idea in its Kantian sense). That idea is the idea of emancipation. What we call philosophies of history, the great narratives by means of which we attempt to order the multitude of events, certainly argue this idea in very different ways ... the *Aufklarer* narrative of emancipation from ignorance and servitude thanks to knowledge and egalitarianism; the speculative narrative of the realization of the universal idea through the dialectic of the concrete; the Marxist narrative of emancipation from exploitation and alienation through the socialization of labour ... These various narratives provide grounds for contention ... But they all situate the data supplied by events within the course of history whose end, even if it is out of reach, is called freedom."[1] According to Lyotard, emancipation interpreted as an Idea of the Kantian form is thus a goal whose function it is to organize, in teleological fashion, the otherwise disorganized political strategies operative at a given time. Just as Reason in Kant gives Ideas to the Understanding (of, for example, a spontaneous causality, or a Supreme Being) that organize and give overall coherence to the realm of independent empirical laws, so too does emancipation organize the different political beliefs of modern thought. All systems of modern thought look to a future in which humanity will be governed by external laws that correspond to its inner, essential nature.

Lyotard unambiguously rejects this image of humanity. The Idea of emancipation is in reality an illusion, a ghost, because it presupposes an essentialist understanding of human subjecthood. Only if at some real level humanity was constitutive of the reality that it inhabited could emancipation be viewed as the species' essential goal. Only if there was a real capacity for self-determination, present but not fulfilled in given societies, would the idea of emancipation make sense. This is an understanding of humanity that Lyotard dismantles. The modern subject has collapsed under the combined weight of failure and opposition from those who have been excluded by its standard definition. If it is now the case that, "the history of emancipation is no longer credible," then it follows that "the status of the 'we' which asks the question [can we still find universal grounds for emancipation] must also be reviewed. It seems that it is condemned (but only in the eyes of modernity is it a condemnation) to remain particular ... and to exclude a lot of third parties ... it must either mourn for unanimity and find another mode of thinking and acting, or be plunged into melancholia by the loss of an 'object' (or the impossibility of a subject): free humanity."[2] Particularity is only a condemnation from the modernist perspective, because modernity was defined by a confusion between the white, male, Western "we" and the universal interests of humanity. The postmodern perspective welcomes this development insofar as a recognition of particularity on the part of all parties is the necessary condition of opening up new possibilities for thought and action. Whatever this new mode of action turns out to be – and Lyotard does not settle very long on any one mode – it must make do without legitimating itself by appeal to a self-determining capacity of humanity. Instead, politics must begin from all the different social positions where selves are situated. In this manner, politics can both develop creative strategies that correspond to changed circumstances and avoid the bloody errors of the past.

This last point is crucial, because Lyotard argues that not only is the essentialist conception of subjecthood obsolete, it has in fact been at the basis of the great political crimes of the twentieth century. Lyotard catalogues these in detail: "Without wishing to decide immediately whether we are dealing with facts or signs, it seems difficult to refute the available evidence of the defaillancy of the modern subject. No matter which genre it makes hegemonic, the very basis of each of the great narratives of emancipation has ... been invalidated over the past 50 years. 'All that is real is rational, all that is rational is real.' 'Auschwitz' refutes speculative doctrine ... 'All that is proletarian is communist, all that is communist is proletarian.' Berlin, 1953, Budapest 1956 ... refutes the doctrine of historical materialism."[3] Lyotard continues on with examples that indicate the failure of the liberal and capitalist metanarratives as well, but the implication of his point is sufficiently clear – humanity has not, and cannot, make itself positively free, and attempts to do so on its behalf result in the opposite of what was intended. This ironic outcome is the case because the modern understanding of freedom is, at root, according to Lyotard, an idea not of freedom but of mastery. The reduction of subjecthood to linguistically constituted subject-positions is thus a critique of the idea of mastery that Lyotard finds at the basis of the modernist understanding of humanity.

Here again he has recourse to general linguistic considerations. Lyotard relates the idea of humanity as subject to the grammatical position of first-person subject. According to Lyotard, the first-person subject-position in a sentence not only denotes who or what the sentence concerns but also who or what regulates the meaning. The subject is the one who intends, who gives birth to, and who controls (or tries to control) the meaning of the statement. Thus, "the position of the first person (the Subject) is in fact marked as being that of the mastery of speech meaning; let the people have a political voice, the workers a social voice."[4] As his examples illustrate, the political analogue of the first-person is mass-based struggle for control over the social environment. Just as meaning is determined by nonsubjective grammatical rules, so too history is governed by a plurality of rules not amenable to democratic or any social control. Refusal to recognize the grammatical point leads to dogmatic attempts at controlling meaning. Refusal to recognize the political analogue leads to terroristic, i.e., exclusivist, political practices. Lyotard's linguistic analysis of the social is designed to rupture the link he asserts between speech and mastery, politics and terror.

As we noted in chapter 2, Lyotard moves increasingly towards an account of language as a productive force that determines and situates speakers. As a dispersed plurality of phrase regimens, language is not amenable to human control. Humans utilize language in different contexts to pursue different ends, but both the contexts and the ends are functions of the rules governing the linkage of phrases, not the rational entailments of essential human interests and capacities. The stakes of this argument, Lyotard contends in the opening of *The Differend*, are "to refute the prejudice anchored in the reader by centuries of humanism and of 'human sciences' that there is 'man,' that there is 'language,' that the former makes use of the latter for his own ends, and that if he does not succeed in attaining these ends, it is for want of good control over language 'by means' of a 'better' language."[5] As we have seen, this prejudice is to be overcome by a pragmatic, linguistic analysis of the social that reveals that human subjects are the product of different language-games, or, as he puts it in this text, phrase regimens. Because humans must speak in order to express what they are, they enter into games where they do not control the rules. There is no autonomy or freedom,, but only heteronomy and determination. There is no escaping this trap, since the only alternative is silence, but this too, according to Lyotard, is a phrase.

Once the humanist prejudice has been overcome, a transformation is possible, an inversion whereby the creative power of language becomes manifest. Humans are dispersed fragments situated by dispersed phrase regimens. The latter carry with them their own instruction for use. Human action amounts to playing with the fragments, but always in a fashion determined by rules immanent to the phrases themselves, because "the phrases that happen are 'awaited,' not by conscious or unconscious 'subjects' who would anticipate them." Instead, phrases "carry their own 'sets of directions' along with them ... they carry instructions as to the end pursued through them."[6] As there are differends (gaps that signify the absence of a mediating principle which could adjudicate equally legitimate claims) separating different phrase regimens from one another, science from morality, one political strategy from another, it follows that there are no valid universal criteria that could define the essential qualities of subjecthood, i.e., produce a collective subject – "humanity" – and, on that basis, ground a global project for a free and rational society. If such a strategy were to be truly human it would require access to an essence that unites the disparate cultures of the globe. The discovery of such an essence would require that one ignore the differends separating one group from the next. The modern understanding of politics sought authorization from a universal interpretation of history, but there are differing interpretations of history, and for Lyotard, as was noted in the previous section, "one side's legitimacy does not entail the other side's lack of legitimacy."

Lyotard believes that if modern, global interpretations of history are abandoned, then respect for the discrete nature of social differences becomes possible. Respect for social differences, in turn, encourages modes of practice that rule out mastery, control, and authoritarianism. From this respect for difference in general Lyotard has attempted to formulate a postmodern justice, and it is this attempt that marks his work as a critique of modernity and not simply a catalogue of its problems. We will explore his postmodern theory of justice in the next chapter. The points that must be kept in mind from this section are that Lyotard equates the modern understanding of subjecthood with totalitarian mastery and that the key to escaping from totalitarian mastery is the elimination of the modern understanding of subjecthood from the basis of political theory and practice. Let us now turn to the the complex history of Foucault's engagement with the problem of subjecthood.

THE DISAPPEARANCE OF "MAN"

Foucault is not only a harsh critic of the notion of subjecthood but also a thinker who, towards the end of his career, refocused attention on the self-creative capacity of the human subject.[7] The present section will focus upon Foucault's critique of subjecthood and the values of self-determination and autonomy that he feels are entailed by that notion. The subsequent section will introduce his rehabilitated notions of subjecthood, autonomy, and power.

Until the "turn" occasioned by his historical analysis of Greek, Roman, and early Christian ethical practices, Foucault was perhaps the most astringent and influential critic of the modernist account of subjecthood.[8] He rejected subjecthood on both methodological and political grounds. As in Lyotard's argument, a crucial link is established between the modernist notion of subjecthood and the desire for mastery and control. During his early career Foucault was driven by the hope of a new day in which a different experience of ourselves, an experience beyond the confines of rational self-identity and collective self-determination, would become possible. Reflecting on his early influences, he wrote that "my encounter with Bataille, Blanchot, and, through them, my reading of Nietzsche [represented for me] an invitation to call into question the category of the 'subject,' its primacy and its originating function. And then, the conviction that an operation of this kind would not make any sense if it had been confined to speculation: to call the subject into question had to mean to live it in an experience that might be its real destruction or dissociation, its explosion or upheaval into something radically 'other.'"[9] In order to access this other in a radical way, Foucault first inquired into the realm of the mad, i.e., those whose experience of the world went well beyond the paradigms of rational thought. In the life of the insane Foucault sought out a "limit-experience," an experience that would "gather the maximum amount of intensity and impossibility at the same time."[10] If this experience could be had, it would, Foucault believed, burst the seams of the rational subject. It is here that he first became fascinated by the practices of transgression, of going beyond prescribed limits, that are central to his politics even after he moves away from his focus on the insane.

Foucault's initial assault upon subjecthood proceeds along two interconnected paths. He aims to disclose both that the self-determining capacity central to the concept of subjecthood is a historically specific posit of anonymous rules governing the formulation of discourse in the modern period and that it is undermined in general by the nonsubjective character of those rules. Given that humanity expresses its purportedly self-creative capacity only by speaking and acting and given that the rules governing speaking and acting are irreducible either to individual intentions or collective projects, Foucault concludes that any capacity for self-determination is a chimera – and a dangerous one at that.

According to Foucault's archaeology of modernity, this period is characterized by the epistemic and historical sovereignty of the subject. That is, the rules defining rational and scientific argument in the period beginning in the late eighteenth century obligated the theorist to ground knowledge in some capacity inhering in the subject. Thus, for Kant the structure of subjective understanding made knowledge of nature possible. For Hegel history was the product of the struggle between self-consciousnesses for understanding and mutual recognition. For Marx human labour was the basis of the historical world and economic value. In each case an active, self-determining essence of human being was at work as the motor of the process. According to Foucault, this self-determining essence did not preexist modernity and is therefore not definitive of a universal human nature. He argues bluntly that "before the end of the eighteenth century, *man* [*sic*] did not exist ... he is a quite recent creature, which the *demiurge of knowledge fabricated with its own hand* less than two hundred years ago" (emphasis added).[11] Kant, Hegel, and Marx did not make any fundamental advances in the understanding of human knowledge and history. What they did was draw valid inferences on the basis of evidence already structured by those unconscious rules that organized knowledge in their period. Their conclusions, according to Foucault, are "truth-effects" relative to the *episteme* in which they worked.

Thus, it is wrong to view as epistemologically or politically progressive the sovereignty attributed to subjecthood in the modern period. Whether construed individually, as in Kant, or collectively, as in Hegel and Marx, the self-certainty of the rational subject, the self-determining capacity of the labouring subject, or the self-creative character of the species as a whole were made possible as ideas by the rules of the epoch, and they must disappear when those rules change. Foucault replaces the sovereign subject with discursively constituted subject positions. What we discovered in the previous chapter with regard to the relationship between sciences and the rules of their formation also holds with regard to subjects. Subjects are in fact subject positions in a discursive practice and thus determined by the rules that structure the discourse. These rules "should not be confused with the expressive operation by which an individual formulates an idea [or] desire." On the contrary, a discursive practice is "a body of anonymous, historical rules, always determined in the time and space that have defined a given period, and for a given social ... area, the conditions of the operation of the enunciative function."[12] Thus, in the archaeological decentering of the subject the rules governing discursive practice determine and situate the subject. These rules are not the conscious product of the efforts of the human species, and they cannot, as a consequence, ever be brought under democratic social control.

The decentering of the subject that this position entails proceeds by means of an inversion, not a supersession, of the modernist relationship between subject and object. For Kant, through Hegel to Marx and beyond that to phenomenology, the object has been made dependent upon the subject. That is, objects are understood as external to, but not independent of, the theoretical and practical activity of human beings. The philosophical and political goals of modernity are summed up in the slogan "overcome the duality of subject and object." In its most politically sophisticated expression, Marxism, overcoming this duality required the construction of a society in which productive activity returns from alienation and manifests itself as what it essentially is, a historically developed capacity for self-creation. The duality of subject and object is overcome, because the objective world is no longer an external limitation upon action but rather the collective product of the citizens of that society, and it is recognized as such. The overcoming of the duality of subject and object is identical to positive freedom. People in a positively free society are not limited by the institutions and productive systems of their society, because both are the outcome of the labour and democratic deliberations of the citizens. The collective product of their labour produces the substance upon which individuals draw for their self-creative activity. There are of course limitations here, but the limitations are immanent to the talents and capacities of the individuals and not imposed from without by class differences. What I can do in such a state is not limited by systematically enforced power imbalances but only by what I, as this person with these talents, can do.

For Foucault, on the other hand, rather than an object-constituting subjectivity there is a subject-constituting objectivity (discursivity). Since Foucault inverts the order of precedence between subject and object, it follows that he must also abandon the idea of positive freedom as self-creation that the priority of subject over object privileged. As we know, Foucault understands society and history as a plurality of dispersed networks of power, institutions, and events in which numerous and distinct subject-positions are determined by those networks of power. Thus, the light begins to dim for the self-determining subject, and on the horizon appears the polychromatic postmodern dawn. In prophetic voice Foucault announces the death of the subject: "In the rumbling which shakes today, perhaps we have to recognize the birth of a world in which the subject is not one, but split, is not sovereign, but dependent, is not an absolute origin, but a function ceaselessly modified."[13] The self-determining capacity of humanity is fractured by this rumbling into the various discursive formations in which humans are variously inserted. Michael Sprinker notes incisively that Foucault's argument aims to make "clear that the apparent self-constitution of the human subject in history is illusory, since all the various discourses, including the discourse of man as historical subject and producer of discourse itself, are produced by language, which has a life, a being, a power of production of its own."[14] Thus, not only is the subject relative to the rules of the modern *episteme;* the very rules that make it possible also make its essential function as the sovereign creator of its own conditions of existence impossible.

The modern period structured discourse such that all knowledge appeared to be grounded in some subjective capacity. The subjective grounding of determinate modes of objectivity has a paradoxical effect, according to Foucault. The positing of the subject as the ground of knowledge is simultaneously the positing of the subject as an object of knowledge. That is, it becomes possible to ask what it is about "man" that allows it to know nature and to create history. On this basis develop the human sciences that take humanity as their object. In being thus transformed into an object, humanity discovers that where its freedom should be there are only determined rules and limitations. Speech follows rules, labour is determined by the laws of the market, and behaviour is governed by rules immanent to the biological organism. Foucault asks, "Will the history of man ever be more than a sort of common modulation of changes in the conditions of life (climate, soil fertility, methods of agriculture, exploitation of wealth), of transformations in the economy (and consequently in society and its institutions), and of the successive forms of usage of language?" If our history is not more than the sum total of objective events, then it follows, Foucault adds, that "man is not himself historical: since time comes to him from somewhere else, he constitutes himself as a subject of history only by the superimposition of the history of beings, the history of things, and the history of words."[15] Thus, Foucault concludes that because subjecthood has no content apart from its objectification and because these objectifications are determined by rules that do not originate with subjecthood and because these rules are historically variable, subjecthood cannot be a transhistorical world-constituting agency. There is no subject of history. "History has no 'meaning.'"[16] There are no criteria to which one could appeal in an effort to judge whether or not we have become more or less rational or more or less free.

The shift to genealogy and the analysis of power relations does not initially alter anything fundamental in this argument. If anything, genealogy is an intensification of the decentring of the subject, for now Foucault argues that the rules governing discursive practices are one and all enmeshed with ever-circulating networks of power. The analysis of power relations is still guided by the idea that "one has to dispense with the constituent subject, to get rid of the subject itself ... to arrive at an analysis which can account for the constitution of the subject within an historical framework."[17]

What changes in Foucault's genealogies is that a new critical voice emerges. The subject is no longer simply the posit of anonymous rules but, rather, the deliberate production of the disciplinary apparatus (prisons, schools, etc.) that structures the social formation. This production extends beyond the production of individuals as determinate objects of knowledge. Power constructs individuals to the very depths of their being. Here it is appropriate to recall Peter Dews' comment cited previously, in which he notes that for Foucault "subjectification" as the process of normalization is a necessary precursor to subjection. In the prison and the factory, through various practices of confession and self-examination, people are constituted so as to believe in an inner truth definitive of human being. Foucault argues that "the obligation to confess is now relayed through so many different points, is so deeply ingrained in us, that we no longer perceive it as an effect of power that constrains us; on the contrary, it seems to us that truth, lodged in our most secret nature, 'demands' only to surface."[18] This practice goes back to the Christian confession of the Middle Ages and has an obvious modern counterpart in psychoanalysis.

There is more at stake here, however, than whether or not there is an inner truth to individuals. Foucault's argument entails the conclusion that there is no capacity distinct from objective power relations definitive of human beings. As the quotation above illustrates, the very thought that one is more than what one is made to be by power is itself an effect of power. Subjecthood cannot therefore be the ground from which a free society could be constructed. A society of self-determining beings is neither possible nor desirable. The very idea of subjecthood is rather a constraining production of the apparatus of power itself. He contends that the word subject has two meanings: "subject to someone else's control or dependence, and tied to his own identity by a conscience or a self-knowledge. Both meanings suggest a form of power which subjugates and makes subject to."[19] It follows from Foucault's argument that there is no essential depth to human being; there are no underlying human capacities that could be distorted or alienated or repressed. Commenting clearly on this implication, David Ingram notes that "Foucault does not hesitate to draw what, for a critical theorist, appears to be a damning conclusion: if power insinuates itself into the very discipline constitutive of self-identity, then it is impossible to know rationally one's true humanity independently of power's distorting effects ... there is no 'false consciousness' but only blindness to the irrecusable historicity, conditionality, and otherness of one's own subjectivity."[20] It is not that it is impossible to know one's true humanity, but rather that there is no true humanity to be found beyond the operations of power that constitute us.

For Foucault the decentring of subjecthood seems a positive development in that it creates hope for a politics beyond the dangers of modern totalizations. Like Lyotard, Foucault argues that at the root of the worst totalitarian excesses there lies the figure of humanity as subjecthood. He claims that "we know from experience that the claim to escape from the system of contemporary society so as to produce the overall programs of another society, of another way of thinking, another culture, another vision of the world, has led only to the return of the most dangerous traditions."[21] This point is made even more forcefully in Foucault's review of André Glucksman's *Les Maîtres Penseurs*. Glucksman argued that the very notion of positive freedom, understood to mean collective self-determination, leads necessarily to totalitarianism. Sounding surprisingly like the conservative philosophers Karl Popper, Isaiah Berlin, and Friedrich Hayek, Glucksman asserts an essential identity between Stalinism and Nazism. Foucault, even more surprisingly given his radical intentions, welcomes Glucksman's argument. He unambiguously links Stalinist terror to the attempt to ground political philosophy in objective truth: "With the Gulag, one did not see the consequences of an unfortunate error but the effect of the "truest" political theories."[22] It was Marxism's "scientific" status, its belief in laws of history that could be known and manipulated to serve collective ends, that caused Stalinism. The argument that Foucault supports contends that if there really were such laws, and if they really could be bent to universal purposes and if the fulfilment of these purposes would finally resolve the contradictions of human history, then those who know them would be justified in taking any measures to bring that situation to pass. The Gulag follows necessarily from this argument because those who stand in the way of the construction of socialism are not just enemies of the state but enemies of humanity. Eliminating them is thus both necessary and justified by the end their elimination will facilitate. The same logic underlay Nazism. Although it took a much more circumscribed view of who was "human," it nevertheless justified the extermination of others by appeal to their inhuman nature. It is a desire to avoid such monstrous crimes that motivates Foucault to abandon "the programs for a new man that the worst political systems have repeated throughout the twentieth century."[23]

The practical political consequences of Foucault's critique of subjecthood will be pursued in the next chapter. The points to keep in mind as we move to examine Derrida's deconstruction of the idea of subjecthood is that Foucault, like Lyotard, argues that the modern idea of subjecthood is in reality the product of more fundamental social processes and that, insofar as the idea has been employed as the basis for unified political struggle, it is the reason why those struggles have tended to result in totalitarian outcomes. As we will now see, Derrida's assault upon the idea of subjecthood reaches nearly identical conclusions.

THE SUBJECT AS A FUNCTION OF LANGUAGE

Like Foucault, Derrida's critique of the notion of subjecthood starts with the subject as the basis of knowledge and ends with a critique of political programs rooted in an essentialist understanding of the human being. The problem with the epistemological subject, as we noted in the preceding chapter, was that it rested upon an exclusion of the primacy of the signifier. If one examines this exclusion critically one discovers signifiers where the originary acts of consciousness should be. Clear and distinct ideas (Descartes), Categories of the Understanding (Kant), or Hegelian Ideas are one and all signs. As such they play according to their own rules. Signs are primary, consciousness and self-consciousness are secondary effects of linguistic operations. Language, Derrida argues, "is not a function of the speaking subject. This implies that the subject (in its identity with itself ... its self-consciousness) is inscribed in language, is a 'function' of language, becomes a *speaking* subject only by making its speech conform – even in so-called 'creation' or in so-called 'transgression' – to the system of the rules of language as a system of differences, or at very least ... to the general law of *différance*."[24] The general law of *différance* holds that meaning is never present, since it must be given through signs, the function of which is to signify the absence of that which should be present. Thus, the subject – rational, self-identical, and self-creative – insofar as it can become conscious of itself only through signifying activity, can never bring itself to presence and thus cannot actually be the unified, rational, self-creative being it is said to be by modern thought.

There is thus no question of any essential core definitive of human being. "The subject is always the posit of external forces," Bill Martin, commenting on Derrida, unequivocally maintains.[25] This does not mean, however, that there is no subject. As in Lyotard and Foucault, there are subject-positions or functions, but they do not owe their existence to a defining subjecthood. "To deconstruct the subject," Derrida states, "does not mean to deny its existence." There are subjects, "operations" or "effects" of subjectivity. However, "to acknowledge this does not mean ... that the subject is what it says it is."[26] Indeed, whatever the subject says, it is will necessarily be undermined by the ongoing dissemination of new meanings. As Marian Hobson comments, "the subject is not a unit entity, an in-dividual [sic] in the literal sense of undivided. It is the scene of intersections, of complex competing forces, in a theatre which is that of language."[27] All attempts to ground and define human being can only function as arbitrary restrictions upon this play.

Derrida thus objects to the abstract nature of the modern conception of the epistemological subject, its separation from the content and contexts in which it is necessarily involved in concrete acts of knowing. While the best modern thinkers (Hegel and Marx are especially noteworthy in this regard) also criticized abstract conceptions of self-identity, they nevertheless maintained an essential link with the philosophy of identity insofar as both conceived humanity as defined by a self-creative capacity. Thus, their criticisms do not escape Derrida's deconstructive gaze. In fact, since Hegel and Marx and those who followed in their wake understood self-identity in a worldly sense as the real unity of human beings in a positively free society, their work is most in need of deconstruction. When the struggle for self-identity is understood as a struggle for a world in which all external limitations on the freedom of the subject have been overcome, then the practical dangers of identity thinking make themselves felt. The very effort displays the desire for mastery and control that is definitive of metaphysics. In the following quotation Derrida is making a general point, but it is clear that he has the politics of positive freedom closely in mind when he argues that "the rapport of self-identity is itself always a rapport of violence with the other, so that notions of property, appropriation, and self-presence so central to logocentric metaphysics are essentially dependent upon an oppositional relationship with otherness."[28]

It matters not whether the identity here is individual or collective. Indeed, the passage carries more critical force if the identity is a shared human identity. The desire of metaphysics to master the real, a peculiarly Western desire, plays itself out as the forcible exclusion of concrete others.

Thus, once again one finds the understanding of humanity as self-determining equated with the ground of totalitarianism. Once again the idea of subjecthood, reliant as it is upon the desire to master the forces that determine it, gives rise to a politics of authority and domination. In reference to the uniqueness of the event of Stalinism, Derrida argues that, "Such an event ... in the philosophico-scientific form claiming to break with myth, religion ... has been bound, for the first time and inseparably, to worldwide forms of social organization (a party with a universal vocation, a labour movement, a confederation of states, and so forth) ... Whatever one may think of this event, of the sometimes terrifying failure of what was thus begun, of the techno-economic or ecological disasters and the totalitarian perversions to which it gave place (perversions that some have been saying for a long time are precisely not perversions ... but the necessary deployment of an essential logic present at birth ...) this unique attempt took place."[29] The logic that led to these disasters is the logic of identity thinking applied in the political realm. Derrida, like Lyotard and Foucault argues here that Stalinism was no perversion of the Marxist project but in fact its necessary outcome insofar as that project was defined by the goal of revolutionising the world in accordance with a positive understanding of freedom. What Marxism understood as the attempt to realize the human essence in society Derrida understands as totalitarianism. These struggles, he writes, tried to realize "an emancipatory eschatology that should have respected the promise, the being-promise of promise."[30] The totalitarian outcome is for the notion of human essence, "the deepest wound."[31]

That is not to say, however, that the goal of emancipation plays no role in Derrida's politics. Emancipation is the promise to which he referred in the preceding quotation. That promise, however, should have been (*aurait du*) respected as a promise, i.e., kept always in front of us and not treated as a determinate program for social transformation. It is necessary, he believes, to treat the idea of emancipation as a goal to work endlessly towards, not a program to be realized by a single revolutionary act. As he writes, "It was a matter, then, of thinking another historicity – not a new history ... but another opening of eventness as historicity ... to open up access to an affirmative thinking of the messianic and emancipatory promise as promise: as promise and not as ontotheological or teleoeschatological program or design ... This is the condition of re-politicization, perhaps of another concept of the political."[32] This new politics is therefore premissed upon a repudiation of the essentialist, teleological understanding of humanity and its history, not in the name of abandoning history but in the name of an affirmative history and a respect for the openness of the future. Whereas modernist politics rooted in an essentialist understanding of the subject tries to close off historical possibility by forcing it to conform to its projects and plans, Derrida's "other" concept of politics is defined by its refusal to impose positions on the excluded groups that it supports. I will explore this other logic of political theory in the next chapter. At this point, let us take stock of what we have learned thus far.

Postmodern criticism believes that its disclosure of social complexity brings to light a crack in the edifice of modern theory through which its most fundamental problems can be perceived. In particular, it argues that the foundational understanding of human subjecthood cannot survive the postmodern analysis of social phenomena. Modern philosophy believed that humanity had essential characteristics and that if these characteristics could be isolated, then they could serve as grounds for the explanation, evaluation, and conscious transformation of historical events. In brief, history could be seen as the struggle for emancipation, and the conclusion of this struggle would arrive when a society defined by an institutional structure that confirmed and expressed the self-determining nature of human being had been created.

If, however, as the postmodern analysis claims to prove, the idea of a human essence is a historically specific and tendential hypostatisation of meaning, then two conclusions follow. One: there is no such thing as an essence that could fulfil its mandate as an essence. Although there are definitions *called* essences, they are not "real" essences, that is, they do not actually express the fundamental character of the things of which they are purportedly the essence. Two: rather than being the ground of emancipation, the function of the concept of human essence is to legitimate the exclusion of different groups and possibilities from the house of freedom. In short, the essentialist idea of human subjecthood is the ground not of emancipation but of totalitarianism. Henceforth, in an effort to minimize the oppressive practices characteristic of the West, human subjecthood must be considered as nothing more than the posit of forces external to human beings, and history understood as an ongoing dissemination of differences forever beyond the control of humanity. Thus, the positive principle of the politics inherent in the work of Lyotard, Foucault, and Derrida is that emancipatory politics must start from the idea that social differences are fundamental and take as its goal the maximization of the sites of social and cultural difference.

4 Postmodern Freedom

If it is the case that the totalitarian disasters of the modern period can be traced back to the idea of mastery inherent in the modernist concept of subjecthood, then postmodern politics, if it is to live up to its self-given radical mandate, must be scrupulous in avoiding a reinstantiation of modernist values in its politics. If postmodern thought were to simply reinterpret the values of self-determination and self-creation, then it would merely be a renovation of modern theory, and not the first light of the new dawn that we have seen it proclaim itself to be. The general stakes of a new politics are nicely outlined by Keith Pheby in his aptly named text *Interventions: Displacing the Metaphysical Subject:* "in as much as deconstruction resists entrenchment, resists being defined univocally by the dominant culture, it cannot fail to strike a transgressive posture when confronted with the hegemony of Western rationalism and its technological domination of the earth."[1] While transgressive *postures* are much in evidence, whether these can be transformed into effective checks against the forces of exclusion is less certain. There may be some truth to the linkage established between metaphysics and oppression, but the postmodern road stretching beyond metaphysics may in fact contradict the values in the name of which it undertakes its criticisms. In this chapter I will extract the core political principles of postmodern radicalism that follow from its deconstruction of the modern subject.

FRAGMENTED JUSTICE

I begin the investigation of postmodern politics by recapitulating a theme developed in the previous section. The attempt to deduce political practice from a philosophy of history is, Lyotard argues, inherently terroristic. He argues that "the social web is made up of a multitude of encounters between interlocutors caught up in different pragmatics. One must judge case by case ... I am not saying that all these positions are equivalent, far from it, but they all partake of a similar attitude toward what one could call 'rationalist terrorism' in matters of history and political decisions. That is, it is not true that a political decision can be derived from a reason in history."[2] In Lyotard's estimation terror flows from the attempt to deduce politics from a purportedly rational and universal standpoint. Any "human" project (Marxist, liberal or otherwise) can constitute itself only by the exclusion of other possibilities. The attempt to rationalize this exclusion does not differentiate these projects from an irrational, groundless terror but only makes the terror more insidious; a "humanist" terror all the more awful because sanctioned, and thus undetectable by, the dominant theories of critical political philosophy. Lyotard's efforts to escape the omnivorous rationality of modernity revolve around the defence and extension of nonuniversalizing forms of discourse. This is an essential point that runs throughout his always changing critical strategies.

In his "pagan" writings of the 1970s Lyotard opposed to rational humanism the specific practice of "small narratives." Small narratives were characteristic of all the diverse points of struggle that emerged after the Second World War. The defining trait of the new movements was, according to Lyotard, that they refused to legitimate themselves by appeal to any universal standard deduced from a philosophy of history. The groups involved in these movements, including women, gays and lesbians, and oppressed ethnic minorities, bore names that "were not listed on the official register" (n'étaient pas porté au registre officiel).[3] As he describes them, "These struggles are the struggles of minorities intending to remain minorities and to be recognized as such ... by interdicting their cultures, their *patois*, one desires to destroy their affirmative power, their 'perspective,' in the Nietzschean sense, that traces each of these struggles in a non-cumulative time."[4] Like Derrida, Lyotard is primarily concerned with an affirmative response to an otherness that summons, an otherness that is not just a step on the road to a universal reconciliation but whose being is constituted by its difference. These minority struggles do not move in an historical continuum established by a metanarrative.

They are immediate events that arise in response to particular exclusions. They manifest the distinctness of the group rather than one inflection of the universal voice of humanity. Contrary to the schemas of essentialist philosophy these small struggles seek only to make manifest particular voices and to strike immediate blows against the forces of exclusion.

If one seeks to reduce these struggles to some general historical schema, one thereby destroys their essentially affirmative character. This is so because these struggles stem from, "a different space, a different logic, a different history from the ones in which Platonism and Judaism combined have searched, and still search, under the authority of Jacobinism, Leninism, Trotskyism, Maoism, liberalism, in order to consign these spasms and thus neutralize them."[5] "Platonism and Judaism combined," i.e., universal theory, destroys the radical character of these struggles by situating them as a moment in a general historical process (the rationalism of Plato is united with the absolute normative presence of the Jewish God in universal theories – God (reason) speaks and those under its authority follow). That is, their radicality is defined by their rejection of inclusion as a meaningful value. What such struggles assert is not the desire for inclusion in a whole thought to be fundamentally just but, on the contrary, the injustice of the idea of a whole into which differences fit as parts. Thus, the very effort to understand such struggles, to comprehend them, is the essence of injustice from Lyotard's perspective.

Thus, one must not suppose that what is realized in such struggles is an underlying human essence repressed by social forms opposed to the existence of that essence. Oppressed minorities are not created because of "inhuman" social conditions. That is, minorities are not oppressed because social dynamics repress a fundamental trait that they share with everyone else. On the contrary, minorities are constituted linguistically as different social positions lacking all essential connection to one another. Lyotard argues that "minorities are not social ensembles, they are territories of language. Every one of us belongs to several minorities, and what is very important, none of them prevails. It is only then that we can say that society is just."[6] The principle of justice does not provide criteria to decide which minorities are oppressed and which are dominant. It simply stipulates that the maximum diversity of linguistic territories be maintained. This principle, essential to the politics of difference, is concerned not so much with what a minority believes as with those beliefs being different from the norm, outside the established territories of theory and practice. Its essential concern is with maximizing differences, not reconciling them or building links of solidarity.

From Lyotard's perspective, then, radical politics amounts to an affirmation of the multiplicity of justices. If there is no valid way of deducing a single all-encompassing ethical-political program, then one must tolerate divers programs whose natures are relative to the territory of language in which they respectively operate. As James Williams argues, "the aim of [Lyotard's] politics will be to testify to the existence of differends against those theories and actions that deny them ... [he] champions the possibility of many different and equally right concatenations entering into the conflict over a same initial phrase event."[7] Only by affirming a maximum openness of possibilities for action can rational terrorism be avoided. As Lyotard himself argues, " there is first a multiplicity of justices, each one of them defined in relation to the rules specific to each game. These rules prescribe what must be done so that a denotative statement, or an interrogative one, or a prescriptive one, etc., is received as such and recognized as 'good' in accordance with the criteria of the game to which it belongs ... Justice here does not consist merely in the observance of rules ... it consists in working at the limits of what the rules permit, in order to invent new moves, perhaps ... new games."[8] Hiding behind Lyotard's affirmation of an irreducible plurality of justices is a very radical idea indeed. If he is correct, then the dominant critical philosophies of the last two hundred years are in fact the sources of the very oppression they have sought to comprehend and supersede.

What Lyotard affirms is a society of maximum openness to difference. He presents this society as a bulwark against the tyrannical rule of instrumental reason and capitalist efficiency. As Steven Best and Douglas Kellner have argued, there is a certain common frame of reference between Lyotard and the critical theory of the Frankfurt School. Both are concerned with mitigating the destructive effects of hegemonic instrumental rationality.[9] Unlike Frankfurt School critical theory, however, Lyotard resists identifying an agent who could effect decisive social transformations, and he does this for reasons that we know to be essential. Such an account of agency or subjecthood is the very basis, Lyotard believes, of the instrumental rationality he decries. Resistance to the destructive effects of the rule instrumental reason must therefore be passive. This passivity becomes more and more pronounced in Lyotard's work.

In his later work the preservation of hope and the possibility of resistance to the tyranny of efficiency have pushed Lyotard further and further away from a critical engagement with social dynamics. By 1988 he had left behind the belief that new links could be forged between genres and embraced the more pessimistic view that "all politics is a program of administrative decision-making, of managing the system."[10] The system itself has become an organism driven by an immanent evolutionary dynamic of self-differentiation. It extends itself by eliminating the "native indeterminacy" that is characteristic of people before they have been subsumed by one or another sector of society. Indeed, Lyotard speculates that the insidious drive of new information technology is to do away with the inefficient human body altogether. He muses that "the importance of technologies constructed around data processing resides in the fact that they make the programming and control of memorizing, i.e., the synthesis of different times in time, less dependent on the conditions of life on earth."[11] This drive towards a disembodied, electronic mind that could more efficiently manage ever more complex social systems proves once and for all that the Enlightenment link between reason and freedom has been broken. Information technology and related media do not "proceed from the reason of mankind, say, of the Enlightenment. [They result] from a process of development, where it is not mankind at issue, but differentiation."[12]

Paradoxically, however, despite the all-encompassing nature of technical evolution, Lyotard still holds out some hope for resistance. The only chance we have to escape from the logic of efficiency is to retreat *inward*, to a nondifferentiated subjective space that Lyotard calls "the inhuman." He means by "inhuman" two things. First, he means the drive inherent in technological rationality towards freeing itself of inefficient human material. He also means by "inhuman," however, the nonrational elements of human being and culture that stand as bulwarks to technological osmosis. In this sense it is, in the words of Gary Browning, "an embodied existence in the world, that stirs human beings to strive against their own imagination and reason, and feel the sublime."[13] In this sense the inhuman is a positive element in relation to what humanity has become in the contemporary world – a mere function of the various subsystems of which society is composed. The inhuman is feeling rather than thought, emotion rather than ratiocination, consciousness of the body rather than self-consciouness. This interior space of "native indeterminacy" expresses what Lyotard "has always tried, under diverse headings – work, figural, heterogeneity, dissensus, event, thing – to reserve: the unharmonizable."[14] Only in that which is absolutely undeveloped or undetermined can some sort of salvation from the society of efficiency be found. But if the desire that motivates this inward retreat is more than simply a desire to be left alone and is rather a desire not to be determined by the forces of "rational terrorism," then it is a desire for self-determination. The subject itself withdraws to this interior space that Lyotard calls "inhuman." Yet even though the name "inhuman" suggests that Lyotard has forever bidden farewell to the subject of humanism, the motivating desire of his retreat is the essential value of humanism, self-determination.

Perhaps, then, this return of inner subjective space in Lyotard casts his previous work in a new light. Perhaps he brings into the open what had been presupposed throughout, namely, some subjective capacity distinct from the normalizing functionalism of contemporary society. After all, contemporary society was always judged to be oppressive. He always championed *invention, affirmative* narratives, and new linkages between phrase regimens. If there were no distinction between subjecthood and external social dynamics, then the criticisms he levels at society, including his criticisms of the modernist character of subjecthood, could not appear as criticisms. It is true, as Browning argues, that "Lyotard's general depreciation of the value of stable consensual norms ... [is a] questionable [response] to the complex contextual conditions inspiring concrete forms of resistance."[15] In an argument that is deeper than that criticism, however, one must ask what grounds and explains Lyotard's very affirmation of resistance. If all capacities definitive of human being are nodes constituted by discourses that are in principle uncontrollable or ungovernable by humanity in accordance with rational and universal principles (if, indeed, as we have seen him suggest, such strategies of universal governance associated with humanism are the "essence" of totalitarianism), then there are no grounds to criticize the logic of efficiency as oppressive or restrictive or destructive, since nothing is affirmed to exist in the absence of this dynamic. This contradiction in Lyotard's work is symptomatic of a general contradiction facing radical postmodern political criticism. As such, further exploration of it will be deferred to part 2 of this text. Let us now turn to see how this same tension arises in Foucault's work.

THE TRANSGRESSIVE GESTURE

If diverse and contradictory interpretations by a plethora of commentators are one sign of great theoretical ingenuity and importance, and I believe that they are, then Foucault is a thinker of first-rate importance. More so than either Lyotard or Derrida, Foucault has been subjected to numerous incompatible interpretations, even by those who support his work. Habermas questions the coherence of the normative grounds of Foucault's critique of power, while David Ingram argues that Foucault provides a more incisive account of power than does Habermas but that their respective arguments are compatible.[16] Michel Druron judges Foucault to be a nihilist, while Deborah Cook sees Foucault as rescuing philosophy from nihilism by affirming the uniquely self-creative ethical powers of concrete individuals.[17] Ernesto Laclau and Chantal Mouffe see in Foucault the source for a renaissance of democratic theory, while Michael Clifford and Steven David Ross judge Foucault to be gesturing to a completely new form of radical politics that does not require contact with old democratic values.[18] Aron Keikel sees in Foucault an affinity with Heidegger's critique of technology, and Mark Poster finds in Foucault the groundwork for a critique of the means of communication characteristic of the computer age.[19] Mark Bevire sees two Foucaults, one an exuberant and not entirely coherent critic of autonomy and agency, the other a composed and ethically insightful supporter of agency against autonomy.[20] This list is by no means exhaustive, but it gives the flavour of the debates surrounding his work. Foucault was pleased by this multiplicity of interpretations and took it as a mark of success.[21]

Common to all these differing interpretations is the belief that whatever it is that constitutes the specific radicality of Foucault's politics, it is decisively related to his archaeological and genealogical decentring of the subject. While he approached the decentring operation differently over the years, it was (until his last works) this effort to decentre the modernist subject that most engaged him. As he claims in a retrospective comment on his work: "the goal of my work over the last twenty years ... has been to create a history of the different modes by which, in our culture, human beings *are made* subjects" (emphasis added).[22] Note that he does not say, "how human beings actualize their subjecthood" but, rather, "how they are made subjects." If they are made subjects, then subjecthood is not a defining human capacity but a social construct. If they are made subjects by external dynamics that mould, shape, and determine inert human material, and Foucault situates his work against this process, then the decentring of subjecthood is also a critique of subjecthood. Foucault was not content merely to analyse this process: he rebelled against it; he saw it as a reduction of humanity to a mere object of disciplinary power. Yet if Foucault is a critic of the objectification of human being by disciplinary society, he must oppose to this society some understanding of the human being not simply as capable of resistance to it but more as essentially subject. Only if some essential capacity for self-determination is presupposed does the critique of disciplinary society make ethical and political sense. Indeed, in the final chapter we will see that Foucault, like Lyotard, eventually restores some of its lost capacities to the subject in an effort to clarify the grounds of his critique of modernity. Once again, this restoration leads to the suspicion that some notion of subjecthood was presupposed all along by the critique of institutions and power. Before examining the shape of the rehabilitated notion of subjecthood in Foucault, however, it is necessary to chart the development of his politics, in order to see what he felt a radical practice not grounded in subjecthood might look like, to highlight the normative and political tensions that this account contains, and to illuminate his specific contribution to the general themes of the politics of difference.

First, it bears repeating that throughout his work Foucault explicitly rejected a political practice based on an essentialist understanding of human being. Even late in life, after he had restored a notion of the subject to his work, he reaffirmed his distrust of essentialist characterizations. He says that he has always "been a little distrustful of the general theme of liberation, to the extent that, if one does not treat it with a certain number of safeguards ... there is the danger that it will refer back to the idea that there does exist a nature or a human foundation which, as a result of a certain number of historical, social, or economic processes found itself concealed, alienated, or imprisoned in and by some repressive mechanism."[23] This hypothesis, Foucault claims, cannot be admitted without the most rigorous examination. In the previous sections we have seen how rigorous Foucault's examination of this hypothesis has been. Consistently interpreted, his original estimation of the effects of power would rule out entirely any such nature or essence. The purported essence was reduced to the status of a historically contingent product of different disciplinary powers. In the absence of an essential capacity for self-determination Foucault thus offered a politics of "transgression."

This notion of transgression has always been a major concern of Foucault and is perhaps the core of the specific radicality of his thought. In its initial formulation (never entirely surpassed) transgression was described in terms of overcoming self-identity and the rational values associated with it. Foucault's rejection of any politics that derives its legitimacy from its being entailed by a human essence makes his work resistant to facile assimilations to democratic and egalitarian political paradigms. The experience of the "radically other" that he mentions in regard to his attraction to Blanchot, Bataille, and Nietzsche is neither necessarily nor obviously amenable to democratic or egalitarian principles. Indeed, in his initial discussions of transgression, the opposite would seem to be the case. That is, transgression strikes out at all universal normative limitations upon activity. He argues that "transgression contains nothing negative, but affirms limited being ... but correspondingly, this affirmation contains nothing positive, no content can bind it, since, by definition, no limit can possibly restrict it. Perhaps it is simply an affirmation of division; but only in so far as division is not understood to mean a cutting gesture, or the establishment of separation or the measuring of a distance, only retaining that in which it may designate the existence of difference."[24] The entire article proceeds in this elusive fashion, but if one keeps in mind Foucault's understanding of the normalizing drive of modern society, good sense can be made of it. Like Derrida, Foucault argues that this discourse always constitutes itself by marking off an "outside." For Foucault this outside, originally, is formed by those "limit-experiences" that he associated with the work of Blanchot et al., experiences of madness, erotism, anything in which one "loses one's self." These are not negative in the Hegelian sense of being dialectical sublations of a practice inadequate to its concept; they are not "higher" moments of a general process. Nor are they "positive" in the sense of being fixed and determinate practices whose function is the realization of a definite desire. They are discourses and practices that erupt and affirm the distinction between reason and the outside.

The hero of transgression in 1972 is not humanity but language. It is this transgressive language that begins to speak in the opening created by the "disappearance of Man" – of dry rationalism and moribund humanism. This space has not yet been filled with anything determinate but, rather, constitutes the possibility of thinking in a different fashion. "It is no longer possible," he argues, " to think in our day other than in the void left by man's disappearance. For this void does not create a deficiency ... It is nothing more, and nothing less, than the unfolding of a space in which it is once more possible to think."[25] It is essential that this new way of thinking not be restricted by any type of rationalist or humanist limitation. Thus, *The Order of Things* concludes with baroque prophecies about the creative power of language supplanting humanity and all the values associated with humanism. However, the metaphorical prophecies of the early works constitute a passing phase. As Foucault's thinking came to be more and more interested in the relation between power and knowledge, his politics became more focussed and concrete. The political function of genealogy is to articulate the local knowledges that Western rationalism has ruled out over the centuries as merely local, unscientific, or too dangerous for public dissemination. Transgression thus becomes harnessed to a practical project that consists in disrupting the hegemony of official knowledge: "By subjugated knowledges I mean two things: on the one hand I am referring to the historical contents that have been buried and disguised in a functionalist coherence or formal systematization ... On the other hand, I believe that by subjugated knowledges one should understand ... a whole set of knowledges that have been disqualified ... [that are] beneath the required level of cognition or scientificity ... a differentiated knowledge incapable of unanimity and which owes its force only to the harshness with which it is opposed to everything around it."[26] As examples one might supply the knowledge of the schizophrenic, the street-person, the "pervert." While there are obvious affinities with Lyotard's idea of "small narratives," there are no self-evident affinities with any practice that would unambiguously resist the "most dangerous traditions" that have resulted from essentialist conceptions of humanity. Absent the universal grounds supplied by an essentialist understanding of human being, there are no reasons Foucault could give that would rule out the psychopath as a transgressive hero engaged in the constitution of a knowledge harshly "opposed to everything around it." It must be added that Foucault does not make any effort, at least until the end of his life, to establish limits to transgression.

Even so, this understanding of transgression is a fitting counterpart to Foucault's Orwellian vision of the social as an omniscient and omnipotent machine of power. If all public institutions are conceived of as analogous to a prison, if broad-based strategies of resistance also rest upon disciplinary power (since the member of a political group must either abide by group decisions or leave), then such "mad" strategies appear as the last resort of individuals trying to flee the normalization factory that is society. As his work progresses still further this concern with the individual, formerly identified as nothing but the product of power, gains essential prominence.

However, as this concern with the individual expresses itself, it forces Foucault to reconsider the heritage of the Enlightenment. The slogan "Release subjugated knowledges" is replaced by Kant's enlightened motto "Know thyself." Foucault will thus attempt to rearticulate reason and freedom, but not in a humanistic, universalistic fashion. In fact, he contrasts his idea of autonomy to the overarching themes of humanism. He argues that "it is a fact that, at least since the seventeenth century, what is called humanism has always been obliged to lean on certain conceptions of man borrowed from religion, science, or politics ... I believe that this thematic ... can be opposed by the principle of a critique and a permanent creation of ourselves in our autonomy."[27] While this may be true, one might ask why it is a problem that humanism should borrow a conception of man from religion or science or politics. Where else would it get such a conception? Moreover, with the exception of the Renaissance, humanism has not been a discourse in its own right separate from other domains but rather a general philosophical orientation that supervenes on specialized domains of research. There is no "science of humanism" but rather the idea that science should pursue humanistic ends – the improvement of the material condition of the species as a whole. There is no "religion of humanism" but rather the idea that humans should realize God's love (it matters not which God one believes in) in their conduct towards one another. There is no "politics of humanism" but rather the principle, variously construed by liberals, socialists, and conservatives, that human civilization should manifest what is best and highest in ourselves.

The ultimate critical-political import of an essentialist humanism will be the topic of part 2. For the moment Foucault's argument must be pursued further. First, let us recall that Foucault distrusts the idea of liberation because he claims that it rests upon an essentialist notion of subjecthood and because it has led historically to greater oppression. Thus, he replaces liberation with transgression, in order to obviate this problem. Transgression does not remain attached either to mad writings or to subjugated knowledges but increasingly comes to be identified with a critical attitude on the part of individuals, or what he calls a "philosophical ethos." This ethos "may be characterized as a *limit-attitude.* We are not talking about a gesture of rejection. We have to move beyond the outside-inside alternative; we have to be at the frontiers ... it seems to me that the critical question today has to be turned back into a positive one – in what is given to us as universal, necessary, obligatory, what place is occupied by whatever is singular, contingent, and the product of arbitrary constraints? The point, in brief, is to transform the critique conducted in the form of necessary limitations into a practical critique that takes the form of a possible transgression."[28] How is this critique related to the "permanent creation of ourselves in our autonomy?"

This is a complex question. The analysis of Foucault's arguments concerning power concluded with the discovery that the "individual is not a pre-given entity." Individuals were said to be the products of power relations, and society was conceived of as a factory for the production of individuals who tow the line. In this scenario there is clearly no room for a notion of autonomy, or if there is, it would have to be understood as one more product of power, something power creates in people, so that, while thinking themselves free, they in fact simply accept the manner in which they are constructed by the apparatus of power. Although Foucault does not use the example, one might think here of the slogan "freedom to choose," the defining ethos of consumer society. One believes oneself to be free when buying consumer goods, and it is true that there is no direct external force that causes one to buy one item rather than another. However, the "autonomy" exercised in this domain is in fact constituted within a coercive market economy, a manipulative system of advertising, and media-sponsored peer pressure to conform. Here power works at a surreptitious level, insidiously making people conform even as it causes them to believe that they are freeing themselves from external, determining forces. However, because Foucault criticized the system of power that produced this notion, one suspects that, as in the case of Lyotard, some notion of self-determining subjecthood was being presupposed all along as the unstated foil against which contemporary society is criticized. If that is the case, then the turn towards an explicit notion of autonomy in the later works may be interpreted as an effort on Foucault's part to clarify the normative foundations of his work. Even so, this notion of autonomy is not designed to be a rehash of "humanist" values.

To articulate a notion of autonomy that is not humanistic would appear to be a rather difficult task. One of the keys to the success of such an effort would be to avoid grounding the capacity for autonomy in an essential human capacity, to make it an emergent quality and not something pregiven in a definition of human being. This seems to be what Foucault tries to do in "What Is Enlightenment?" He argues that "if we are not to settle for the empty affirmation or the empty dream of freedom, it seems to me that this historico-critical attitude must also be an experimental one ... this work done at the limits of ourselves must, on the one hand, open up a realm of historical inquiry, and, on the other, put itself to the test of reality, of contemporary reality, both to grasp the points where change is possible ... and to determine the precise form this change should take."[29] Thus, critique is not a matter of giving a definition of human being and proceeding to deduce from that definition political systems that would be adequate to the meaning of human existence. On the contrary, the critical attitude is contextual and attuned to the specificities of each case. Thus the disdain for totality is reproduced here at the political level. Ultimately, the critical attitude disengages the individual from the apparatus of power by illuminating the impoverished manner of existence constituted within it. Such a critical reflection is the formal condition of possibility of the "permanent creation of ourselves in our autonomy." Freedom here would be an ongoing experimentation with our limits on the margins of the social machine. Or would it?

Notwithstanding his celebration of the emergent capacity for a "permanent creation of ourselves," Foucault nevertheless agrees that "the following objection would no doubt be entirely legitimate: if we limit ourselves to this type of always partial and local inquiry or test, do we not run the risk of letting ourselves be determined by more general structures of which we may well not be conscious and over which we may have no control?"[30] This is a strange comment. Foucault's initial analysis of power operated at this very depth, which he now feels could be overlooked. The point of the first theory of power was that no aspect of human existence escaped the disciplinary apparatus. Now he entertains objections to the effect that his notion of autonomy ignores deep-seated social structures and dynamics. His initial analysis of power left no room for autonomy but was a thorough-going investigation of deep institutional structures and dynamics. Thus, to make room for autonomy, Foucault had to rework his analysis of power.

Whereas formerly no effort was made to distinguish power, force, and domination, such distinctions become crucial in Foucault's last works. Foucault thus asserts that "there cannot be relations of power unless the subjects are free. If one or the other were completely at the disposition of the other and became his thing, an object on which he exercised an unlimited violence, there would be no relations of power. In order for there to be relations of power, there must be on both sides a certain form of liberty."[31] This new position implies, however, that human beings are not simply subjects in some contexts (that subjecthood is identical simply to the empirical practices through which we shape ourselves) or not simply capable of modifying the relations of power but are to be defined essentially as subjects, as in essence self-determining. This position seems to admit that the essentialist understanding of subjecthood that Foucault formerly identified as the deep cause of oppression is the necessary presupposition of theory designed to understand and supersede oppression.

The newly discovered freedom attaching to subjects raises questions not only about the coherence of Foucault's analysis but also about the nature of this freedom itself. In "What Is Enlightenment?" one is presented with a picture of autonomy as the emergent property of a critical attitude towards society. In the interview from which the above passage is drawn and which was conducted in the same year, 1984, as "What Is Enlightenment?" was written, a different picture emerges. Here freedom is transcendental, at least functionally, insofar as it is the condition of possibility for the existence of empirical power relations. In this same interview Foucault contends that "liberty is the ontological condition of ethics."[32] Ethics is a domain defined by those autonomous practices – what he calls technologies of the self – that, in the future, ought to stem from the critical attitude. However, rather than being an emergent quality, autonomy or liberty is now posited as a presupposition of the possibility of ethical action. It is thus difficult to agree with Foucault when he says, in the same interview yet again, that "What I refused was precisely that you first of all set up a theory of the subject."[33] That was true of the work whose task it was to decentre the subject. However, that decentring landed him in the quagmire of an analysis of power that, in showing how power was completely constitutive of individuals, left no *coherent* room for genuine resistance. In order to make good his desire for resistance, he was led back to the question of the *subject as a potential ground of resistance*. However, liberty of subjects is now an "ontological presupposition"; that is, clearly not something deducible from merely local, particular empirical analyses. Hence, we have returned to a theory of the subject, and a self-determining subject at that.

While Lyotard is pessimistic and Foucault is optimistic about the possibilities of resistance, their politics share a deeper bond. Both look to small-scale minority struggles as the agents of resistance and both take as their goal the proliferation of sites of opposition and difference. Even deeper, both predicate their new radicalism on the rejection of the modern understanding of the human essence as the capacity for self-determination. Just because each rejects self-determination as the essence of human being and simultaneously supports struggles against what they take to be the most oppressive features of society, both appear to be guilty of a very serious self-contradiction. In Foucault's case, his very decentring of the modernist account of subjecthood appears to presuppose the essence of the concept. Foucault takes a stand on the side of the voice of the mad, the marginal, and the midwife because he feels that they have something worthy to say. If, as he claimed in the mid-seventies, power is all-constitutive, then these discourses would also have been constituted by power and thus would not be genuine points of resistance to it. That they were posited as points of resistance entails that, to some extent, these discourses are not merely local irruptions against power but in fact stem from something deeper: a universal capacity on the part of human beings as such to struggle for free conditions of existence. Struggles, local or global, are meaningful as struggles against oppression only if they are not what Foucault says they are and ought to be, i.e., only if they stem from an essential human power of self-determination. While affirming the struggles, Foucault at the same time denies that subjects have any essential capacity through which they could determine themselves. He thus appears to try to mend this problem by reinstantiating a notion of subjecthood and by reworking his account of power. However, this reworking does not solve the "normative confusion" (there are no grounds to criticize the effects of power because power constitutes both the given system and the character of resistance to it) a confusion that exists in his first attempts, since no universal criteria are allowed to govern experimentation.[34] Nonetheless, the unbounded character of experimentation is perhaps his most radical political gesture. The deep-seated problems attending it and the manner in which subjecthood is presupposed by the critique of subjecthood – indicated but not yet fully substantiated – will be attended to in chapter 8. But at this point let us turn to Derrida.

WRITING RESISTANCE

The previous chapter concluded with some citations that displayed with admirable clarity the connection that Derrida believes to exist between essentialist accounts of human history and totalitarian politics. The political core of deconstruction and its affinities in this regard to Lyotard and Foucault were thus also made manifest. What must now be illuminated is the meaning of the positive and affirmative character of deconstruction in the political realm. The ultimate question here is, if, as Derrida asserts, truth, freedom, and subjecthood are values that have led necessarily to totalitarianism, what are the deconstructive values (values that are not merely parasitical on the old ones) that will at least allow one to remain vigilant in the struggle against oppression?[35] Or, if not that, how can one remain vigilant against totalitarianism in the absence of values?

It may prove useful to recapitulate the essential connection posited by Derrida between violence and metaphysics. Philosophy and the political discourse it has entailed (characterized by ongoing efforts to identify freedom and reason) have constituted themselves only by virtue of the exclusion of "the other." This has been a central theme from the earliest days of deconstruction. Take the following citation drawn from the 1968 piece "The Ends of Man" as exemplary of the essential political thrust of Derrida's work. He argues that a "radical trembling can only come from the *outside*. Therefore, the trembling of which I speak derives no more than any other from some spontaneous decision or philosophical thought after some internal mutation in its history. This trembling is being played out in the violent history of the West to its other, whether a 'linguistic' relationship ... economic, ethnological, political, military relationship etc."[36] The trembling of which he speaks is, in general, the trembling of rational humanism confronted with what has been excluded. In the particular context of 1968, one might think of the "outside" that prompts such trembling as the wars in Algeria and Viet Nam.

The relations of the West with its outside are the enduring political focus of Derrida's work. The history of Europe, Derrida contends, is the history of a confusion. Europe has always confused its own trajectory with the proper trajectory of the human species as a whole: "Europe has also confused its image, its face, its figure, and its very place ... with that of an advanced point, call it a phallus if you will, and thus, once again, with a heading for world civilization or human culture in general."[37] The culture of Europe has purchased its progressivist self-understanding only at the cost of excluding moments of otherness internal and external to itself. Internally, Europe's self-understanding marks off and excludes the feminine as other, while externally it marks off non-Western cultures in general as other.

Derrida's metaphor of the phallus indicates that for him the exclusionary tactics of the West are essentially masculine. The radical trembling that comes from the geographic outside is duplicated on the inside by the emergent voices of women. As he explains, "The discourses of Nietzsche, Joyce and the women's movement which you have identified epitomize a profound and unprecedented transformation of the man-woman relationship. The deconstruction of phallologocentrism is carried by this transformation ... But we cannot objectify or thematize this mutation even though it is bringing about such a radical change in our understanding of the world that a return to the former logocentric philosophies of mastery, possession, totalization or certitude may soon be unthinkable."[38] The critical import of the idea of the feminine is not felt so much directly at the level of practical politics but at the deeper (and, for Derrida, more important) level of our experience of that which is not-self. The feminine is the opposite of the masculine relationship to otherness. Whereas for the masculine ego the not-self is a threat, a limit to be surpassed and incorporated, the feminine represents an openness to the other, a welcoming.[39] A thinking that moves beyond mastery and possessiveness is certainly to be welcomed. The problem, however, concerns the relationship between those others who are mastered and a thinking beyond mastery. From the perspective of the oppressed, welcoming the other would entail welcoming the oppressor. Derrida's attempt to ground a radical politics in feminine forms of openness runs into trouble when it attempts to think the other side of the political equation, that is, when it tries to say something positive about the struggle against oppression. This problem becomes clear when we consider his analysis of the other essential site of exclusion, the former European colonies of Africa and Asia, paradigmatically South Africa.

Derrida's writings on apartheid are his most passionate, polemical, and forceful works. Apartheid, he contends, is the culmination of European history, the brutal objectification of its contradictory heritage. Here the liberal rule of law was employed in a constitutionally valid manner to legitimate the most barbarous state racism. It is necessary to quote him at length on this point. He writes, in reference to an art exhibit exposing the history of apartheid that the "exhibition expresses and commemorates, indicts and contradicts, *the whole of Western history*. That a certain white community of European decent imposes apartheid on four-fifths of South Africa's population and maintains (up until 1980!) the *official* lie of a white migration is not the only reason that Apartheid was a European 'creation.' The primary reason, however, is that here it is a question of state racism ... The juridical simulacrum and the political theatre of this state racism have no meaning and would have had no chance outside a European 'discourse' on the concept of race ... No doubt there is also here ... a contradiction internal to the West and to its assertion of its rights. No doubt that Apartheid was instituted and maintained against the British Commonwealth ... But this contradiction only confirms the occidental essence of the historical process."[40] The contradiction is that a universal discourse on rights is used to legitimate the exclusion (legitimate because constitutional) of the vast majority of the South African population. It is unthinkable without a discourse on race, for obvious reasons. Derrida also seems to imply here and confirms in "The Law of Reflection" that one can also turn this discourse on rights around once again and employ it as a critique of the racist restriction of rights to whites only.[41] That is, one can oppose the "spirit of the Law" (equal rights for all) to the letter of the law ("all" means all whites). Indeed, Derrida supports the very argument that Nelson Mandela presented to the South African court during his trial for treason. However, in the passage above, the liberal critique of Apartheid "confirms the occidental essence of the historical process," whereas Mandela, using the same conceptual tools, is effecting a "true critique." If this is the case, then Derrida's support for the latter and critique of the former would rest upon the same concept of race that he denounces, since the criteria of true critique would lie not in the concepts employed but in the cultural heritage of the one who articulates the critique. Derrida's critique would thus undo itself through its very articulation.

This is a general problem that affects the postmodern attempt to think oppression and resistance to it without grounding this thinking in a concept of human self-determination. On the whole, the various sites of oppression generate a critique of that oppression that activates concepts such as self-determination, human rights, and equality and that have employed violent means to acquire them. The postmodern critique of the West, as we have seen, depends upon a criticism of subjecthood and desires to open itself to the voice of the other. When the other speaks the same language as the language being criticized by postmodern critique, that critique is caught in a double bind – it must either be silent, and thus allow the same problematic categories to hold sway, or dictate to the other what language it should speak. This contradiction will be explored in detail in chapter 7. But let us return here to Derrida in order to see whether he has a way out of this seeming dead end.

As Derrida's work develops it seems to wrestle more and more with working out the ethical and political implications of the deconstruction of metaphysics. What is perhaps most interesting in Derrida's account is that he actually attempts to ground the political commitments of deconstruction. While there may be nothing outside the text, while all signifiers may play, that is, disseminate new meanings in an unsaturable fashion, Derrida nevertheless claims that there is one thing that is undeconstructible: responsibility. He argues that "The philosophical determination of this responsibility, its axiomatic concepts (for example, the will, property, subject, the identity of a 'me' free and individual, the conscientious 'person,' the presence-to-self of an intention, etc.) can always be discussed, questioned, displaced, critiqued, and, more radically, deconstructed. It will always be in the name of a more demanding responsibility, one more true to the memory and the promise, always beyond the horizon, of the present."[42] At the root of deconstructive practice, therefore, is this responsibility. It is in the name of responsibility that one deconstructs the metaphysical grounds of previous characterizations of responsibility. This responsibility is always responsibility to the other, and it is the "foundation" of deconstructive justice. One does justice to the singularity and integrity of the other not, first and foremost, by following rules and laws, but by remaining open to the other's address. It is the responsibility to remain open that charges the decision to respond to the call of the other with real ethical depth. As Geoffrey Bennington argues, "Derrida believes that a decision is only a decision to the extent that it cannot be programmed ... a decision that was determined by prior theories or reasons would not be a decision."[43] Responsibility is thus grounded in silence, in the capacity to hold oneself open, to listen, and to decide anew every time an ethical-political crisis arises. Derrida elaborates in one of his most recent texts: "This non-response conditions my responsibility, there where I alone must respond. Without silence, without the hiatus, which is not the absence of rules but the necessity of a leap at the moment of ethical, political, or juridical decision, we could simply unfold knowledge into a program or a course of action. Nothing could make us more irresponsible; nothing could be more totalitarian."[44] Following the thought of Emmanuel Levinas, Derrida understands by "other" the infinite world that is the other person. In every instance of ethical decision the deciding self has a two-fold relation to otherness: to the first other, towards whom the responsibility is exercised, and to what Derrida calls the "third," the other who acts as witness. The reality of the other always exceeds the knowing capacity of the self, which is why responsibility to the other must be lived by remaining open to the other, refusing the conceit that would claim to know absolutely what the other is or is facing. To make such a claim is to violate the difference that separates always self and other, to absorb the other into the self. To speak in the name of the other is thus always wrong, "because it is a determination of that someone."[45]

In thus invoking an undeconstructible responsibility, Derrida offers to a certain extent a means of limiting the play of signifiers without foreclosing altogether on play. Insofar as deconstruction is responsible to the other, there is a normative limitation established upon instances of deconstructive reading. An irresponsible usage would be the merely frivolous undoing of a given argument. A responsible usage, on the other hand, would undo the totalizing claims of a given argument in an effort to allow other possibilities to speak themselves in their own language. Bill Martin provides an excellent explanation of the meaning of Derridean responsibility and openness. He argues that "no other can speak the language of the same. The enforcement of this language (sometimes by straightforwardly authoritarian, even fascist measures, i.e., English-only laws, sometimes by what Marcuse calls 'repressive tolerance') is a way of keeping the other silent – and of admitting the possibility (in fact the counter-possibility) of the other only if the other submits to the 'Logic of the Same.' Letting the other speak, therefore, means actively resisting the pre-dominance of the same and its identity logic."[46] Real openness demands that one genuinely listens to what the others have to say about themselves. Only in this way can the full radicality of deconstruction be appreciated. No currently extant political discourse is "adequate to the radicality of deconstruction."[47]

Thus, the affirmative, positive moment of deconstruction must be expressed in a passive openness, the openness evoked in Derrida's notion of responsibility. As he explains, deconstruction is a "positive response to an alterity which calls, summons, or motivates it. This other, as other than self, the other that opposes self-identity, is not something that can be detected or disclosed within a philosophical space with the aid of a philosophical lamp ... It is within this rapport with the other that affirmation expresses itself."[48] As a living relationship between individual selves responsibility is thus fulfilled when the self permits the other the space and time the other needs if he or she is to speak in his or her own name. As a practical public politics responsibility is fulfilled when a politics of fixed programs and determinate projects is subordinated to a "messianic" politics of the promise.

This promise is a promise of emancipation. Like the Jewish understanding of the messiah, the saviour who is *yet to come*, Derrida sees emancipation as a promise that must always be kept in front of us. In *Spectres de Marx*, Derrida identifies this promise as the living core of Marxism. In 1968, when the students of the Western world rose in solidarity with the Maoist armies of Southeast Asia, Derrida consigned Marxism to the garbage heap along with the rest of humanist philosophy. Then, in 1993, when everyone else had abandoned Marxism *tout court*, Derrida appeared on the scene in order to reexamine it and to extract from it, "the spirit of the Marxist critique."[49]

This critical spirit is not found in any determinate argument that one could find within Marxism but rather in its dream of a free, just, and equal society. This dream is messianic and in order for it to produce positive effects, it must be distinguished from any political program that would posit it as a realizable goal. Derrida argues that "What remains ... as deconstructable ... is, perhaps, a certain experience of the emancipatory promise; it is perhaps even the formality of a structural messianism, a messianism without religion ... an idea of justice – which we distinguish from law or right and even from human rights – and an idea of democracy – which we distinguish from its current concept and from its determined predicates today."[50] Thus, from Derrida's perspective democracy is less a determinate system of government and more a relationship between self and other such that the other is always within a space from which he or she can name himself or herself. Here again, the problem that posed itself in relation to Lyotard and Foucault reappears. While Derrida's rejection of actual systems of democracy in favour of a democratic relationship between self and other is a solid critical position, it is difficult to understand its critical import unless that conception of democracy rests implicitly on the notion of human self-determination that he has deconstructed. If deconstruction teaches that the "subject is not always what it says it is," if meaning is never saturable, then not only the self but equally the other can never name itself. If it cannot name itself, if it is not defined by a capacity for self-determination, then deconstruction cannot distinguish between oppressive and nonoppressive contexts. To be oppressed means to be wrongly silenced, but Derrida's argument advanced the position that subjects were spoken by language; they could never truly speak for themselves. Moreover, Derrida cannot coherently distinguish between democratic and nondemocratic systems, since democracy, no matter if it is understood as a political form or a relationship between self and other, presupposes a capacity for self-determination on the part of people that democratic societies express and confirm.

Although Derrida is clearly concerned with unshackling people from oppressive, socially imposed categories, he fails to see that this project presupposes that humans are not essentially "functions of language" but must be something in virtue of themselves. Although he rejects a facile celebration of difference as the goal of deconstruction, he ultimately leaves us with a merely passive form of openness to a future that can never be realized. "Once again, here as elsewhere, wherever deconstruction is at stake, it would be a matter of linking affirmation (in particular, a political one), *if there is any*, to the experience of the impossible, which can only be a radical experience of the perhaps."[51] To simply affirm the possible in the face of the injustice of the actual, however, fails just that responsibility to the other that Derrida himself identifies as the core of deconstruction. While such radical openness to possibility will certainly prevent one's own practice from becoming totalitarian, it is difficult to see how it can play any role in preventing the world from becoming so.

If Derrida's work in particular and postmodern radical politics in general is to contribute to a freer world, it must confront the question of the deconstruction of subjecthood. Put straightforwardly, the question is, if language and power determine human needs, interests, and capacities, then on what basis can the politics of difference argue that minority groups are excluded and oppressed? The only cogent answer to this question – minority groups are excluded and oppressed because their self-determining capacity is denied by the given society – is one that the critical moment of postmodern politics denies itself. The critical moment of that politics is the deconstruction of the subject. The subject is the human being understood as essentially self-determining. If human beings are not essentially self-determining but are always functions of forces external to them, then there is no conceptual ground for the distinction between an oppressed and a free state. To be oppressed is to be made into something you are not by forces that you do not recognize to be legitimate. Thus, the capacity to experience oppression presupposes the capacity to distinguish between yourself as endowed with the capacity to shape your identity and world and forces in the world that are opposed to your so doing. Hence, to the extent that the politics of difference is oriented by the goal of releasing the excluded others of our world from that exclusion, it presupposes the very concept of subjecthood that its critique of modernity rejects.

Part 2 will systematically criticise the postmodern politics of difference by elaborating upon the contradictions we have noted in part 1. I will begin by sharpening our understanding of those contradictions by briefly examining two influential attempts at developing a practical and programmatic politics of difference.

PART TWO

The Contradictions of the Postmodern Politics of Difference

5 Realizing Postmodern Politics

The ramifications of the radical politics of difference are all-pervasive. The self-assertion and clash of social, cultural, and national differences in large part define the stakes of political struggle today. In the Western world, marginalised groups continue to struggle against exclusion and often legitimate their struggles by appeal to the validity of their cultural differences. Their struggles have been central to the changing cultural landscape of the last thirty years. The consequences of difference-based conflict, however, are not unambiguously positive. In the Middle East, Palestinians and Israelis battle over space for the security of their national differences. In the Balkans, the relatively stable cosmopolitanism of the Tito years disintegrated into the firestorm of nationalist conflict. In Canada, the last fifteen years have seen the reawakening of the sovereignty movement in Quebec, as well as the rebirth of Aboriginal activism. Postmodern strategies of critique, in grappling anew with the logic of the multiple relationships of exclusion and domination characteristic of the modern world, are clearly of preeminent contemporary significance. As the problem of the marginalisation and oppression of minority groups is very far from being solved, the renewed efforts of postmodern thinkers and political activists to articulate novel approaches to questions of pressing local and global concern stand at the theoretical forefront of the struggles for a better world.

The postmodern politics of difference have been able to capture the radical imagination because the old vocabulary of universalist politics has broken down. This collapse has affected the radical universalism of Marxism most of all. Stanley Aronowitz is correct when he argues that "what has occurred in the last quarter century is that, on the assumption that the working class shares in the general level of material culture, class has been removed from the politics of subalterity and has been replaced by new identities."[1] The universalism of the old left has been replaced by the politics of difference, and this substitution has been justified by appeal to the deconstructive philosophical strategies examined in part 1. In order both to emphasise the political implications of those philosophical strategies and to bring into sharper relief their inadequacies as radical political categories, the present chapter will examine two attempts to develop practical political arguments from postmodern philosophical premises: the first, a deconstruction of Marxism, the second, a deconstruction of liberal democracy. The first and perhaps most influential attempt to concretize postmodernism as a radical politics was the "post-Marxism" of Ernesto Laclau and Chantal Mouffe.[2] The most important attempt to apply a deconstructive reading to the traditions of liberal democracy is the work of Iris Marion Young. We shall examine each in turn. This step in the argument is essential, because although Lyotard, Foucault, and Derrida have obvious ethical-political concerns and although each alludes to the significance of his work for a critique of the present, none attempts to concretely spell out his work as practical politics.

POST-MARXISM AND THE POLITICS
OF DIFFERENCE

Ernesto Laclau and Chantal Mouffe's 1985 text *Hegemony and Socialist Strategy* was the first systematic effort to translate Foucault and Derrida into the language of radical political practice.[3] Its goal was to revitalise moribund socialist politics by redescribing its aims according to the deconstructive logic of postmodern criticism. It bid farewell to the central themes of Marxism – the centrality of the working class to the project of liberation, the essentialist understanding of labour as positive human freedom, and the primacy of socioeconomic relations over political struggle – but claimed that in so doing it was true to socialism's deeper emancipatory message, what Derrida called its "promise." Laclau and Mouffe's project was excited by the emergence of new political agents (women, gays and lesbians, the environmental movement, people of colour) whose theory and practice seemed to confirm the death of universalist politics. The political vitality of these movements, according to Laclau and Mouffe, was due precisely to the fact that their practice followed from their sense of difference and specificity. They claimed not to be speaking for humanity (as Marxism pretended to do) but for their own constitutive differences. Laclau and Mouffe attempt to systematize the politics of difference by elaborating a theory of what they call radical and plural democracy that breaks with the essentialism of Marxism but preserves its emancipatory promise.

Laclau and Mouffe begin by arguing that the problem with Marxism was that it was rooted in the essentialist understanding of subjecthood. Because it understood the human essence as self-determination, and self-determination to find its privileged expression in labour, Marxism historically demanded that working-class interests take precedence in radical movements. Marxism thus developed on the basis of exclusionary relationships with other oppressed social and cultural differences. The demand to either subordinate themselves to the struggle for socialism or disappear spelled doom for Marxism when, in the 1960s, women, African-Americans, and gays and lesbians moved their specific demands to the front of the radical agenda.[4] Because of its oppositional relationship to otherness, Marxism found itself cut off from this new kinetic political energy and thus became obsolete. The future of radicalism, Laclau and Mouffe insisted, now lay with singularity and difference, not unity and universality.[5]

The problem with universality is that it is rooted in an essentialist theory of subjecthood, and essentialist theories of subjecthood confused freedom with rational mastery of that which is not-self or object. Derrida makes this point very clearly. He argues that "the modern dominance of the principle of reason had to go hand in hand with the interpretation of the essence of beings as objects, an object present as representation (*Vorstellung*), an object placed and positioned *before* a subject. This latter, a man who says "I," an ego certain of itself, thus ensures his own technical mastery over the totality of what is."[6] The political interpretation of this understanding of reason and freedom led to a politics of experts whose purpose was to interpret for the masses their essential interest. Laclau and Mouffe follow Derrida, Foucault, and Lyotard in the belief that politics as expertise inevitably leads to politics as rational terrorism. They hope that if the basis of the politics of expertise in the essentialist understanding of the subject is deconstructed, then new forms of democratic political struggle might emerge.

The defining value of those new struggles is pluralism. Postmodern pluralism does not mean, however, *e pluribus unum* (out of many, one). On the contrary, the specific difference of postmodern pluralism is that it maintains separation between the differences that are constitutive of the social formation. Its point is not to unify around a centre but rather to free social differences form all centralising forces. As Laclau and Mouffe argue, "the alternative of the left should consist of locating itself fully in the field of the democratic revolution and expanding the chains of equivalents between the different struggles against oppression. The task of the left therefore cannot be to renounce liberal democratic ideology, but on the contrary, to deepen and expand it in the direction of radical democracy."[7]

Rather than trying to subordinate different groups and struggles to an overweening political logic radical democracy seeks only to "expand the chains of equivalents" between different political actors. In simpler terms, what Laclau and Mouffe hope for is dialogue between different sites of oppression out of which temporary alliances and movements can be forged. Each group, however, would retain its separate existence. In practice radical democracy would take the form of a loose coalition between marginalised social and cultural differences. Solidarity would not oblige any group to give up its independent organizational structure or unique political goals.

In order for groups to work together in ways that will enable them to preserve their independence, the metaphysical foundation of modern politics must be deconstructed and rejected. Laclau and Mouffe draw upon Foucault's notion of "subject-position" in their critique of the essentialist understanding of subjecthood. They state that "whenever we use the category of 'subject' in this text, we will do so in the sense of 'subject-positions' in a discursive structure. Subjects cannot, therefore, be the origin of social relations – not even in the limited sense of being endowed with powers that make an experience possible – as all 'experience' depends upon quite precise discursive conditions of possibility."[8] Laclau and Mouffe here reassert the defining postmodern argument that human beings cannot be defined by reference to any essential nature. Instead, humans are made to be what they are by the social positions they occupy. Thus, there are no "human beings" but only blacks and whites, workers and owners, women and men, gays and lesbians. To be a woman or a black Canadian is not a function of one's own self-determining capacities encouraged or limited by social and cultural dynamics. Rather, it is a function of those social and cultural dynamics (discursive conditions) pure and simple.

The expected political returns from the deconstruction of the subject are as follows. The universal grounding of Marxism in an essentialist theory of the subject privileged the working class over other oppressed groups. However, in reality it was not the working class that was privileged but the expert interpreters of working class interests, the Party. Workers could not in practice be trusted to understand their own essence (they failed to free themselves from antirevolutionary beliefs), and thus they required enlightened masters to clarify their own essence and its political entailments for them. The expert interpreters were endowed with the power to decide between the essential and the inessential, the human and the inhuman. Whichever interests fell outside the program of the experts became, *ipso facto*, inhuman. If, however, the idea that humans are essentially subjects is dropped, then the belief in "objective interests" (interests that follow from the human essence) also collapses. That collapse is a gain for democratic theory, because it purportedly frees other oppressed groups from the dogmatism of expertise and permits the type of free negotiation between groups that Laclau and Mouffe believe to be necessary to the revitalisation of radical democracy.

From their perspective a radical democracy is a society in which formerly marginalised or oppressed groups are freed from the "subaltern" social positions they formerly occupied. The political movement necessary for the construction of such a society is a coalition, or series of coalitions, between different groups, each of which maintains organizational autonomy. The condition for the development of such coalitions is the freeing of radical theory from a universal understanding of human interests, needs, and capacities. While it is certainly true that in the particular case of organized Marxism very serious problems could be found in its relationship with other oppressed groups, Laclau and Mouffe's attempt to use the deconstruction of subjecthood to free radical politics from those problems runs into the immanent contradictions of its philosophical underpinnings. At the level of practice, they must confront the question of why, if groups are distinct and separate, they would form coalitions in the first place. Coalitions between oppressed groups presuppose just what the politics of difference denies, namely a shared set of interests, needs, and capacities. More deeply, their deconstruction of the idea that human beings are subjects undermines the conceptual grounds necessary for a coherent understanding of oppression. This structural incoherence is evident in Mouffe's latest work in which, without backing off at all from the deconstruction of the subject central to the politics of radical pluralism, she warns the reader of the consequences of a radical conception of pluralism. Thus she argues that, "viewed from an anti-essentialist perspective ... pluralism is not merely a fact, but an axiological principle ... constitutive *at the conceptual level* of the very nature of modern democracy." Without tempering her allegiances to the deconstruction of universal normative grounds, however, she adds that her radical pluralism "does not allow a total pluralism," a pluralism that valorizes all differences, because such a total pluralism, "prevents us from recognizing how certain differences are constructed as relations of subordination."[9] Her qualifications here make sense, however, only if they are rooted in an essentialist understanding of the subject. A nonarbitrary distinction between legitimate and illegitimate differences depends upon a conception of human being as self-determining. Illegitimate differences are precisely those that deny the subjecthood of others while claiming for themselves exclusive access to the grounds for the maintenance and development of cultural differences.

Mouffe, however, does not depart from the deconstruction of the subject developed in *Hegemony and Socialist Strategy*. There, recall, she and Laclau argued that the subject was always in reality a subject-position. Subjects were not even endowed with the capacity to render an experience possible. But oppression is not simply a function of social structures, it is also, and crucially, an experience on the part of some members of society that their life horizons are being shaped by forces opposed to their freedom. An Aboriginal person whose hopes for the future are dashed by poverty and entrenched racist assumptions is not simply a subaltern subject position; he experiences himself as oppressed. This experience, however, cannot itself be a function of the subject position he occupies, because otherwise oppression would be something external to the oppressed subject and thus not definitive of his very being as an oppressed person. More seriously, his liberation from that oppressed position (should it occur) would also be external to his being, and thus not his own act, i.e., not real liberation. While Laclau and Mouffe's conception of radical democracy is a consistent elaboration of the postmodern themes of tolerance and pluralism and while these values are essential to the advance of democracy and freedom in the contemporary world, they in fact presuppose just that conception of self-determining subjecthood that they and their postmodern philosophical premises deny. I will return to this point with a more complex analysis of the subjective conditions for the experience and overcoming of oppression in the penultimate chapter. At this point let us examine the analogous problems faced by Iris Marion Young's attempt to translate the deconstruction of subjecthood into a more critical and postmodern understanding of liberal democracy.

POSTMODERN CITIZENSHIP

Whereas Laclau and Mouffe are concerned with rescuing the socialist project from what they see as the dogmatic implications of

Marxist essentialism, Young hopes to rescue the liberal-democratic idea of citizenship from its essentialist interpretation. Both seek to advance the practical aim of postmodern thinking, namely, the creation of a world in which all those groups who have been silenced by being consigned to the inessential side by metaphysical thought gain, or regain, their proper voice. As Young explains, "metaphysical thinking makes distinctions and formulates accounts by relying on such oppositions [subject/object, knowledge/opinion, essence/accident], where one side designates the pure, authentic, good, and the other the impure, inauthentic, bad."[10] The resolution of this problem must involve a nondialectical reversal in which the excluded differences manifest themselves, not as higher expressions of an underlying essence, but separately and each in its own right. She argues that "the metaphysics of presence represses or denies difference ... As I understand it, difference means the irreducible particularity of entities, which makes it impossible to reduce them to commonness or bring them into unity without remainder."[11] That is, there is no underlying human essence that would unite different oppressed groups or explain what constitutes their oppression. Groups are "irreducibly particular." This particularity is denied both by manifestly exclusionary theory and practice and by universalist recipes for change like Marxism and traditional liberalism, which appeal to a repressed human essence (reason or creative labouring activity) in their critiques.

Thus, Young attempts to reconceive of oppression as the theoretical and practical denial of group difference. "Where social group differences exist," she contends, "and some groups are privileged and others are oppressed, the propensity to universalize the particular reinforces the oppression."[12] To universalize the particular means to make one form of oppression the master form and to demand that all oppressed groups conceive of their oppression according to the master categories. In Young's view, however, this strategy simply exacerbates the social structures that are responsible for oppression. The struggle against oppression must be one through which the "irreducible particularity" of the voices of the specific oppressed groups is cultivated.

The main target of Young's criticism is the abstractly universal liberal idea of equality. The classic liberal understanding of equality demands that concrete differences be ignored in the adjudication of claims over political representation, legal protection, and the exercise of rights.[13] One stands before the law not as a black man or a white woman but as a citizen, a rational being defined by universalizable interests, not irreducible particularities. This abstract universality has been challenged by the new social movements that Young supports. "The assumed link between citizenship for everyone, on the one hand, and the two other senses of citizenship – having a common life with and being treated in the same way as other citizens – is itself a problem. Contemporary social movements have weakened the link. They assert a positivity and a pride in group specificity against ideals of assimilation. They have also questioned whether justice always means that law and policy should enforce equal treatment for all groups. Embryonic in these challenges is the idea of *differentiated citizenship*."[14] Differentiated citizenship means that rights and duties will be distributed relative to group differences. This differential distribution of rights and duties need not violate equality, Young believes, because it makes up for substantive disadvantages that oppressed groups face. For example, it would be no injustice to men to give women extended maternity benefits, because men do not have to face the same emotional and physical challenges of pregnancy.

While there is nothing problematic from my perspective with the idea of group-differentiated rights (many of which already exist), there are decisive problems with the philosophical grounds upon which Young asserts their legitimacy. Because Young accepts the deconstruction of identity according to which the specific difference of things is established not by an inner essence but by differential relations with other things, she threatens to undermine the coherence of the notion of group upon which her critique of oppression depends for its sense. She seems to assert at one and the same time that there is no such thing as a group and that contemporary society is defined by the manifold ways by which it oppresses different groups. "Whether unequal or relatively equal, difference as otherness conceives of social groups as mutually exclusive, categorically opposed. This conception means that each group has its own nature and shares no attributes with those defined as other. The ideology of group difference in this logic attempts to make clear borders between groups and to identify the characteristics that mark the purity of one group from the characteristics of the others."[15] Young rejects this position and wants not only to argue that groups are not defined by some peculiar nature or essence but also to insist upon the "irreducible particularity" of groups. She argues on the one hand that the problem is that groups conceive of themselves as mutually exclusive and on the other that the beginning of a solution to the problem of intergroup conflict is to develop representative bodies in which all oppressed groups have standing as distinct oppressed groups.

Despite the fact that she never turns her back on the claim that groups are "irreducibly particular," she grounds her program for reform not in the name of that irreducible particularity but rather under the banner of deliberative democracy. On the one hand, then, she argues, still rooting her position in Derrida's deconstruction of metaphysics, that "the representative does not stand for or refer to a substance or essence of opinion and interest which it is his job to describe."[16] On the other hand, she argues that group representation is one key means of redressing the historic underrepresentation of "women ... racial, ethnic, or religious groups ... working class people."[17] What, however, is the representative of a specific group to represent if the essence of the group in question is deconstructed? Young would respond that the interest of the group emerges and changes through the process of deliberation that differential representation enables. Again, I have no quarrel with the democratic credentials of her conclusion but rather with the grounds upon which she asserts it. If minority *groups* need special representation, then they must exist and be defined by reference to some interest, call it substantial or essential, that is not allowed to be expressed in the given society. Young's attempt to use deconstruction for democratic ends simply leads to confusion. This wavering between opposed positions without mediation is once again a function of trying to conceive of group differences in the absence of a strong notion of subjecthood.

Young is rightly concerned by the fact that where differences are understood to follow from fixed underlying identities, intragroup differences will be denied. We can see just such a problem within Quebec. For example, in his now infamous "l'argent et la vote ethnique" (money and the ethnic vote) speech following the defeat of the 1995 referendum, the Quebec premier, Jacques Parizeau, implored his supporters to "never forget: three-fifths of us voted 'yes.'"[18] Anglophones and allophones, even if they support the nationalist agenda, are always suspect from this position that counterposes "us" and "them" in absolute terms. This exclusive conception of difference, as we will see, results not from an essentialist conception of subjecthood but rather from cutting off the struggle of, in this case, the Québécois from its universal grounds in a concept of human being as self-determination. Young, however, far from appealing to this underlying universal logic as the solution to her problem, charges it with being the problem in the first place. She understands group struggle not as a development out of the universal human capacity for self-determination but as a response to exclusionary universals. Then, however, she confronts the problem that where groups assert their particularity, they run up against other groups asserting their particularity, and the struggle against oppression degenerates into a struggle between groups, each claiming an absolute right to difference. Her solution is to develop a relational understanding of difference. She writes: "The relational conception of difference does not posit a social group as having an essential nature composed of a set of attributes defining only that group. Rather a social group exists and is defined as a specific group only in ... interactive relations with others. Social group identities emerge from the encounters and interactions amongst people who experience some differences in their way of life and forms of association ... Group identity is not a set of objective facts, but the product of experienced meanings."[19]

This interpretation can be true, however, only at the cost of negating the "irreducible particularity" of oppressed groups, which was, recall, the value that Young's political philosophy sought to promote. If group identity is always constituted relationally, then in different relations the identity of that group will change. This implication threatens to undermine both her affirmation of the value of particularity and her critique of oppression. Once again forces outside the oppressed group itself are responsible, in essence and not simply in fact, for the identity and life horizons of the group. Groups are defined; they can never be self-defining. But the struggle against oppression is precisely a struggle for self-definition, and that struggle is not unique to some groups: it is, as I will argue, the very essence of human being. The problem for social criticism is not, therefore, to comprehend the irreducible particularity of groups but to demonstrate how group difference is a product of the universal human capacity for self-definition, how the present constitution of the globe subordinates this struggle for self-definition to the operations of socioeconomic forces fundamentally opposed to this positive human freedom, and how the attempt to promote differences from the perspective of a philosophy that takes difference and not universal identity as basic is both incoherent and self-contradictory.

The first four chapters of this book traced the emergence of a new radical political philosophy from the deconstruction of essentialist conceptions of human subjecthood. We saw that the ethical-political core of postmodern radicalism is the irreducible value of difference. Lyotard, Foucault, and Derrida argue that the metaphysical grounds of modern political philosophy are opposed to the free elaboration of differences. Concretely, this opposition manifests itself in the exclusion of others who, for whatever reason, do not measure up to the standards of human being encoded in the essentialist idea of subject.

While Lyotard, Foucault, and Derrida are clearly oriented by the desire to free those excluded others from their imposed silence, none attempt to elaborate a systematic politics designed to overcome the problems they take to be definitive of the contemporary world. Laclau and Mouffe and Iris Marion Young start from the deconstruction of the modern conception of subjecthood and attempt to develop from it a practical politics of difference. While their targets are different, their goals are the same. However, given that their starting point is incoherent, their politics cannot without self-contradiction promote the values that guide them.

In the remaining three chapters I will link theory and practice together in a detailed criticism of the contradictions of the politics of difference. First, we will demonstrate that pluralism is a coherent value only if it is conceived from the perspective of an underlying universal human identity. Next, I will argue that the struggles of oppressed groups are necessarily grounded in that universal understanding of the essence of human being as the capacity for self-determination that postmodern radicalism denies. Finally, I will reveal that the postmodern politics of difference must in fact presuppose the idea of subjecthood as self-determination if it is to make sense as radical politics. That this idea must be presupposed is the strongest proof that a radical politics conceived of on the basis of the deconstruction of subjecthood is self-confuting. The renewal of radical theory and practice depends therefore upon a revitalised critical-humanist understanding of humanity's essential self-determining nature.

6 Is Radical Pluralism a Coherent Idea?

Stated positively and not as a critique of modernity, the politics of difference is a series of efforts to create the conditions for the unfettered elaboration of social, cultural, ethnic, and gender differences. Honi Fern Haber calls the practical politics of difference "radical pluralism," a term I will adopt for the remainder of this chapter. She argues that radical pluralism is "engendered by the poststructuralist law of difference" and is "a rich resource for developing alternatives to the concepts of subjectivity, identity, resistance, and domination. Because it insists on the recognition of difference, it displaces the hierarchical oppositions that characterize capitalist, patriarchal societies. This means that power can (at least theoretically) belong to those at the margins."[1] While the goal of investing power in the powerless is the correct one, we will see that postmodern radical pluralism is an incoherent platform form which to launch the necessary struggles. *Radical* pluralism, pluralism that takes difference and not identity to be fundamental, can not distinguish between oppressed and oppressive minority groups, nor can it understand the type of group unity needed to successfully struggle against oppression. As we will see, the consistent political implication of postmodern radical pluralism is ever greater social fragmentation and blindness to the deep socioeconomic grounds of oppression. I will explicate this criticism through the example of the struggle of the Québécois for what the postmodern politics of difference denies everyone: self-determination.

Before developing the example, however, it is important to review and deepen our understanding of the practical implications of the deconstruction of identity thinking. Recall that this deconstruction sets its sights against the idea that human beings are defined by a shared essence, that human beings are essentially self-determining beings, that we are (at least potentially in a future free state) a family of differences. It insists rather that we are just ever-shifting differences free from any underlying identity or shared material interest. This approach contrasts sharply with what postmodern criticism took to be the modern approach to the problem of difference. Modern philosophy allowed differences into its equations only insofar as they could be managed by a conception of human essence that organized and limited the play of differences. It allowed differences into the overarching story only in order to all the more securely strip them of their singularity and specificity.[2] Much as radicals are co-opted into the status quo in order to silence them, modern theory allowed differences into its metanarratives in order to domesticate them. What is really at issue in modern philosophy's approach to the problem of difference is thus not liberation of the different from the same but anxiety about unmastered forces and movements. The quotation from Sky Gilbert with which my argument began (introduction) nicely encapsulates the postmodern critique of modern philosophy's relationship to difference. Gilbert's deep point was that the defining motifs of modern thought have infiltrated the margins where the differences lie and have compelled the differences to speak according to a script already prepared for them. This surreptitious rewriting of the content of differences is the "human" face of mastery. If necessary, totalizing thought will forcibly eliminate any distinct element that cannot be assimilated, but it prefers nowadays to assimilate differences by providing the concepts through which opposition to given order will be conducted.

Thus, the subsumption of differences by modern thought is most effective when it convinces the margins to play by the rules that already define the existent world. According to the postmodern critique, political opposition to the given world fails when it roots itself in a concern for clarity, truth, order, discipline. When these categories enter into political discourse, even revolutionary political discourse, the game has already been won by the forces that that discourse hopes to oppose. Rather than confronting the given society with a difference which is unmanageable, that would really shake the society to its foundations, such strategies merely repeat the categories that ensure the perpetuation of the existing society.

94   Contradictions

As a critique of modern approaches to the question of differences, then, postmodernism highlights the repressive and/or violent implications of the concept of essence. As such a criticism, postmodernism has much to recommend it. It is certainly true that monstrous crimes have been committed in the name of civilization and humanity. Where language, gender, or skin colour have been posited as reasons justifying social exclusion and domination, it is necessary to deconstruct those oppositions. But deconstruction of hierarchical oppositions in the absence of a universal concept of human self-determination cannot provide the coherent normative grounds required by emancipatory movements. As we will see, radical pluralism ends up supporting the proliferation of any difference whatsoever and ends up setting groups against themselves, not the forces responsible for their oppression. It is time to put flesh to this skeleton of criticism.

LIBERATION THROUGH SILENCE

What remains to be determined is whether social criticism can begin from difference and still remain critical of a society whose fault is supposed to lie in its exclusion or destruction of differences. If social unity grounded in an essentialist understanding of humanity is the problem, can a radical critique that frees differences from their essentialist reduction be the solution? Concretely, can a society that takes differences, their maintenance and extension, as primary be a society where differences actually are maintained and extended? The first step towards answering these questions is to remind ourselves of how postmodernism characterized itself as a passive overture towards difference.

The postmodern response to otherness, aiming as it does at an appreciation of what differences are beyond the confines of humanist toleration and mutual respect, is, as we have seen, first of all a passive response. If there is an analogue to toleration in radical pluralism, it is the idea of openness. This is evident if we recall the diction utilized by the theorists under investigation when they spoke of what would appear if essentialist thought were overcome. Thus Derrida spoke of the need for a politics that would offer an "expérience de l'impossible,"[3] and of deconstruction as opening up the suppressed "contradiction[s] and difference[s]" of history, in particular non-Western history.[4] Foucault invoked a transgression "unleashed in its movement of pure violence ... toward the limit"[5] and later in his life called upon us to engage in the "undefined work of freedom."[6] Lyotard, meanwhile, saw in postmodern creations the attempt to "present the unpresentable."[7] What unifies all three positions is that each resists categorization, naming, and strict definition. "Is there any worse violence," Derrida asks, "than that which calls for the response, demanding that one give an account of everything, and preferably thematically?"[8] This rhetorical question sums up with crystalline sharpness the core of postmodern openness. There will be no response to the other if by response is meant commentary, thematic packaging, or criticism. Radical openness means listening to what the other has to say, whatever that may be, for the real atrocity occurs when one silences the other before the other has had a chance to speak.

The value of openness thus lies in the silence that defines it. It is neither affirmation nor negation of what the other will say. It holds itself back from commentary, criticism, or agreement, so that something new, perhaps impossible, or even, for Foucault, "violent" may emerge. Yet silence is necessary, for only by holding commentary in abeyance can the categorizing, classifying, limiting thought of modern philosophy be overcome. This silence, however, is motivated by a profound respect for those at the margins. It trusts that, at the very least, they have something to say that cannot be heard if one is too quick to judge and define. Holding judgment in abeyance, therefore, is not indifference or nihilism. Nor is it mere modern tolerance, which listens only in order to package, ignore, and ultimately oppress. Radical openness towards the other is silent precisely so that the other no longer need be silent. Modern tolerance listens only so long as what the other says does not disturb the structure that apportions to the other an already defined space and insists on the protocols that determine what is acceptable to say. Precisely because postmodernism takes differences as basic, it can hear in raw, unbridled form all that modernity has excluded – the feminine, the mad, the gay, the Native.

Openness to the other purportedly gets beyond the enclosures of modern thought by refusing to make demands on the other. If this is an emancipatory political stance, in the sense that a new space for the articulation of difference emerges, it is owing to the silence of the theorist and not to what the other in fact will say. For if the first step towards radical pluralism is silence so that the other can speak, then one must hold one's tongue regardless of what is in fact said by the other. The wrong, the violence, enters into politics when limitations are placed upon the other, even if these limitations are well-intentioned and "humanist." The other is not obliged to be polite or tolerant; the theorist is the one who is obliged to listen. The theorist might not necessarily be obliged to support every utterance of

96   Contradictions

every group who begins to speak, but s/he is obliged to let whatever is going to be spoken be spoken without critical comment.

Again, it is worth citing further textual evidence to support this interpretation. In their most uncompromising formulations each of the three theorists examined here sought a form of practice whose aim was to go beyond modern forms of politics in unanticipated ways. For Derrida this practice was associated with the "nature" of writing once it had been restored to its originally destabilizing character. He argues that "perhaps the desire to write is the desire to launch things that come back to you as much as possible in as many different forms as possible. That is, it is the desire to perfect a program or a matrix having the greatest potential, variability, undecidability, plurivocity, et cetera, so that each time something returns it will be as different as possible."[9] Generalized to the field of politics, his argument implies that the writings or the voices that one encounters must be allowed to produce their own differences through an unbounded process of dissemination. The voice of the other cannot return "as different as possible" if it is constrained by interpretations of that voice that confine it within already well-established political idioms. The plurivocity of the voice of the other can emerge only if the theorist lets this voice be, lets it produce whatever effects it will, according to its own movement.

One finds a similar desire to let the work of the other be, to let it produce novel effects, in Foucault's notion of genealogy. The point of genealogy is not to manage history but simply to chart the many sides of its multiple play of dominations and to position oneself so as to be able to introduce new practices. Foucault insists that " the law is a calculated and relentless pleasure, delight in the promised blood, which permits the perpetual instigation of new dominations, and the staging of meticulously repeated scenes of violence."[10] Foucault does not desire to break out of this movement but rather, so long at least as he speaks of transgression, to operate within it, to effect new ways of going beyond established boundaries in a "lightning flash" that is neither positive nor negative. The point is not what is done but rather the fact that what is done is unforseen and unpredictable.

Lyotard, as well, was centrally concerned with allowing the novel and the unmanageable to be expressed against modern theory. In a retrospective reading of his work, Lyotard identifies this unmanageable element as what he has always sought to illuminate and let speak. He argues that what humanism "crushes" is "what, after the fact, I have always tried, under diverse headings – work, figural, heterogeneity, dissensus, event, thing – to preserve – the unharmonizable."[11] Note that Lyotard says "preserve." In other words, the unharmonizable is already; it is not brought into being by his work. In order for it to produce new effects, one must refuse to attempt to assimilate it to a metanarrative. Again, letting this element be is crucial to what makes Lyotard's work distinct from past forms of theorizing.

If one of the hallmarks of the radical postmodern politics of difference is an intial suspension of judgment, it would seem to follow that the first practical consequence is that the distinction between "progressive" and "reactionary" groups must be given up or at least held in abeyance. That distinction is basic to modernist political theory and thus quite incompatible with a radical politics of difference. Such a political cartography cannot be constructed unless one can identify the essential vehicle that is moving across the historical terrain in one of two directions. That vehicle, the human essence, has been deconstructed and therefore no longer exists as a possible means of orientation in the political landscape. Thus, there is no longer any basis for determining which voice(s) express the more legitimate or valuable differences.

If the distinction between progressive and reactionary must be given up, then it follows that radical pluralism cannot simply side with the groups that have traditionally formed the progressive side of political struggle – workers, women, and racial and cultural minorities. If no social group has the truth but simply has a difference to manifest, and if the manifestation of difference as such is what radical pluralism conceives of as "good," then each group with a specific difference must be allowed its proper voice. Once the criterion of conformity to the true interest of human being has been dropped, one cannot object to the expression of minority differences that, from a modernist perspective, would seem to be backward-looking or to misrepresent the real identity of another group. Backwardness presupposes the desirability of moving forward, and misrepresentation presupposes that there is a truth that discourse can represent. Both those ideas, we have seen, are rejected by radical pluralism.

Thus, it is not at all clear exactly how one is to distinguish between oppressed groups who ought to be supported and oppressive minority groups who ought to be resisted. A more serious problem, however, concerns the ability of radical pluralism to even conceive of the idea of oppressed *group*. As Young paradigmatically emphasized, not only is society composed of different groups, these groups are in turn composed of different subgroups. If the logic of radical pluralism tends towards the fragmentation of all identities, then it follows that, just as the universal "humanity" is the product of a false effacing of differences, so too is the universal "women" or "First Nations" or

"Québécois." Just as no social group represents the truth of human history, so too no subgroup, no avant-garde, represents the truth of a group. Just as radical pluralism must open itself to all possible differences at the level of social groups, so too it must listen to all the perspectives within those groups.

Again it is important to substantiate this inference by returning to the texts themselves. Thus Derrida, speaking of feminism, concentrates not upon what would unify it but rather on its proper goals, which Derrida believes to be the manifestation of the multiple possibilities of sexuality freed from all codes. He thus hopes for a world "beyond the binary differences that govern the decorum of all codes ... I would like to believe in the multiplicity of sexually marked voices. I would like to believe in the masses, this indeterminable number of blended voices, this mobile of non-identified sexual marks whose choreography can carry, divide, multiply the body of each "individual."[12] From this passage it is clear that no one of these voices is more important than any other. What is crucial to Derrida's hope is the multiple, blended, "non-identified" character of the dance as such. To give any one dancer the lead in such a piece would be to undermine what is beautiful about it. All who are involved in such a movement fully partake of it only when they recognize the multiplicity that they themselves are and thus get beyond the binary thought that picks out more and less important elements. To the extent that his choreography would free us from the tyranny of compulsory heterosexuality and the nuclear family, Derrida's argument is sound. However, feminism as such cannot simply be defined by reference to heterogeneity and difference. It emerged against a specific set of problems faced by women as women. If Derrida's deconstruction was applied to *that* identity, then the coherence of the movement would dissolve, because the group that carried the movement would no longer exist as a unified (or potentially unified) subject.

Foucault's politics runs into the same problem. For Foucault, recall, the problem with modern radical politics, especially Marxism, was that it rested upon a scientific claim to have mastered the understanding of history. On this basis the political world could be apportioned into progressive and reactionary segments, which could then be further subdivided into leaders and followers. In this way, non-conforming groups could be marginalised and disempowered. The proper political response to this situation entailed giving voice to all those groups who, because their discourse did not rest upon rational subjecthood, had been refused entry into the struggle. What genealogy struggles against is precisely the idea that society is a whole that can be taken apart and reconstructed by a single social agent.

Foucault argues that "the 'whole of society' is precisely that which should not be considered except as something to be destroyed."[13] This is what genealogy sought to do, not by determining another standpoint from which society could be mastered but by unleashing fragmentary and multiple voices of criticism against society. This goal cannot be fulfilled if, for example, the voice of "women" is substituted for the voice of the "proletariat." The only way to do away with the "whole of society" is to attack it from an indeterminate number of angles. Otherwise, the movement against society will replicate the problematic, totalizing logic of that society. Remember that for Foucault, to get beyond the subject, i.e., the metaphysical ground of totalizing society, meant "an experience that might be its real destruction or dissociation, its explosion or upheaval into something radically 'other.'"[14] To get at this radically other means getting beyond the group identities that characterize us in this society. Otherwise, the other would not be radically so.

Lyotard is more clear and concrete on this score than Derrida and Foucault. Through his engagement with the work of Habermas he was led to the conclusion that "consensus does violence to the heterogeneity of language games." He further explains that "consensus is only a particular state of discussion, not its end. Its end, on the contrary, is paralogy. This double observation (the heterogeneity of the rules and the search for dissent) destroys a belief that still underlines Habermas' research, namely, that humanity as a collective (universal) subject seeks its common emancipation through the regularization of the "moves" permitted in all language games and that the legitimacy of any statement resides in its contributing to that emancipation."[15] Thus, only by fragmenting given language games, rather than constructing higher levels of unity, can one approach a politics that would "respect both the desire for justice and the desire for the unknown."[16]

Thus, if the postmodern critique of essentialist identity is truly radical, then it must question unities such as the "Women's movement" the "First Nations" or "Québécois." Not only that, however, it must also equalize the perspectives and the differences released once those unities have been fractured. To the extent that it insists upon the "singularity" of the other and the imperative to listen, it seems obliged to accept the language of pure difference and its exclusionary consequences. On the other hand, to the extent that it resists exclusionary thinking, the politics of difference seems obliged to deconstruct the language of the oppressed when it takes exclusionary forms, but at the cost of contradicting its imperative of passive openness. By its own logic, radical pluralism thus ends up in an incoherent position.

The example of the struggle of the Québécois will confirm this incoherence.

FROM SILENCE TO ENGAGEMENT

To begin, let us consider the historical position of the Québécois vis-à-vis English Canada.[17] Until the Quiet Revolution and, later, the passage of Bill 101, English was the language of rule in Quebec. Unilingual francophones were among the poorest citizens of Canada, were subject to racial slurs and mockery, were excluded from positions of economic power in their own province, and were generally subordinate to the Montreal-based anglophone elite.[18] The history of this subordination extends back to 1759, but the ideological underpinnings of the oppression of the Québécois are best expressed in Lord Durham's report on the causes of and solutions to the 1837 rebellions. His solution to the rebellion of Lower Canada was assimilation of the French. He asks if "this French Canadian nationality is one which, for the good merely of that people, we ought to strive to perpetuate, even if it were possible?" His response is unequivocal: "I know of no national distinction marking and continuing a more hopeless inferiority ... It is to elevate them from that inferiority that I desire to give to the Canadians our English character ... They are a people with no history, and no literature ... Their nationality serves to deprive them of the enjoyments and civilizing influence of the arts."[19]

On the surface this classic example of the colonial mind-set seems a perfect candidate for deconstruction. It operates with the binary opposition civilized/uncivilized and justifies the elimination of the constitutive difference of the Québécois (their language) by consigning them to the uncivilized side of the ledger. The politics of difference could respond to this and any other example of colonial oppression by affirming the difference of the excluded, demonstrating the tendentious character of the idea of civilization, and working to create a space in which the Québécois could protect and unfold their specific difference. The problem faced by the politics of difference emerges when it shifts its focus from a deconstruction of colonial discourse to comprehension of the discourse and struggles of the oppressed. If it is committed to radical pluralism, it seems to face a problem of accepting the logic of struggle manifest in the history of the nationalist movement. To see why, we must reflect upon the metaphysical and normative underpinnings of that movement.

The history of the Québécois is marked by an ongoing struggle to preserve and develop their culture against the real threat of assimilation into English (Canadian and American) culture. The particularities of that history are not essential here. What is crucial is the normative basis of the idea of the Québécois as an oppressed nation. It is obvious that this universal abstracts from class and gender differences and marks itself off from an outside defined by non-francophone citizens of the province of Quebec. Thus, it would seem that if radical pluralism applies itself consistently, it must deconstruct not only colonial discourse but the discourse of the politically active segments of the Québécois population engaged in the struggle against their oppression. This discourse and practice too contains exclusionary elements of identity thinking that the politics of difference was concerned with deconstructing.

Consider this response to Lord Durham's report: "The government does all it can to frustrate our industry and then tells us, you are not industrious. It seizes assets intended for the schools, discourages education, and then tells us, you are ignorant. It refuses us the posts of honour and profit and then says, you have no wealth, no status. The press it controls, along with all those who benefit from this state of affairs join the chorus: you are lazy, you know nothing, you are poor, you are unimportant ... we stand convicted of lack of industry and want of knowledge, as if the crime and shame were not upon them who are their cause."[20] This argument rests on a binary opposition between "the government" and the French Canadians; it counterposes one fixed identity to another and depends upon the belief that the French Canadians have objective material interests that are thwarted by the policy of the government. Rather than deconstructing this binary opposition or adopting a relational understanding of difference, the critic seizes upon the binary opposition and turns it against itself. It asserts the needs of the Québécois people against the government; it sharpens the opposition rather than deconstructing it. The fact that the nationalist response to colonial thinking rests on binary thinking and sharpens national differences puts it at odds with the deconstructive strategies of the politics of difference.

The same binary thinking is evident in the modern nationalist movement. In an open letter to the Quebec people before the 1980 referendum René Lévesque argued that "for generations, against all odds, we have maintained an identity that sets us apart in North America. We did this after the defeat, then in the assembly of Lower Canada, we did it despite being crushed in 1837 and under the Act of Union, both of which were aimed at cutting us down to nothing, and again under a federal system which has increasingly driven us to minority status."[21] In this reading the assertion of a defined Québécois identity is a victory over the forces first of English colonialism and then of Canadian federalism. This voice of cultural difference asserting itself in binary fashion is still heard today, after the failure of two referendums, in the continuing belief that the full cultural development of the Québécois depends upon securing an independent Quebec. Québécois sociologist Fernand Dumont argues that Quebec has two choices: to accept an official culture programmed in Ottawa or, "inspired by a cultural conception of the nation that is their heritage, give themselves an effective form of political organization."[22] It is not important for present purposes to evaluate the veracity of the argument linking cultural health and political independence. What is important is to note how the assertion of cultural particularity adopts the binary language that is held, by the theorists of the politics of difference to be the language of the oppressors. This seems to oblige the postmodern defender of difference to deconstruct the "us" that is the Québécois, to reveal that it is as exclusionary as the Canadian identity to which it opposes itself. However, if it does so deconstruct the universal "Québécois" in the name of the differences that constitute it, it simultaneously weakens the asserted difference and ceases thereby to let the other speak for itself.

Perhaps the strategy of passivity, of letting the other speak for itself, would be a more efficacious strategy to adopt. While that would solve the problem of encouraging the oppressed national identity to deconstruct itself, it would then leave the politics of difference hostage to the other horn of the dilemma, namely, that it would have no grounds to oppose the most close-minded and xenophobic elements of the nationalist movement. If one understands justice and responsibility simply as heeding the address of the other or as waiting for the lightning flash of transgression, or as maximizing the number of minority positions in a society, one obliges oneself to accept whatever comes along. Both deconstructive strategies put themselves at odds with the conditions of advancing minority differences and respecting the existence of other differences. A more successful strategy must start not from what is particular in the struggles of the oppressed but from what is universal. Let us return to the critic of Lord Durham by way of making a beginning at a sketch of this alternative.

The author begins from the binary opposition between French Canadians and the government, and he clearly wants to advance the interests of the former against the latter. However, he begins not from the singularity or irreducible particularity of the Québécois but rather from something deeper: their need for access to the resources of cultural self-creation.[23] Rather than starting from an insistence upon the absolutely unique character of the Québécois, the passage is focussed on bringing to light the ways in which the material resources necessary for the creation of cultural differences are controlled by a foreign power. More deeply, the quotation rests upon the belief that the Québécois are capable of becoming subjects of their own history rather than objects of a foreign power. It thus presupposes the essentialist understanding of subjecthood as self-determination. The capacity for self-determination is suppressed by the colonial arrangement. That suppression is the motivating basis of struggle. What he demands is access to the resources necessary to make self-determination a reality and not merely a possibility.

One can see this grounding of the particular in the universal reappear in the contemporary context. In the hopes of contributing to the formation of Bouchard's "winning conditions," Jean Côté published a volume of key dates in the nationalist movement designed to awaken in the voters a memory of the struggle of the Québécois against the forces of assimilation. Notwithstanding this aim, Côté grounded his argument in favour of nationalism in the right to self-determination as defined by the UN. He argued that "by its origins, its history, its mother tongue ... its desire to live collectively, Quebec forms an authentic nation ... In 1945 the right of peoples to self-determination was recognized by article 51 of the United Nations Charter."[24] Again, the point is not to deliberate here about whether the UN Charter gives the Québécois the right to an independent nation but to draw attention to the fact that the claim to particularity is rooted in a universal ground. Côté does not argue that the Quebec people have an exclusive claim on sovereignty, but rather he argues that nations have such a right. As we will see in the next chapter, only by focussing upon the universality of the capacity for self-determination can a coherent understanding of struggles against assimilation and colonialism be developed.

From the 1837 Rebellion to the Quiet Revolution and from the Quiet Revolution to the spontaneous demonstrations in support of Bill 101 following the 1988 Supreme Court decision against its constitutionality, the struggle in Quebec has been a struggle for access to the resources necessary to preserve and develop its language and culture. In the 1960s and 1970s, amidst a wave of anti-imperialist struggles worldwide, the nationalist movement was outward-looking and critical. As more and more resources and language-specific legislation have been accumulated in the hands of the Québécois, as Meech Lake and then the Charlottetown Accord were defeated, and as the 1995 referendum narrowly failed, the nationalist movement has increasingly lost its raison d'être. Practical disorientation (not to mention an English press always on the lookout for xenophobes) has allowed narrow-minded and parochial politicians (Yves Michaud comes readily to mind) to assume a prominence not warranted by their politics or their vision. Such parochialism as we see emanating from the some members of the Parti Québécois, however, seems more in tune with the postmodern affirmation of absolute difference. But the insistence on absolute difference must inevitably turn against other differences, contradicting the postmodern affirmation of tolerance and openness, as well as detracting from the struggle over access to the material grounds of self-determination. While deconstructing parochial discourse and false notions of national purity would be an antidote to xenophobia and close-mindedness, if thought through radically, it would equally well undermine the proliferation of differences. To deconstruct social and cultural differences radically would be to destroy completely the group integrity necessary to the existence of differences. Contrary to the deconstructive moment of radical pluralism, the best way to preserve group differences is to ground them in a universal understanding of subjecthood as self-determination.

The politics of difference runs aground precisely because it fails to see beyond the surface level of difference. To be sure, as Will Kymlicka argues, the struggle of the Québécois is a struggle to "name itself."[25] But behind that particular struggle to name *itself* is a capacity *to name* that is not unique to the Québécois but is claimed and shared by all oppressed and exploited minority groups. The moment of particularity is thus grounded in a moment of universality, the struggle of one group is a specific moment in a global struggle against the control of culture-creating resources by another minority acting under the imperative of market expansion. The oppressed, no matter what their name, assert against the structures of oppression not just their name but their capacity *to name* themselves. If there is to be solidarity in the struggle against oppressive conditions, the theory that enables solidarity must not stop at a superficial understanding of differences as basic but must bring to light, indeed, sometimes confront the oppressed with, the shared universal grounds of their struggle. I will develop this point in the following chapter.

This chapter has revealed a basic incoherence in the politics of radical pluralism. More than this, however, it has also given us a glimpse of the normative and metaphysical basis of struggles against oppression. It turns out that this basis is just the capacity for self-determination that the politics of difference denies. If the oppressed were to, in effect, deconstruct the metaphysical and normative basis of their struggle, if, that is, they were to agree that they cannot in fact determine themselves, that they are simply functions of language with ever shifting identities, then the necessary grounds of their struggle would be destroyed. But if, for example, the Québécois had abandoned their struggle to preserve and develop the French language in 1837, or in 1965, or in 1988, Canada would be or would soon become a unilingual anglophone country. A real and vital sociocultural difference would have been lost. Thus, not only in theory but more seriously in practice radical pluralism contradicts itself. Consistently applied it would lead to a diminution rather than an augmentation of social differences.

The fact remains, however, that struggles for the extension of some differences quite often occur at the expense of other differences. The politics of difference is to be commended in bringing this destructive logic to light. However, it is one thing to bring a destructive logic to light, quite another to develop a counter-logic that solves the problem. In the last ten years Canada has witnessed some awful scenes of conflict between its two historically oppressed groups, the Québécois and the First Nations. The path to resolving those conflicts, we will now see, takes us deeper into the essentialist understanding of subjecthood. In the next chapter I will examine this conflict from the perspective of the First Nations, bringing to light the identity between the normative grounds of their struggle and those of the Québécois. I will then set both struggles in the global context of struggles against the homogenizing forces of the global market. In drawing the links between different communities of resistance, the next chapter will supply objective evidence against the postmodern understanding of the normative grounds of minority struggle and more clearly bring to light their universal basis.

7 The Universal Voice of the Other

In the previous chapter we observed the paradoxical outcome of radical pluralist thought. The harder one pushes the radical elements – either differences as absolutely singular or the deconstruction of the identities that define differences – the more one advances conditions opposed to the existence of social differences. Rather than strengthening the position of those on the margins, then, radical pluralism either undermines the unity the margins themselves assert or accepts a belief in absolute differences that encourages the degeneration of struggles into conflicts between oppressed groups. In both cases the politics of differences draws political attention away from the global forces responsible for cultural homogenization. Radical pluralism, thought through consistently, does not secure the conditions for a society that is more tolerant of cultural differences but undermines those cultural differences, because it repudiates unity and universality.

Nevertheless, we have also noted that the self-assertion of oppressed differences can take the form of exclusionary practices. It is the case, for example, that the politics of Québécois nationalism have polarised the opposition between *"pur laine"* Québécois and non-Francophones. The pertinent question is, therefore, how critical philosophy can defend the values both of difference and pluralism without making concessions to the violence of the discourse of racial purity? Contrary to the politics of difference, I will maintain that the only way to accomplish this goal is to begin not from difference but from a critical understanding of a universal human essence. This essence, we have begun to see, is not the tendentious product of a modernist metanarrative but the necessary presupposition of struggles against oppression that is brought to light by the struggles of the oppressed themselves.

By insisting on the humanist grounds of cultural difference, this argument puts itself at odds with the main strains of contemporary critical philosophy,[1] all of which, as we have seen, condemn "the totalizing logic of humanism" for "disconnect[ing] and hierarchically separat[ing]" oppressed identities.[2] Humanism, as we are about to see, is not necessarily totalizing in the pernicious sense Emberly and other theorists of the politics of difference assume it to be. While it is of course true that the idea of humanity has been invoked to justify the exclusion and oppression of the nonwhite, nonmale world, there is a much deeper meaning of the term that is manifest not in the ideology of the oppressors but in the struggles of the oppressed against their oppressors. To discover this sense of humanism, however, one must work beneath the surface level of struggles to the depth of their metaphysical enabling conditions, a strategy that has become taboo in the last thirty years. Nonetheless, a recovery of a properly understood universal metaphysical ground of struggle is the best hope for ending the destructive antipathies of the contemporary world. Once we go beneath the surface, we will discover that the oppressed assert a capacity for self-determination that is not relative or unique to specific groups but is the universal essence of human being and the necessary condition of those struggles themselves. I will bring this deep ground to light by examining some recent struggles of Canada's First Nations, in particular struggles that have brought them into conflict with the Québécois. If these opposed struggles can be shown to follow from a failure to recognize the underlying essence shared by the Québécois and the First Nations, I will have uncovered the framework for a solution to their conflicts and, by extension, other conflicts between the oppressed that mark our world and detract from the struggle for freedom.

THE UNIVERSAL GROUNDS OF CULTURAL DIFFERENCE

It is essential to keep in mind that postmodern criticism argued that the key to understanding the struggles of oppressed minorities was to accept the fact that those struggles did not rest upon universal normative grounds and did not have universal aims. The politics of difference would argue, then, that to interpret minority struggles in a universal fashion runs the risk of distorting the real character of those struggles. The postmodern reading is not without evidence in its favour in the continuing proliferation of difference-based struggles against imposed normalcy, as well as in more classical struggles for national self-determination. It is in the latter, however, that we see the real danger of a politics of difference cut off from its universal grounds. The last ten years have been witness to shocking struggles between groups, each of whom claims to be an oppressed minority. The civil wars in the Balkans are of course the most obvious examples, but Canada has not been spared these conflicts. The clearest example in the case of Canada is the confrontation in Oka, Quebec, between the Sûreté de Québec, the Canadian Army, and the Mohawk Nation. This conflict will serve as the test case for my claims, first, that there is a universal ground for minority struggle that has been overlooked by postmodern critique and (at times) the struggling minorities themselves and, second, that this ground must be brought to light and made into the conscious principle of struggles against oppression as the necessary condition of success.

On first glance the struggles around Oka seem to emphasize the need for the deconstruction of all absolute claims to difference. The Québécois who stoned Mohawks fleeing the army's occupation at Ville Lasalle appear to be a paradigmatic example of the dangers of insisting upon the purity of their differences. On the other hand, from the deconstructive perspective the Mohawk warriors who took up arms might appear equally dangerous to a politics of openness, tolerance, and difference, insofar as they usurped the voice of the whole community.[3] The deconstructive response to a naked conflict of differences would seem to have to follow Iris Young's prescription and set out to break down the hard and fast lines dividing Québécois from Mohawk, to set out to reveal the relational character of the differences, the co-dependence, so to speak, of differences upon one another. Under the glare of deconstructive criticism, suppressed differences within each community (Québécois who supported the Mohawks, Mohawks who preached negotiation, etc.) might have been brought to light and a nonviolent reconciliation might have become possible. Examined closely, however, what such an approach brings to light is precisely what the other side of deconstruction (the side that insists that difference and not identity is fundamental) denied, namely, shared interests across the divisions of difference. Those shared interests are the universal voice of the other that critical philosophy must heed if it is to play a part in advancing the cause of pluralism and tolerance.

On the surface, of course, this universal voice is not apparent. The struggle at Oka (and subsequent confrontations in Southern Alberta,

Gustafson Lake in British Columbia, and, more recently, in Burnt Church, New Brunswick) seems to be rooted in the First Nations' exclusive claim to control the land, which runs up against, again in the case of Oka, the claims of the Québécois to sovereignty and the indivisibility of their territory. Viewed in that light, the struggle of the Mohawks of Kanesatake and Kahnawake goes back more than one century and is grounded in a particular claim to a right to control traditional lands. The arguments to which the Mohawks of 1989 appealed were first formulated in the late nineteenth century. Consider, for example, the words of Joseph Onasakenarat, chief of the Mohawk nation in 1868. He argued that "this land is ours; ours by right of possession; ours as a heritage, given to us by a sacred legacy. It is the spot where our fathers lie; beneath whose trees our mothers sang our lullaby, and you would tear it from us and leave us wanderers at the mercy of fate."[4] There is little in this quotation that would lead one to conclude that there is a universal normative basis for the claim over the land. It bears more in common with Lyotard's understanding of minority struggles as the struggle of groups striving to remain minorities. It makes reference only to the particular, specific history of the Mohawk people.

If, however, we examine the argument of the Mohawks more fully, we see that this claim to the land is not rooted simply in an exclusive "right of possession." That right of possession is in turn grounded in an understanding of the relationship between a people and the earth. The understanding of the earth as the ground of survival and flourishing of all people is a universal normative ground, not a private and exclusive claim of one specific minority. As Johnny Cree, faithkeeper of the longhouse of Kanesatake explains, "[Mother Earth] gives the land and the trees that breathe the oxygen that sustains all life on earth. Her breath is all over the world giving and sustaining life. Without Mother Earth and the trees there would be no life ... We do not have a sense of ownership like the white man. We are the caretakers of the land for our children and for future generations but we are responsible to Mother Earth to see that our children and their children will be able to walk the land and still see the green trees and grass and clear streams that give clean water and fresh air."[5] Cree here appeals not to a particular tradition of the Mohawk people but to a universal value – the earth as the force that gives and sustains all life – to justify the struggles of this particular group of people. This understanding of the earth as the universal life-sustaining force is not unique to the Mohawks of Kanesatake and Kahnawake: it is shared by indigenous peoples around the globe.[6] That universalism is poignantly evident in a photograph that forms part of the photo essay that makes up *This Land is Our Land*. It pictures a small child near the barricades in Kanesatake beneath a homemade sign that reads simply, "All Native people want peace and sovereignty." "Peace and sovereignty," it reads, not sovereignty at any cost and to the exclusion of everyone else. The particular claim to difference made by the Mohawks of Quebec is thus grounded in a universal value, namely, a nondestructive relationship between humanity and nature (remember that the struggle was sparked by the decision of the town of Oka to expand a golf course onto lands sacred to the Mohawk community), and articulated as a particular demand for self-government.

To be sure, the spiritual moment of the Mohawks' struggle is not universally shared with other minority struggles. The specific content of the spiritual claim can be set to one side, however, in order that the form it shares with all struggles of oppressed minorities may come to light. Cree's argument understands the relationship between peoples and the earth as one of nondestructive life maintenance. The particularities of a people, any people, depend for their existence on the availability of resources, through the transformation of which a people defines itself. Here again we see that the basis of the struggle for cultural particularity is not particular but universal, a relationship to the earth as the origin of the resources of cultural difference. The demand for control over the land is thus not a demand made simply on the basis of a private and exclusive right; rather, it is made in universal terms on the grounds that the earth exists for all people and makes available what every culture needs to sustain itself. It argues against the practices of the "white man," but at the deepest level it is not attacking a particular group (the white man *as* white or the Québécois *as* Québécois) but a destructive mode of land use that, as I have implied, is the real cause of cultural homogeneity.

The universal grounds of cultural difference were not lost on some elements of the Québécois people. Madeleine Parent, president of the Solidarité Populaire du Québec, wrote Robert Bourassa, who was premier at the time, denouncing the plan to call in the army and drawing a parallel with the October crisis of 1970 .[7] More instructively, the present premier, Bernard Landry, who was then a PQ opposition member, articulated precisely the identity that underlies the cultural differences dividing the Québécois from the Mohawks. "How can we claim the right to independence," he asked, "and deny that right to the First People? It is not reasonable. It is not logical."[8] Indeed it is not reasonable or logical, but that conclusion follows only from a philosophical perspective that has not bid adieu to reason and logic.

The claim that we are dealing with a critique of socioeconomic forces and not with the particular culture of the white man can be further supported by briefly examining the most famous struggle of indigenous peoples of the last decade, the Zapatista Rebellion in Mexico. The indigenous people of Mexico, like the indigenous people of Canada, also faced economically motivated threats to their traditional lands. The grounds of their resistance are instructive insofar as they are the same as the grounds claimed by the indigenous people of Canada and, as we will see, the Québécois.

On 1 January 1993, the North American Free Trade Agreement (NAFTA) came into effect. While North American capital celebrated the securing of a free-trade zone stretching virtually from the North Pole to the equator, workers, social activists, feminists, and indigenous populations sensed that the increase in the freedom of capital promised by NAFTA meant an increase in their own servitude. Although capital had secured for itself a trade bloc capable of competing against the European Community (EC) and the growing power of the Pacific Rim, for workers and others marginalised by the market, NAFTA represented yet another diminution of their power and rights. While protest was on the whole rather quiet, in the jungle of the Chiapas region of Mexico shots rang out and villages were seized by the Zapatista Liberation Army. "Today we say ENOUGH IS ENOUGH. We are the inheritors of the true builders of our nation. The dispossessed, we are millions, and we thereby call upon our brothers and sisters to join this struggle as the only path, so that we will not die of hunger."[9] Thus was war declared on the Mexican state and, by extension, on North American capital on the day that NAFTA took effect. This was no arbitrary act, however. The Zapatistas argued that their revolt accorded with the Mexican Constitution and flowed from the underlying freedom definitive of human beings. Their declaration rejects "any attempt to disgrace our just cause by accusing us of being drug traffickers, drug guerrillas, thieves, or other names that might be used by our enemies. Our struggle follows from the Constitution, which is held high by its call for justice and equality."[10] The declaration concludes with the observation that the people who have undertaken the struggle are "full and free" and that the struggle seeks to create a political and economic system in which this freedom is concretely realized.

Although the Zapatistas emerged from the specific circumstances that endangered the very survival of the indigenous population of Mexico, they did not, as the above document makes clear, rest their struggle on this particularity but rather sought universal foundations in the notions of justice, equality, and freedom. This was not, as

Lyotard claims anti-imperialist struggles are, "struggles of minorities intending to remain minorities and to be recognized as such."[11] Luis Hernandez argues that "the great virtue of the Zapatistas has been that their discourse is sufficiently wide to be interpreted by many sectors according to their own interests and objectives. At a moment in which nobody was betting on great change, in which there was enormous skepticism about possibilities of bringing about satisfactory change through revolution, the January 1 insurrection was a breath of fresh air blowing from the South ... The uprising seems to want to tell us that we don't have to conform to the way things are going, that the particular authoritarian and vertical form of modernization is not necessarily the only path."[12]

The global outlook of the Zapatistas is passionately confirmed in the words of their leader, Commander Marcos: "Marcos is gay in San Francisco, black in South Africa, an Asian in Europe, a Chicano in San Ysidro ... a communist in the post–Cold War era."[13] In other words, Marcos is not a "territory of language" but a link in a chain of struggles forged by the outsiders and the oppressed against liberal-capitalist society. Marcos reconfirms this global, universal outlook in an interview concerning the effects of capitalist globalization on marginal cultures. Against the myth of openness that sustains fantasies of the progressive effects of globalization, Marcos argues that "the world is becoming more closed, and it's becoming increasingly intolerant, and it's causing absurd fundamentalisms to proliferate. They're absurd, it's nothing else. And look ... the one promoting it is the man with money ... saying that suits me, because the fragmentation works for me. We are saying that what's going on here is a world war. They are destroying land like never before, riches like never before, they are eliminating populations like never before."[14]

Marcos' point is clear. What threatens indigenous culture and particularity is not universal rationality or an essentialist conception of subjecthood but rather the forces of capitalist globalization. Responses that rest on the radical assertion of differences are the reflex of the imposed homogenization of the globe, but they are powerless to resist it insofar as they remain dispersed. Instead, local cultures under threat must work down to the common source of their problems and draw on their common strength – the very power the postmodern politics of difference denies – the power of self-determination.

The globalism of Marcos's position is hardly surprising given the global source of the particular problems the indigenous population of Chiapas faces. NAFTA was a step in the present restructuring of the North American economy in response to the increase in competitive pressures. The same forces that threatened the Mohawk Nation (profit-driven expansion onto sacred land) threatened the indigenous population of Mexico. But those same forces are responsible for threatening the specific differences of the Québécois, even though the leaders of the Québécois nationalist movement are for the most part fully integrated into the system of capitalist market relations. What these facts reveal is that the axes of struggle today are fundamentally between not different cultural groups but different understandings of life. On the one hand are the *human* values of self-differentiation, toleration of otherness, and pluralism, all of which presuppose a system of resource appropriation based on need, and on the other are the market values of exploitation, privatisation, and profit maximization. In order to understand this claim, however, we must bring to light the way in which the struggle of the Québécois to maintain their language and the struggle of indigenous communities to maintain their land base both rest upon an understanding of the essence of human being as self-determination and how this universal essence can form the ground of solidarity rather than division.

This ground can be disclosed by comparing the object of struggle in each case. For the Québécois, their goal has always been to create conditions in which the French language is secure. For the Mohawks, their struggle has been for a secure land base. As everyone knows, these two struggles have brought the two communities into conflict. The deep cause of the conflict is a failure in both groups to see the common source and common goal of their struggles. The common goal has often been recognized at the political level. As Kymlicka argues, "the demands of the two groups share an important feature: they rest, at least in part, on the sense that both are distinct nations or peoples whose existence predates that of the Canadian state. As nations or peoples, they claim the right to self-determination."[15] What is most often overlooked, however, is the shared nature of the threats their right to self-determination faces and, more deeply, the grounds of this private *right* to self-determination in the universal *capacity* for self-determination.

In both cases the communities have historically lacked the material securities for their cultural differences, because someone else has controlled the resources necessary for cultural survival. Consciousness of the fact that the resources for cultural survival have been controlled by groups opposed or indifferent to cultural survival gives rise to a consciousness of oppression. The Québécoise who is forced to speak English or the Mohawk who sees her land swallowed up by a golf course becomes aware in that experience of being determined by forces external to what she takes to be her fundamental identity. If both simply insist on their identity to the exclusion of its material grounds, then conflict between the two is possible. If, however, both refer to the structure of the experience of oppression, a deeper identity of interests becomes apparent. In both cases the members of the group are conscious of not-being what they take themselves to be essentially. Both struggles are possible because both groups are not in fact what they are in essence, self-determining. Both groups are shaped by forces opposed to the specific difference constitutive of the community. But what makes those specific differences possible – the capacity for self-determination, subjecthood – is not unique to either group but is a human capacity variously articulated.

The underlying ground of the struggle for cultural difference in the human capacity for self-determination is most beautifully evoked in the work of Lee Maracle. Maracle, a member of the Stoh:lo Nation of British Columbia, has long been a fighter for Aboriginal and women's freedom. She does not give into the disintegrative logic entailed by the postmodern understanding of difference. That is, she does not assert her womanhood against her Aboriginal identity and her Aboriginal identity against racist traditions. Instead, she expressly articulates her identity as an Aboriginal woman as the reality of her human being. Thus she argues that "the denial of native womanhood is the reduction of a whole people to a subhuman level."[16] It drives the people to a subhuman level precisely because it denies to them what is most human, and what is most human is no particular feature of Natives, of women, or of Native women but rather the capacity to determine themselves. Maracle writes that "until we are also seen as people we are not equal and there can be no unity between us. Until our separate history is recognized and our need for self-determination satisfied, we are not equal."[17]

For Maracle humanity is neither a particular feature of a particular identity nor an abstract universal invented by the colonizer in order to justify his rule but rather the necessary basis of resistance to colonialism. In claiming her humanity she claims back from the coloniser the power to determine her identity. Her humanity is expressed in this power to resist, the power to assert against the oppressive determining force of colonial racism her ability to create herself. Human being is thus in Maracle's eyes the power to create differences in a context of mutuality and freedom. Acting on the basis of this humanity means in part recovering her "separate history," but the recovery is for the sake of new creations. Cultural differences are not the products of symbolic codes that merely position subjects within them; they are the living creations of subjects who have secured the conditions for a free existence: "culture changes ... and it will do so as long as people busy themselves with living. It is a living thing."[18] Insofar as culture is an expression of a people's "busying themselves with living" the interest in cultural difference is a human concern, and thus Maracle declares her solidarity with "ordinary white folk" and with other oppressed minorities throughout the globe.[19]

Twenty years before Maracle's text, Harold Adams, a Métis scholar and activist from Saskatchewan, declared that a forward-looking Native nationalism would usher in a "new humanism" that would establish the conditions for "new cultural developments" not only within Native communities but in the white world as well.[20] The nationalist Guy Laforest also justifies the struggle of the Québécois on humanist terms. In his view it is not a struggle against other differences but a struggle for the conditions in which new differences can be created on the basis of mutual respect and interaction.[21]

Let us at this point contrast the underlying identity between oppressed groups in a concept of human being as the power of subjecthood, as the power of self-determination, with the understanding of cultural difference definitive of the postmodern politics of difference. We have seen in the previous chapter that postmodern theory adopts two opposed understandings of difference. Both, as we will now see, are in definite tension, indeed, contradiction, with the expressed understandings of oppressed groups in struggle. On the one hand, postmodern theory insists on the absolute singularity of cultural difference. To be sure, there are always voices in cultural groups who insist on the group's purity, but these voices can hardly be accepted if one's overriding goal is to promote tolerance and protect difference. Because that is its overriding goal, postmodern theory is forced to the opposite approach to difference: to deny absolute singularity and to deconstruct discourses of racial or ethnic purity. This approach, however, ends up deconstructing the very differences that it is the goal of postmodern theory to defend. In both cases postmodernism maintains that in no case are differences the products of self-determining activity, because their defining deconstruction of the concept of subjecthood concludes with the claim that all differences are the function of symbolic codes that determine, and are never determined by, active human beings.

The oppressed themselves, as we have seen, do not simply base their claims to difference by insisting on the specificity or uniqueness of their differences. That is, they point to universal normative grounds to legitimate their struggles. As Charles Taylor argues, "the development of modern notions of identity has given rise to a politics of difference. There is, of course, a universalist basis to this as well ... Everyone should be recognized for his or her unique identity ... with the politics of difference, what we are asked to recognize is the unique identity of this individual or group."[22] Thus, the Québécois have not simply insisted on their private right to speak French, they appeal to a "right" to self-determination that is universally recognized as a legitimate claim. The Mohawks do not simply appeal to a right to possession; they go further and ground that right in an understanding of the earth as the fundamental ground of all life. Those rights make sense, however, only if there is a real capacity shared by both groups (and historically denied by the oppressor groups) to determine their own cultural horizons. Hence the universal basis of claims to difference is the essential capacity of human beings to become the creators of their own life-horizons. Minority groups enter into struggle when social conditions contradict that essential nature.

The postmodern politics of difference, however, stakes its claim to radicality on a denial of subjecthood and a deconstruction of all ideas of the human essence. In other words, the politics of difference sets itself against the necessary ground of the struggles of the oppressed groups it purports to support. If it is true that the understanding of human being as essentially self-determining is inevitably exclusionary and oppressive, then the struggles of the oppressed, which are precisely struggles for self-determination, must be adduced as part of the problems plaguing the modern world. But those struggles become exclusionary and oppressive when they are not consciously rooted in the universalist understanding of human being. That is, when the groups in struggle fail to understand that their specific differences are in essence moments of an underlying human capacity for self-determination, they conflict with other struggles for the same. For the same. That is the crucial truth to be gleaned from this comparison of the ground of the struggles of the Mohawks, Zapatistas, and Québécois. All stem from the same contradiction between the essential capacity for self-determination and social conditions that determine them from without, i.e., oppressively. Both aim at the same general solution – social conditions that express rather than deny that essential self-determining capacity.

POSTMODERNISM'S DOUBLE BIND

The politics of difference recommends itself as more attuned to specificity and difference, and yet in concrete instances of struggle to preserve and extend differences, the groups in question appeal to universal goals and values and set themselves against social conditions that thwart their capacity for self-determination. If Young, for example, is right, and postmodern thought "critiques ... the logic of identity because ... [it] denies or represses the particularities and heterogeneities of sensual experience," then she must extend this critique to oppressed peoples who also ground their struggles in the "logic of identity."[23] To do so, however, would be to set herself against the very groups she hopes to support. Not to do so, on the other hand, puts her at odds with the philosophical deconstruction of identity thinking that motivates her politics. This 'double-bind' affects the politics of difference generally.

The politics of difference cannot both affirm struggles against oppression, as it does, and deny that these struggles are rooted in the capacity for self-determination, which it also does. To understand this claim at the necessary philosophical depth, we must entertain a digression on the meaning of the terms "self" and "other." These terms are not unique to postmodernism but extend back in the history of philosophy to Hegel's *Phenomenology of Spirit*. What the postmodern use forgets is what Hegel took to be essential, that the difference between self and other is the result of a one-sided understanding of selfhood. In other words, the difference between self and other is really a matter of hidden identity. Bringing this hidden identity to the surface does not entail the subordination of the other to the self or the reduction of difference to an identity without remainder but expresses, rather, an achieved equality between unique and self-determining individuals.

There can be no *essential* difference between self and other, because the positions are completely reversible. Let us take a clear political example. Consider the colonial relationship as a relationship between self (the coloniser) and other (colonised). From the perspective of the coloniser, the colonized is other. Yet, from the perspective of the colonized, the coloniser is other. Together, both categories have universal extension; apart, each implies the other. As such, there is no substantive difference between them. What is different is that the colonizer does not recognize in the other what cannot in substance be recognized by postmodernism: the capacity for self-determination. Postmodernism attempts to maintain this distinction between self and other as the basis of its critical project. But it does so by contending that the other stands on the side of "difference." We have seen, however, that this postmodern position, thought through, is incoherent. It presupposes what it denies, namely, a capacity on the part of the other to assert its proper identity against the forces that oppress that identity. At the same time, the reality is that actual struggles against oppression do not base themselves on a claim to the possession of pure difference but rather on a claim to a shared humanity, a capacity for self-determination that is violently denied the oppressed. If one approaches this struggle from a certain interpretation of the Hegelian perspective on the relation between self and other, one can both understand the specificity of the other and account for why the other tends to situate its discourse within a universal framework.

What one witnesses in the struggle between self and other is not a conflict between "the logic of difference" and "the logic of the same," but rather a struggle between two forces, one of humanity, one of denying this humanity in the other. This struggle is characterized by Hegel as a "struggle to the death" in chapter 4 of *The Phenomenology.* There he notes that "what is 'other' for it [self-consciousness] is an unessential, negatively characterized object. But the 'other' is also self-consciousness; one individual is confronted by another individual."[24] What postmodernism characterizes as a necessarily unbalanced relationship is, in fact, a relationship of unrecognized equality in a shared human essence. This equality can be recognized only after each proves to the other his or her essential freedom. Hegel continues: "Thus the relation of the two self-conscious individuals is such that they prove themselves and each other through a life-and-death struggle. They must engage in this struggle, for they must raise their certainty of being *for themselves* to truth, both in the case of the other and in their own case. And it is only through staking one's life that freedom is won."[25] Before their antagonistic relationship each posits the other as unessential, merely other. Once the struggle has been joined, the underlying equality in essence, the fact that each proves himself or herself a self, an active, self-determining force, emerges and breaks down the apparent difference between the two.

This abstract characterization is certainly no substitute for concrete empirical analysis of definite struggles. Nevertheless, it discloses an issue of profound metaphysical importance, particularly in the context of the postmodern attempt to conceive of struggle apart from this underlying essence of the human subject. Lest it be thought that I am falsely imposing a modernist "metanarrative" on struggles that are not amenable to this Hegelian reading, consider for a moment how Franz Fanon, arguably the greatest theorist of anticolonialist struggle, conceives of the grounds of struggles against oppression. Commenting on the Algerian civil war, Fanon argues that it is at the moment when the colonized person recognizes his or her humanity, the universal expressed in the particular, that s/he begins to resist: "General de Gaulle speaks of the 'yellow multitudes' and Francois Mauriac of the black, brown, and yellow masses that will soon be unleashed.

The native knows all this and laughs to himself every time he spots an allusion to the animal kingdom in the other's words. For he knows he is not an animal, and it is precisely when he recognizes his humanity that he begins to sharpen the weapons with which he will secure his victory."[26] When the native recognizes his humanity what he recognizes is that he is not "other" but "self," not an object fit to serve but a subject fit to determine his own horizons. Moreover, he proves this not only to himself but to the colonizer, i.e., the one who tries to reduce the native to the status of mere object.

Furthermore, Fanon does not believe that anticolonial struggle is simply concerned with the particular freedom of the colonised or with merely preserving non-Western cultures against the onslaught of oppressive modernization. He argues instead that "all the elements of a solution to the great problems of mankind have existed at one time or another in European thought. But the action of European man has not carried out this mission which fell to him ... Today we are present at the stasis of Europe ... Let us reconsider the question of the cerebral reality and the cerebral mass of all mankind, whose connections must be increased, whose channels must be diversified, and whose message must be re-humanized."[27] Fanon, theorist from Martinique and militant in the Algerian War of Liberation, does not see that the ground of anticolonialism is the minority character of the oppressed, nor does he conceive of emancipation as an increase in the fragmentation of the globe into smaller and smaller differences. Fanon reaches a conclusion in direct opposition to that of the postmodern politics of difference but perfectly in line what I am arguing for – the struggle for national self-determination is a struggle waged in the name of the *humanity* of the oppressed and for the sake of the full expression of the cultural differences that concretely define what *human* being is. Lewis Gordon, commenting on Fanon, explicates these critical-humanist implications. He argues that by "identifying European man *qua* European man, we, following Fanon, signal the importance of decentering *him* as the designator of human reality. But this does not mean that the project of constructing or engaging in human science must also be abandoned. Instead, in the spirit of Fanon's call for radicality and originality, the challenge becomes one of radical engagement and attuned relevance."[28] In other words, the point is not to abandon the universal foundations of the critique of oppression but to make the abstract universal "man" (which is nothing more than the particular idea of European man falsely generalized and imposed on others) into a concrete universal (the self-determining capacity of human being realized as a multiplicity of freely interacting cultures).

In a related vein, Cornell West brings to light the universal human capacity underlying what he calls the "cultural politics of difference." His focus is on the struggles of marginalised groups to reclaim and transform the representations that have been imposed upon them by the culture of the oppressors. He is thinking of the manifold artistic practices by which women, gays and lesbians, and African Americans, amongst others, have, over the last thirty years, sought to change their social standing by transfiguring the images through which they are represented to the popular consciousness. Although what is contested in each struggle considered singularly is something particular (the representation of woman as handmaiden to man, the African-American man as dangerous, etc.) underlying and connecting them all as a form of *politics* is a universal value. West argues that "the most significant theme" of the cultural politics of difference is "the agency, capacity, and ability of human beings who have been culturally degraded, politically oppressed, and economically exploited." He continues, maintaining that "this theme neither romanticizes nor idealizes marginalised people. Rather, it accentuates their humanity and tries to attenuate the institutional constraints on their life-chances."[29] Like Maracle, West neither reduces humanity to particular differences nor elevates one difference to the status of universal truth. Instead, humanity is identified with the culture-creating capacity of the oppressed: their ability to consciously transform their situation.

The fundamental point of this section is that the struggles of the oppressed are not really struggles between self and other but in fact struggles between two selves, one of which, the oppressor, refuses to recognize the selfhood of the other (the oppressed). What becomes manifest through the struggle is that the free development of each position requires the transcendence of the unequal relationship. By proving itself in victory, the formerly oppressed side proves itself to be in essence human, that is, the same as what the oppressive side asserted itself to be: a subject capable of ruling itself. What is changed is that the one-sidedness of the oppressor's claim to difference has been overcome. In showing itself to be a people capable of self-determination, the oppressed people destroys the oppressor's claim to difference. "Otherness," then, is really a concept that belongs to the thinking of the oppressor. The struggle of the oppressed is a struggle to make manifest precisely what the oppressor denies. Success in such struggles opens the way for reconciliation, reciprocity, and mutual recognition of a common humanity underlying the activity of creating new cultural forms.

Thus we return to the examination of the central problem. If the struggle between self and other is a struggle between two selves, one of which is struggling for what the other already has – the material and institutional means of self-determination, then the postmodern conception of this struggle contradicts not only the nature of the struggle but also itself. If postmodernism insists that the other must remain other, then it is once again telling the other what it should be; it is once again imposing a discourse (which, we might add, was also developed in Western universities) upon non-Western peoples. By presupposing that the arguments it has made against modern political criticism are applicable to the zones where exploitation and oppression are most extreme and by ruling out the efficacy of radical economic and political transformation in these zones, postmodern critique can wrongly substitute itself for the actual character of the historic struggles against imperialism. It ignores the fact that no one has forced the discourse of critical humanism upon the oppressed, that they themselves have taken up the notion of human essence as self-determination and applied it concretely in their own situation. To the extent that postmodernism is a radical critique of essentialism, therefore, it is in contradiction with what the oppressed say for themselves and is thus in contradiction with itself, since it holds that the other "cannot speak the language of the same" or is a "minority seeking to be recognized as such." If it presses forward with this analysis, therefore, it is in practice telling the other what the other is. It also deflects attention away from the basic, global causes of oppression.

For the Mexican teenage woman being poisoned in a factory in one of the Maquiladoras, Marxist political economy may have a great deal more relevance than the deconstruction of the subject. Indeed, she might benefit from reading a text that tells her that she is linked by her situation to sweatshop workers in Indonesia and on Spadina Avenue in Toronto and that together, by forging the links of solidarity on the basis of the humanity denied to them, they can one day become in actuality what they are in essence, free beings. As Kate Soper argues, "revelling in the loss of progress is a Western metropolitan privilege which depends upon living in a state of grace where no one is starving you, no one is torturing you, no one even denying you the price of a cinema ticket or tube fare to the postmodernism conference."[30] It is possible that in a liberal democracy, where tolerance is already to some extent an operative value, the deconstruction of the subject *may appear* to offer the possibility of increased pluralism, but in contexts where these formal guarantees have not been achieved, such a deconstruction would deprive groups of the concepts for struggle *that they themselves* lay claim to.

In either case, the relationship between self and other is wrongly conceived and the struggle against the material grounds of oppression is not advanced.

What has become apparent is that the essential problem underlying the postmodern position is that its desire to listen to the other as the other would speak itself implies emancipation from external forces that determine the other but also criticizes the only foundation upon which emancipation can be coherently conceived – a defining capacity for self-determination. The belief that the other has something to say and that this cannot be heard today calls forth the idea, manifestly criticized and deconstructed, that human beings have the capacity to determine themselves and the society in which they will exist. Nevertheless, just that idea is held to be behind "the worst political systems ... [of] the twentieth century," and for that reason it is deconstructed.[31] In so deconstructing this idea, however, postmodernism deconstructs the very grounds upon which the other could speak *freely*. The feminist theorist Nancy Hartsock asks a pertinent question in this regard. "Why is it," she questions, "that just at the moment when so many of us ... begin to act as subjects rather than objects of history, that just then the concept of subjecthood becomes problematic?"[32] Kirstie McClure, although she ultimately rejects the notion of subjecthood she invokes, reveals the ultimate problem with the deconstruction of the human capacity for self-determination. "Just when marginal and oppressed people are asserting their rights as political subjects is no time deconstruct the categories ... to do so is to become complicit with the neo-conservative agenda."[33]

The politics of difference is not, of course, neoconservative in its goals. Its problem lies rather in a systematic confusion about the nature of subjecthood and the political implications of the concept of human essence. This confusion, which will be explicated in detail in the final chapter, results in a pervasive failure on the part of postmodernism to think through the necessary grounds of the concept of oppression. Failure to see that oppression presupposes an essential difference between what people have the capacity to become and what they are in fact made to be, the difference between subjecthood and subject-position, led to the belief that oppression could be overcome without this occurrence being viewed as the release of oppressed subjective capacities. The idea of freedom in postmodern philosophy is the maximization of subject-positions. However, as subjecthood is reduced to subject-position, the idea of freedom becomes incoherent, because all subject-positions are determined by dynamics that are beyond human control.

Let me stop at this point in order to sum up the results of the present chapter. The central problem examined here stems from the contradiction between the postmodern claim that universal history and essential subjecthood are exclusionary modes of thinking and the actual use made of these very notions by different groups struggling against Western imperialism. The claim that modernist theory and practice are oppressive is contradicted by the appeal made to these very modes by actual groups in struggle. This implies a contradiction in the postmodern argument as soon as it is put into practice in any act of solidarity with struggles against oppression. Support for such struggles entails support for principles that are the antithesis of postmodern principles. Thus, the specific content of postmodern politics is negated in proportion to the support lent to struggles which employ universal ideas of history and subjecthood.

On the other hand, if postmodern thinking resists such an outcome and criticizes such struggles, it falls into a second contradiction. That is, it will contradict the claim that others must be allowed to speak in a voice of their own choosing. The middle path between these two contradictions, i.e., attempting to isolate, from within what appears to be a modernist discourse, elements that are in fact radically different, either returns postmodernity to the incoherence of radical pluralism or it again runs up against the fact that when the oppressed speak they manifest a capacity for self-determination and a desire for a different world, one which corresponds to this capacity.

The more fundamental question remains. What is it that explains the concern postmodern thinking shows towards oppressed and marginalised people and groups? If, as the postmodern analysis shows, all subjects are in fact discursively constructed subject-positions with no capacities proper to themselves, what is it that allows postmodern thinking to even conceive of an oppressed subject-position? At root, all positions are equally determined by forces beyond individual and collective control. At root, there is no basis upon which one could determine the difference between an oppressive and a free society. If there is no normative value to the idea of humanity, then there is no normative weight to the notion of inhumanity either. In other words, there are no social systems that are fundamentally opposed to human freedom, because human freedom has no meaning if humans are mere positions determined by social dynamics. Human freedom, as I will argue in the next chapter, must mean more than the unbounded proliferation of sites for the production of differences. The production of differences must be tied in a fundamental way to an essential capacity to produce those differences. While postmodernism affirms the production of differences, it cannot connect this to a capacity to self-consciously create differences without contradicting its deconstruction of subjecthood.

However, it is clear that there is genuine concern for the amelioration of social and political problems among the major postmodern thinkers. The critique of the modern idea of subjecthood is essentially political. This idea of the subject as the creator of its own reality, the politics of difference argues, is the cause of the marginalization of nonconforming groups. However, as I will now argue, this critique makes sense only if human beings have a shared capacity to determine the social environment. Only if there is something proper to humans themselves that is repressed but not destroyed by society can oppression or marginalization be coherently conceived. In other words, by concerning themselves with questions of oppression and marginalization, postmodern thinkers presuppose subjecthood as *that which demands that differences be expressed*, even as their deconstruction argues that this capacity is a destructive fiction. Only if subjecthood is presupposed do the political concerns of postmodern thought make sense. Some capacity that ought not to be oppressed or marginalized is presupposed by those concerns as the ground against which they take on their normative meaning.

8 The Return of the Repressed

In part 1, through a close reading of the work of Derrida, Foucault, and Lyotard, I disclosed the philosophical groundwork for a radical politics of difference. That groundwork is defined by four core principles: that human being is not defined by any essence; that the modern understanding of the human essence, subjecthood as self-determination, is the metaphysical ground of the exclusion and oppression of nonconforming others, that there is, in the words of Gayatri Spivak, "an affinity between the subject of imperialism and the subject of humanism";[1] that to "free" those excluded and oppressed others from their exclusion and oppression is the main task of postmodern political philosophy; and that in order to further this goal, postmodern radical philosophy must take difference, not identity, as fundamental to the constitution of human society. In the transitional chapter 5 I examined two attempts to translate the deconstruction of subjecthood and identity thinking into political practice and concluded that those efforts faced serious problems of coherence, because they rested upon the philosophical groundwork defined by part 1. In the preceding two chapters I have explicated two basic contradictions that follow from the attempt to realize a postmodern politics of difference. First, either postmodernism accepts the singularity of the oppressed and thus commits itself to having to listen to discourses of racial and ethnic purity that contradict its defining openness to and tolerance of all others, or it sets about deconstructing those claims and violates its commitments to allowing the other to speak for itself, as well as undermining the coherence of the very differences it seeks to protect. Second, regardless of which strategy it adopts, postmodernism confronts in the discourse of the other not simply claims to difference but universal grounds for these claims in the form of demands for self-determination. In other words, struggles against oppression are always struggles for self-determination, but the politics of difference is rooted in the deconstruction of just that capacity for self-determination. Here, in the final chapter, I must fully spell out the meaning of the shared universal essence of human being that I have relied upon, explicate its necessary function in critical political philosophy, and demonstrate that if the politics of difference is to be adequate to its values, then it must have presupposed this very idea of the human essence even as it worked to deconstruct it.

To be clear, this final chapter will argue that the values promoted by the politics of difference are coherent as values and can be advanced in the world only if they are grounded in a universal understanding of human subjecthood. As universal, this essence points towards a society where the use of resources is freed from the homogenizing effects of market forces and is instead utilised to produce human value – the engendering of the self-creative capacities of human beings in their uniqueness and specificity. Human being is self-differentiating by its very nature. To invoke the essence of human being is to defend the capacity to create cultural differences against social, economic, and political forces opposed to them. The essential ground of the production of human value, our self-creative capacity, cannot be restricted to some groups only on the basis of particular social, cultural, or economic distinctions. The full exercise of this capacity implies a global civilization where invidious distinctions are overcome, not in the name of humanity as a generic mass, but so that differences can be freely manifested; that is, it implies a global civilization where the differences that are manifested do not require the elimination of other differences as a precondition of their manifestation.

But postmodern criticism distinguishes itself as criticism by deconstructing this essence. In so doing, however, it deprives the oppressed of what they themselves claim when they fight back against the source of their oppression. What is more, it transforms all struggles that seek to change reality according to self-given plans into delusional battles. That is, because subjecthood has been reduced to discursively constituted subject-positions and because this discursive constitution is said to be both necessary and unchangeable by changed human activity, all struggles that claim to struggle for freedom, i.e., the overcoming of external, uncontrollable forces constituting the subject, are based on the false and dangerous belief that humans can actually structure their societies in ways that conform to their essential nature. Consistently interpreted, the politics of difference is grounded in a metaphysics that teaches us that our fate is to be determined, never determining.

As this problem is explored in this final chapter, the conclusion that postmodern political criticism is at root self-confuting will force itself upon us. By siding with the oppressed against the oppressors, postmodern thinking must presuppose the capacity for self-determination as essential, even though it gains its distinctiveness by denying that this capacity for self-determination is a real, shared, human capacity. If the radical claim of postmodernism is true – that subjecthood is a function of language and culture and thus not foundational – then it loses all positive political value. If, on the other hand, postmodernism is to aid in the realization of the values that it espouses, it must presuppose this capacity.

As this argument is the cornerstone of this critique of postmodernism, it will prove useful to once again briefly recapitulate the conclusions of the postmodern deconstruction of subjecthood. Recall, then, that for Foucault the subject is a "function ceaselessly modified," that for Lyotard the subject "free humanity" quite simply "does not exist" and that the self is a post "through which various types of messages pass," while for Derrida "even in so-called creation the subject is a function of language," one, moreover, "which is not what it says itself to be." The basic problems are summed up clearly by Kate Soper. She argues that "if the experience of individual men and women is viewed as unessential to their existence then the category of 'concrete individual' ceases to have any reference to *human* beings; within the confines of such a theory, we can no longer speak of individuals as dominated by social structures or in need of liberation."[2] The present chapter will be concerned with explicating the essence of human being upon which Soper's criticism implicitly relies.

THE METAPHYSICAL GROUNDS OF CONSCIOUSNESS OF OPPRESSION

Rather than seeing it as a process in which general social structures unfold, break down, and regenerate, postmodern thinking, as has been illustrated, conceives of history as a plural, open-ended process of displacement. The problem with modern accounts of history is that they are rooted in an understanding of human subjecthood that privileges mastery over novelty. If this grounding concept of subjecthood can be overthrown, then history will be restored to its fullness and open-endedness. The question remains, however, whether or not this postmodern claim can retain any critical-political sense in the absence of foundations within the subject. If not, then postmodernism will not be able to speak meaningfully of marginalization, domination, or oppression. That this is in fact the case will become evident if some consideration is given to the nature of oppression and to the requirements for even conceiving of it. These requirements, I will argue, are lacking in radical postmodern thought insofar as its radicality is defined by the deconstruction of subjecthood. Let us now explore why this is the case. Since the notion of "the marginal" is often employed in postmodern discourse, let us begin with a reflection upon what it is to be marginalised.

The margin of a page divides it into the space where the body of the work is composed and the space where comments, afterthoughts, and notes for revision are jotted down. Ofttimes the Muse inspires after the work has been completed, and thus the margin can contain more interesting insights than the draft of the work contained by the standard space for composition. So too with the social margins, especially according to postmodern thought. The outsiders, those on the wrong side of the thin red line, often contain more interesting, valuable, and critical insights than those written in society's official spaces.

Thus, to be marginalised means, first of all, that someone or some group is ruled out by "normal" society. There are two political possibilities provoked by marginalization. The first possibility is that the marginalization is self-imposed. The atheist marginalizes him/herself from organized religion. The Beats marginalised themselves from American society in the 1950s. The Dadaists turned their backs on European "civilization" around the period of the First World War. In such cases, because these groups rule themselves out, there is no political problem. Marginalization does not become domination or oppression.

The second possibility is one where official society actively structures the marginalization of a group that it deems unfit for participation in the life of civil society. Rather than embracing their exclusion, groups so treated resist. They demand social changes that will end the marginalization and thus allow the groups' members to articulate their identity freely. As we have seen, Canada's two historically marginalized peoples, the Québécois and the First Nations, when they have entered into struggle, have demanded increased access to the necessary resources – money, political representation and power, information, public institutions (day care, schools, etc.) – through which they can concretely express, develop, and extend themselves. This type of marginalization and these types of struggles are of primary interest here. In particular, one needs to ask, what are the fundamental conditions of possibility for the emergence of resistance.

Jana Sawicki offers a sound starting point from which to address this question. She argues that "oppression must be experienced before it can be resisted."[3] Thus, the question is, what are the conditions for the possible experience of oppression? An example may prove a useful aid to answering this question. Let us consider a recent report on the socioeconomic status of different immigrant communities of colour in Toronto.[4] This report proved what had long been suspected, namely, that immigrants of colour in Toronto face much higher levels of poverty and unemployment than white Canadians. Let us suppose a member of one of these communities tries to mobilise the economically marginalised immigrant communities. What are the conditions of her first coming to consciousness of the problem and what are the grounds upon which her struggle can be organized? At first glance there seem to be two crucial elements involved. First, the person experiences her specific difference as a member of a community of colour, a "dominated subject-position" if you like, as a barrier to inclusion. Second, she experiences the given socioeconomic structure as the authoritative subject-position that situates her, her community, and other communities of colour in an economically marginalised position. So far everything can be accounted for by postmodern analysis. The conflict could be conceptualized as a conflict between the discursively constructed position of "member of a community of colour" and the discursively constructed racism of Canadian capitalism at the dawn of the twenty-first century. Neither subject-position, however, contains anything that would lead to resistance. A dominated position is dominated because it is constructed by the dominant position in the service of the dominant position. Now, if people were simply functions of their positions, then those in dominated positions would be identical to their construction by the dominant position. Someone within such a position, therefore, would experience only her relative position in society and nothing in addition to this position by which she could become conscious of being *oppressed*. There would be nothing beyond the position itself, within the dominated person, to ground a consciousness of oppression that could lead to resistance. If there is to be struggle *against* this position, there must be a ground for this struggle that is not included in the discursively constructed dominated position. But what is this ground? It cannot lie within the dominated position, for the reasons cited above. It cannot, for postmodernism, lie outside of the oppressed position, for that would once again imply that there is something more to people and societies than discursive positions. Thus, if the struggle is to be a struggle of, by, and for those on the margins, then this ground must lie within those who are in fact on the margins.

If one resists, one must not only experience one's *position* as dominated, one must experience one's *self* as dominated. The wrong of domination can be explained only by reference to its effects on the self-creative capacity of the dominated human being. There could be no accounting for this wrong if people were mere functions of the positions that they occupy from moment to moment. What then explains the wrong? It must be that added to the experience of exclusion is the experience of some potential to do what you are excluded from doing. Oppression is wrong because it denies people the capacity to express what they in fact are truly capable of. The wrong stems from the fact that the oppressive construction of the oppressed lies about the nature of those who are oppressed. The lie is universal – that the oppressed have themselves to blame for their inferior position, that they are incapable, for intrinsic reasons, of ruling themselves.

This capacity for self-determination that is manifested by the oppressed when they enter into struggle against their oppression is not, however, just another discourse. To so interpret this struggle is to deny, once again, the truth of the oppressed that the oppressed themselves manifest when they enter into struggle. No matter how minute such struggles are, whether they are for a community centre in St James Town in Toronto, for native fishing rights in New Brunswick, or for protection of the French Language Charter in Quebec, they always, and must, assert against the oppressor what the oppressor denies. The experience of exclusion as wrongful therefore emerges from a consciousness of a contradiction between what the official line says the oppressed are capable of doing and what the oppressed themselves reveal themselves to be capable of doing. In order to mount resistance to a situation deemed wrong, therefore, one must not only experience the situation as wrong, that is, against one's human capacity for self-determination, one must also really possess this capacity to fight against the situation.

One is reminded here of Fanon's comment to the effect that the Native begins to resist at the very moment s/he recognizes his or her humanity. While external political discourses (Marxism, human rights, etc.) may be essential in structuring a fight-back, before this can happen the people who will wage the struggle must recognize an identity between what the oppositional discourse says they are and can do and what they themselves know they are and can do. One must understand oneself as a subject, in the sense given by the concept of subjecthood as the capacity for self-determination.[5] Without consciousness of this capacity and the corresponding drive to realize it in action, resistance would not arise. People would simply accept the situation. However, if in struggling against oppressive situations people draw upon their capacity for self-determination, then the struggle in question is not just a struggle of one particular group against another particular group. That is, a struggle against oppression is not just a struggle to secure the identity of the particular group. It is, rather, a moment in the struggle for the freedom of all human beings impelled by the underlying interest in self-determination they all share. I have said throughout that the capacity for self-determination is not a capacity that can be restricted to specific groups of human beings. That strategy is the strategy of oppressive thinking, which legitimatizes oppression by claiming that only some humans (whites, men, etc.) are capable of ruling themselves and determining their own lives. If struggles against oppression are not to repeat this sectarian logic, then they must go beyond particularity towards a universal basis. That is, they must recognize that the particular identity for which they struggle is in fact one manifestation of the universal capacity for self-determination. In order to clarify this relationship, it is important to determine the precise meaning of the concept of essence in this regard.

ESSENTIALISM AND RADICAL CRITICISM

The first point that needs to be established is that essence here does not denote a transcendent, ideal, ahistorical substance. Like humanity itself, the concept of essence has a history, one in which the transcendent character of essence is progressively concretized. The rejection of a transcendent status for the concept of essence occurs very early in the history of philosophy in Aristotle's criticism of the Platonic theory of Forms. Rather than employing a static model, Aristotle conceived of essence as the active principle guiding the development of real things. His teleological concept of the development of substance adds to Plato's notion the ideas of process and activity.[6] Essence is not a timeless form but rather the highest possibility of things, which must work itself out in reality. While a great step forward, Aristotle's notion of essence is marred by his teleology. Because his understanding of development is teleological, the manifestation of essence proceeds according to metaphysical necessity. That is, the essence *must* work itself out to its completion, for it is of the nature of essence to fulfil itself in reality.

A historical concept of essence, while maintaining the crucial idea that essence is an active force whose realization would represent the fulfilment of a goal, must deprive essence of metaphysical necessity. That is, if essence is to change from being a potential whose fulfilment is necessary by definition to being a tool of social criticism, it must leave behind teleology and become historical. Essence still denotes the highest potential of that of which it is the essence, but the fulfilment of this goal is no longer metaphysically necessary. Fulfilment depends upon the self-activity of those who are characterized by the essence. Herbert Marcuse understands the meaning of essence as the grounds of social criticism better than anyone else in the history of twentieth-century philosophy. He argues that "when the materialist dialectic as social theory confronts the opposition of essence and appearance, the concern for man which governs it gives the critical motif in the theory of essence a new sharpness. The tension between potentiality and actuality, between what men and things could be and what they are in fact, is one of the dynamic focal points of this theory of society. It sees therein not a transcendental structure of Being or an immutable ontological difference, but a historical relationship which can be transformed in this life by real men."[7] In becoming historical, the concept of essence leaves its metaphysical transcendence and becomes a human capacity to reconfigure the given according to self-chosen plans. While this capacity must operate under given historical conditions, it is not reducible to them. Nor, however, is it anything outside of nature and history.

The essence of human being is the capacity to reflect upon, evaluate, and change social structures when they become barriers to the freedom implied by that very capacity. *That* people fight for freedom in widely different historical and cultural contexts proves that they are essentially free. *What* people fight for in those different contexts weaves a historical tapestry of the content of human freedom. As Marcuse argues, "the truth of this model of essence is preserved better in human misery and suffering and the struggles to overcome them than in the forms and concepts of pure thought."[8] We thus know that slavery is contrary to the human essence, because slaves have risen up against their masters in both the ancient and the modern world. We know that a free society must remove all sexist barriers to the freedom of women, because women have risen up against those barriers. We know that a free society demands equality for gays and lesbians, because gays and lesbians have risen up against homophobia and exclusion. We know that a free society must permit the autonomous development of indigenous cultures, because indigenous people around the world have risen up against their violent absorption into modernity. We know that a free society demands accessible public spaces and equal opportunity for the disabled, because the disabled have risen up against oppressive medicalization and socially imposed barriers to their life-activity. We know, ultimately, that a free society provides access to life-sustaining and life-enhancing resources not mediated by the ability to pay, because this struggle for resources underlies all particular struggles of the oppressed and exploited.

Thus, the notion of human essence as self-determination identifies the objective barriers standing in the way of positive freedom. If the essence of human beings is self-determination, then, as a tool of critique, it identifies the material and institutional barriers (poverty, racism, sexism, etc.,) standing in the way of self-determination in specific social contexts. Humans are free when they can exercise this capacity for self-determination as they see fit, subject to the condition that others are equally free to do the same. As such, critique rooted in this notion of essence must take account of the real differences operative in different societies in its critical evaluation of those societies. As Terry Eagleton writes, "To be *some* kind of cultural being is indeed essential to our humanity, but not to be any particular kind. There are no non-cultural human beings, not because culture is all there is to human beings, but because culture belongs to their nature. Human nature is always incarnate in some specific cultural mode, just as all languages are specific."[9] The point is not to reduce the human to a generic standard but to identify the underlying basis for those specific cultural differences and thus establish a universal standard for the criticism of what stands in the way of free self-creation.

This transformative capacity operating in different environments is what creates cultural differences, but it cannot be reduced to these differences themselves. Yet, ironically, this reduction is just what postmodernism entails in its drive to bring the presentation of differences to the very heart of critical politics. Rather than being a project to overcome reductionism and enable the free articulation of social and cultural differences, postmodernism, thought through consistently, implies that humans are merely the products of their environment.

While this is true, it remains of the utmost importance to determine why empirical identity depends upon the essential capacity of self-determination. The argument advanced here against postmodernism claims that because postmodern thought deconstructs the notion of human essence, it simultaneously deconstructs the oppressed, whom it nevertheless hopes to support. To deny that humans are distinguished by their capacity to deliberately alter circumstances, to insist, on the contrary, that humans are material always already altered by circumstances, is to undercut the distinction between oppressed and oppressor. All are equally under the sway of language or power or signs. It is language or power that determines our horizons and projects. Be that as it may, the need for a universal human essence as the ground of struggles waged in the name of a particular empirical identity has not been fully justified.

In the foregoing argument, the difference marked out was a difference between what an oppressed group understood itself to be essentially and what oppressive society forced it to be in existence. Phrasing it thus leaves open the possibility that "essence" here means nothing more than the empirical identity of the group. While this identity obviously has a profound role to play in any act of resistance, it is not the essence of the group. If empirical identity and essence are conflated, then the argument against postmodern thought would reproduce the first problem of postmodernism. That is, it too would be forced to accept the logic of any struggle for difference, including struggles that were destructively exclusive of other social differences, and it would be unable to intervene in disputes between differences. All distinctions would be equal, and struggles would devolve into an unending cycle of positing and deconstructing given identities. In the case of Oka, for example, it would have to accept both that the town of Oka had the right to expand the golf course and that the Mohawks had the right to resist it. But the idea of self-determination is not a descriptive term applied to any act of any group: it is normative and critical. Thus, if the critique of postmodern thought is to have any purchase, it must disclose why the notion of a universal human essence is necessary for the existence of discrete identities.

A beginning to the argument may be made by borrowing a turn of phrase from Marx. People can define themselves as African-Canadians, lesbians, or anything else they like, but in each case they display a capacity for self-determination that is distinct from the means, language, and so forth, through which it is *expressed*. In general, humans are distinct as a species because we display this capacity to determine ourselves and to alter reality according to these self-given concepts. In the process of thus transforming external reality, we also, and fundamentally, transform ourselves. That is the meaning of Marx's claim in the Sixth Thesis on Feuerbach that "the essence of man is no abstraction indwelling in each separate individual, in its reality it is the ensemble of social relations."[10] While this claim was interpreted by the French structuralist-Marxist Louis Althusser to mean that Marx had abandoned his earlier humanism, the truth is the opposite.[11] What this claim means is that humanity is what it makes itself to be. Just as the essence of man is "no abstraction," neither is "the ensemble of social relations." These too are the product of human historical activity. The truth of this interpretation can be established by quoting the Third Thesis. Marx writes, "the materialist doctrine about changed circumstances ... forgets that *circumstances are changed by men* ... The coincidence of changed circumstances and of human activity or self-change can be conceived and rationally understood only as *revolutionary practice*" (emphasis added).[12] Thus, the human essence is to be equated not with any static predicate – "rationality," "goodness," and so forth – but rather with the active capacity to change our environment and ourselves according to our own projects and ideas. As Marcuse understood, this is not a reduction of humanity to a single, exclusive category;, it is in fact a release of humanity from all one-sided, ahistorical categorizations.

Thus, the postmodern criticism of essentialism, that it depends for its existence upon the exclusion of practices and people who have historically been excluded by Western society, is invalid. This criticism would be valid *if* the necessary result of the essentialist argument was the elimination of differences. That is, if essentialism sought to eliminate differences by subsuming them under an abstraction ("humans are essentially self-interested," for example), then postmodern thought would be correct – this is a dangerous misunderstanding of human being. However, the function of essence in critical thinking is not to reduce humanity to an undifferentiated mass but rather to understand how differences come about and, more importantly, to adjudicate the conflicts that inevitably arise *over* differences. Let us reexamine the argument with which this chapter opened in light of this abstract characterization of the essence of human being.

Considered in general, a struggle waged in the name of a specific difference is a conflict caused by the imposition of a system upon a group by an external authority that does not take into account the identity, capacities, and goals of the group upon which that system is imposed. If this imposition is resisted, not only does the group in question assert its identity against the external authority's definition, it also asserts a general capacity to determine its own conditions of existence. However, this capacity cannot be restricted to certain groups only. If the Eritrean community organizes against the structural barriers placed in the way of the freedom of its members, it does not thereby assert that only Eritreans and not Somalians are capable of transforming their situation. Likewise, if the Somalian community organizes and struggles for increased access to needed resources, it is not drawing on a capacity specific to the Somali community. Both groups face the same problem and draw upon the same capacity when they resist the structures imposed upon them. If critical theory privileges difference over this deep human identity, it unwittingly repeats the basic structure of imperialist thinking. Such thinking presupposes that only certain sections of humanity have the capacity to rule themselves. The history not only of anti-imperialist struggles but also of the women's movement, the labour movement, and the gay and lesbian movement has proven imperialist thinking fallacious. Each of these struggles has proven that the groups formerly judged inadequate to the task of self-determination are, in fact, adequate to that task. That is, they have proven themselves human in the sense in which Fanon employed the term – capable of resistance and self-rule.

Thus, postmodern thought, which has set itself the task of undermining imperialist modes of thinking cannot, in truth, do without this ontological ground, namely, that human beings are, by their nature as human, defined by their capacity for self-determination. If, as postmodernism believes, differences should be multiplied, this belief can gain political value only if it *expresses* the idea that what is in fact manifested in a struggle against exclusion is the universal capacity for self-determination. If this capacity were not universal, then either postmodernism's affirmation of difference would be politically meaningless (difference would be just the principle of social relations and not a desirable state of affairs that must be actively created), or it would have to claim that not everyone was fit for the life of difference but only certain privileged marginal positions.

For the most part and to its credit, such elitism is not openly affirmed in the postmodern argument. However, if domination is resisted, then there must be, if my argument is valid, a universal criterion from which to make the judgment that the situation so resisted is wrong. Resistance is legitimate when it is a response to a situation of oppression, and only a universal criterion can determine when a situation of exclusion is oppressive. For example, to exclude men from a healing circle designed to deal with the ravages of sexual assault is an exclusion, but it is not oppressive. It is not oppressive, because it does not deny to the men so excluded anything necessary for their all-round development. On the contrary, it gives to the women a space necessary for healing and therefore something essential to their all-round development. In order to make such a judgment, however, a universal criterion that decides between wrongfully and rightfully excluded differences is necessary. That criterion states that exclusion is oppressive and therefore wrong when a group with preponderant social, political, and economic power exercises that power in a systematic way to deny, denigrate, or destroy in another or several groups the capacity to determine themselves freely. So in the case of Oka, for example, this principle entails the conclusion that the expansion of the golf course onto sacred lands is not justifiable by appeal to the principle of Québécois self-determination. Golf is not an essential part of the culture of the Québécois; sacred lands are an essential part of the culture of the Mohawks. It is thus no loss to the specificity of Québécois culture if the golf course does not go through, but it is an essential loss to the Mohawks if their sacred lands are lost.

As I argued in chapter 6, such a criterion is lacking from the radical postmodern position. Nevertheless, one would hope that pluralist thinking would not affirm groups who are opposed to pluralism, yet it lacks grounds for coherently doing so. If, on the other hand, one operates from a universalist platform, one needs only to support struggles whose goal is the removal of barriers to self-determination, which entails struggles against groups and social dynamics whose project is to deny self-determination. Thus, the critical humanist position does not stop at simply siding with one group over another when collisions of differences occur. In bringing to light the ground of cultural difference in a shared capacity for self-determination, critical humanism encourages different groups to look beneath the manifest differences to their common human source and thus establishes at least the possibility of solidarity between differently identified groups in a struggle for secure access to the resources necessary for active self-creation.

Thus, operating from the foundation of a capacity for self-determination, one is not obliged to listen to ethnic purists of any culture or male misogynists arguing on the basis of "masculinity" or heterosexuals asserting their "right" to heterosexuality. The discourse of ethnic purists, for example, denies that self-determination is a universal human capacity in favour of ethnic particularity and thus undermines the grounds of its own legitimacy. It rules itself out of consideration as a genuine struggle against oppression. It is "inhuman," since it denies what history shows to be the case – other races, given the opportunity or, better, forcibly creating that opportunity for themselves by defeating the purported "master race," are as capable of ruling themselves as the group that claims an exclusive right to self-determination. Self-determination, it should now be clear, is a normative concept. It does not simply describe human behaviour. Instead, it judges that behaviour according to its implications for the actor and those affected by the act. Any act justified by appeal to this concept of self-determination that denies in the other what the actor claims for itself is self-contradictory, oppressive to the other, and thus not a genuine act of self-determination.

A critical humanist philosophy thus concerns itself with identifying the general barriers to human self-determination and works to overcome these. To the extent that people gain more equal access to resources and democratic modes of political participation, to that extent they become free to create themselves according to their specific character and to transform that specific character. However, if a group appeals to this universal ground, it thereby imposes upon itself an obligation to work for the common good, rather than only for its own particular good, to the exclusion of everyone else. The critical humanist position points to those moments in history when groups in struggle for the freedom to determine themselves consciously identified with other groups in struggle and all voices together spoke in the name of human freedom as empirical evidence of the validity of its claims. Through such conflicts a shared history of struggle is forged that links the oppressed and the exploited. Through these real links the essence of humanity is historically developed and expressed. Given "ensembles of social relations" are challenged on the basis that they do not permit the full self-realization of all the members of that society. Each specific struggle, if it is successful, overcomes another limit standing in the way of a universal, positively free society characterized not by homogeneity but by the free development of specific differences, a society where "the free development of each is the pre-condition for the free development of all."[13] In this manner an essentialist understanding of humanity is anything but reductionist. It is, on the contrary, the only coherent means of developing a pluralist society that does not undermine its own foundations.

Now it is true, of course, that the articulation of differences will have to involve the use of language. However, if language or, more generally, cultural dynamics is the cause of difference, then difference has no political or ethical value; it is no longer something whose manifestation can be identified as of essential importance to the people who manifest the difference. If difference exists just because society is divided into different domains and if it proliferates just because the meaning-generating capacity of language is by definition unbounded, then postmodern thought is nothing more than a description of a state of affairs. Manifestation and exclusion would be nothing more than the banal logical point that by asserting x I exclude y, and so on, *ad infinitum.* Since we must speak and, in speaking, affirm one thing rather than another, there would be no escaping domination and exclusion. At root, domination would have nothing to do with political systems; it would simply be a defining feature of our existence, more of an existential horizon than a political problem. While there would still be room for a vigilant scrutiny of our words, there could be no question of ever escaping the cycle of exclusion, no question, therefore, of ever reaching the nonexclusionary form of thought postmodernism invokes. Our relationship to such a cycle of exclusion would be analogous to our relationship to our natural death. Death becomes a problem only when it occurs unnaturally, as the result of alterable social causes like poverty, disease, or state-sponsored murder. Natural death is an existential horizon of human finitude, important but not a relevant political problem.

The same can be said for language. If its exclusions and categorizations become political and ethical problems, it is only because there is a human reality that these exclusions distort and constrain. That is, if in applying a category to a group I do, in Derrida's words, a "violence" to that group, this can only be because the category that I have applied to them does not in fact grasp the full reality of that group. If such categorization is violent, it is because it actively excludes the *real* nature of the group in question. If language and culture determine us absolutely, that is, if we are but functions of language and culture even when we think we are engaged in the act of creation, then there is no real nature against which we can determine whether certain categorizations are appropriate or not. In that case, we could not talk about categorization as violent either, since we could never determine whether we have in fact excluded something that should be included. In that case, the ethical-political concerns of postmodernism become impossible to explain.

Postmodern philosophy argues that the dynamics of meaning creation in language undermines the capacity for rational self-determination. Because the subject can not be without expressing this being and because this expression has to go through the detour of language, the subject finds itself embroiled in dynamics over which it has no control. Hence the conclusion that the subject is a function of language. This conclusion, however, misunderstands the nature of subjecthood. Subjecthood, as we have seen, is not a static, ahistorical, exclusive abstraction; it is the capacity for self-determination that enables humanity to resist all situations where it is reduced to mere functions or objects of external powers, including the powers of culture and language. No critical theory that works in the service of overcoming the oppressive barriers placed in the way of minorities can make sense without it. As we will now see, this capacity must have been presupposed all along by the main theorists of postmodern deconstruction as the normative ground of their deconstruction of it.

THE RETURN OF SUBJECTHOOD IN POSTMODERN CRITICISM

The truth of the claim that subjecthood is a capacity for self-determination can be determined from a brief rereading of the major thinkers who have concerned us in this work. In each case one finds that crucial elements of the modernist notion of subjecthood reenter their work. If each was himself forced by the logic of his argument to qualify the critique of subjecthood and if the entire edifice of postmodern criticism was "based" upon that deconstructive critique, then the return of this notion would prove more surely than any formal argument on my part that subjecthood is an unsurpassable foundation for critical thinking that hopes to have a positive impact on the struggle against oppression. This claim must now be textually substantiated.

Foucault is the obvious starting point since, as has been touched upon throughout this investigation, he explicitly revives the concept of the autonomous subject in his later writings. This revival is at least in part a response to the inability of his early work to distinguish between "facticity and validity."[14] However, his return to a conception of self-determining subjecthood is not accompanied by an explicit renunciation of the transgressive, local, and antiessentialist modes of political struggle that he said could develop only after the concept of subjecthood had been abandoned. In other words, Foucault fails to recognize that in rehabilitating a strong conception of subjecthood, he in fact undermines what he took to be radical and critical about his work, namely, that it demonstrated the link between essentialist conceptions of subjecthood and totalitarian configurations of power and created the possibility for new modes of political struggle. If it proved true that a conception of subjecthood as self-determination is a necessary presupposition of critical philosophy and political practice, then it would not be true, as he argued for two decades, that the modern subject is both the product of power and the grounding principle of its disciplinary uses.

One of the most sustained attempts at understanding the role of subjecthood in Foucault's later work is Deborah Cook's *The Subject Finds a Voice*. Cook agrees that without a concept of subjecthood Foucault's project is normatively incoherent. Cook, however, like Foucault, does not seem to recognize the problems Foucault's rehabilitation of the idea of subjecthood causes for the specific radicality of his early work. Cook contends that Foucault's rehabilitation of the subject "calls for a reinterpretation, though not a rejection, of his ideas of power and knowledge."[15] Like Nancy Fraser, Charles Taylor, Michael Walzer, and Jürgen Habermas, Cook begins from the claim that the early work was hampered by the absence of a foundation for free ethical practice, which Foucault implicitly deploys against contemporary systems of the circulation of power.[16] The last works, she argues, fill in a gap in, rather than fatally compromise, the political positions of the early Foucault: "with his idea of *rapport-à-soi* [relation to self], Foucault has found his way out of the impasse in which he floundered when he claimed that power and knowledge are abstract, neutral, and in no one's hands. His notion of the self would allow him to attribute historical events to moral agents – that is, to give power back to subjects."[17] The *rapport-à-soi*, Cook contends, is a "transcendental historical"; that is, like the critical-humanist interpretation of subjecthood, it is an underlying condition of specific practices through which empirical identities are forged.[18] While I agree that the ethically self-constituting agent would correct the "normative confusion" of his analysis of power, I would argue further that it could do so only at the cost of negating every novel insight that archaeology and genealogy has claimed to offer about the way in which power constitutes subjects. The reinterpretation that Cook proposes would in effect amount to a rejection of his analysis of power, insofar as that analysis leads to the practical conclusion that resistance has to be by way of giving oneself over to cultural dynamics, because it was the modern attempt to control them that underlay "the worst political systems."

Cook tries to work around this problem by contrasting Foucault's rehabilitated notion of the subject with the "ahistorical and autonomous character of 'man' and of the subject."[19] Thus, it is perhaps the case that the subject that reenters Foucault's work is not the subject decentred by his earlier efforts. If that was the case, this figure would not necessarily undermine his analysis of power and knowledge, but it would permit the type of reinterpretation Cook offers. Cook, playing on the affinity between Foucault and Nietzsche, attempts to justify just such a claim. She argues that "just as Nietzsche provided Foucault with a way out of phenomenology, so too he provided Foucault with the tools to burst open the bars of the iron cage [of power/knowledge]. All historical instantiations of subjectivity are inscribed in forces of power and forms of knowledge, but individuals nonetheless also have the power to constitute themselves through various forms of self-mastery ... another Nietzschean idea. Those subjects who actively resist colonisation by rejecting the techniques and norms imposed upon them by the apparatus are the more creative and autonomous members of disciplinary society."[20] In trying to distance Foucault's rehabilitated concept of the subject from the traditional philosophical account, however, Cook forgets her own interpretation of the *rapport-à-soi*. The relation-to-self is what enables any subject to resist, to make itself. It is thus this *universal* capacity to relate to oneself, and not any specific set of practices, that explains resistance. It was this universalism, however, that Foucault always rejected. Thus, the potential for autonomous ethical self-creation, even if we conceive of it, as Foucault does, as "the creation of ourselves as a work of art,"[21] is now rooted in the general form of subjecthood so trenchantly criticized by Foucault. Howsoever the creation of ourselves is conceived, it must be rooted in a capacity to create; otherwise we would not be creating ourselves, but rather we would be created. Either humans have an essential capacity to create themselves or they do not. Foucault at one point claimed they did not, in his later works he clearly believed they did. Cook is right to argue that the idea of the subject returns in his later works and also to insist that it must if his work is to make political sense. My complaint is that she does not connect this return to a criticism of the intrinsic incoherence of the radicality of Foucault's early politics of transgression, which, as we have seen, was rooted in the deconstruction of the modern subject.

Cook contends that the rehabilitated subject in Foucault's work provides the grounds for resistance and emancipation. She writes that "this idea that we create ourselves in our ethical activity is of paramount importance for Foucault's work. It is one which allows Foucault not only to make claims about the role of subjects in history, but also about resistance and the prospect of our emancipation from disciplinary society."[22] If the subject is what allows Foucault to make claims about resistance, then the entirety of his genealogical work, which does away with the subject, is politically incoherent, not just because it is not consciously rooted in a foundational idea of the subject but also because he takes the deconstruction of the subject to be the radical core of the work. It is the critique of subjecthood that allows the subjugated knowledges to become manifest. If the subject is necessary for resistance, then all the elements of Foucault's work that he takes to be novel and different from modern political philosophy are revealed to be self-confuting. At the end of the day Cook's argument, as well as Foucault's own trajectory, proves the central positive argument of the present work: subjecthood in the form represented by the best of modern philosophy is necessary for coherent critical politics that aim to ameliorate the conditions of the dominated and oppressed.

The effects of this incoherence run through Foucault's entire corpus. There is a constant oscillation between the decentring of subjecthood and political positions that presuppose that very capacity. This is the case even in the earliest, most "transgressive" works that concerned the manner in which rationality marginalized the insane. Take, for example, the following interpretation of Goya's *The Madhouse:* "The man in the tricorne is not mad because he has stuck an old hat upon his nakedness, but within this madman in a hat rises – by the inarticulate power of his muscular body, of his savage and marvellously unconstricted youth – a human presence already liberated and somehow free since the beginning of time, by his birth right."[23] The content of this freedom may be distinct from the social structures envisioned by Hegel or Marx or Mill (which were each distinct) as expressive of freedom, but the fundamental difference between dominating power and capacity for self-determination is present. The madman is free because the "human presence" is manifest. It is this *human* presence that is "liberated and somehow free." Moreover, this presence is not specific to this individual, since the presence "has existed from the beginning of time," while this person clearly has not. The essential role of that which is specific to humanity is thus clearly presupposed by the notion of freedom invoked here, regardless of the fact that this is manifested by a "madman" rather than a philosopher, a worker, or a cultivated liberal citizen.

The presupposition of a capacity for self-determination is even more evident in Foucault's magisterial history of the prison, *Discipline and Punish.* In a work that, as we have seen, argues that disciplinary society manufactures normalized beings down to their very core, Foucault nevertheless concludes with a call to arms: "in this central and centralized humanity, the effect and instrument of complex power relations, bodies and forces subjected by the multiple mechanisms of 'incarceration,' objects for discourses that are themselves elements for this strategy, we must hear the distant roar of battle."[24] This is a splendid conclusion. However, the argument of the text asserts that there is nothing within the individual that could resist power: power is omnipotent and omnipresent. If that were the case, then there would be no one capable of waging the battle that Foucault hopes to incite.

Recall that even in the period when he was developing his notion of the subject, Foucault still maintained that he was suspicious of the notion of liberation because "there is the danger that it will refer back to the idea that there does exist a human nature or human foundation."[25] If, however, this foundation is lacking, then the ontological basis for resistance is undermined. Foucault himself realized this, judging from the fact that he himself restored a "human foundation" for his ethical and political concerns. In so doing, however, he in fact brought forth what was presupposed by his earlier political positions, positions that, nevertheless, hoped to do without the foundation that they required. He solved the problem, but his work thus became a variation on the theme of self-determination, not a radical transgression of it.

The strongest evidence of this is provided in one of Foucault's last interviews. We have seen how critical disengagement from the apparatus of power is the crucial step in becoming an autonomous individual. The source of this disengagement is thought. "Thought is not what inhabits a certain conduct and gives it meaning," he writes; "rather it is what allows one to step back from this way of acting or reacting, to present it to oneself as an object of thought and question it as to its meaning, its conditions, and its goals. Thought is freedom in relation to what one does, the notion by which one detaches oneself from it, establishes it as an object, and reflects on it as a problem."[26] This is a truly astounding comment from someone who wrote in 1977 that the essential problem of philosophy in the last 150 years is "how not to be Hegelian."[27] For the definition of thought given above is exactly what Hegel gives in the *Logic*. There Hegel writes that "man is not content with a bare acquaintance, or with the fact as it appears to the senses, he would like to get behind the surface, to know what it is, and to comprehend it. This leads him to reflect."[28] The link that ties Foucault to Hegel is the idea that thought is freedom in relation to the object of thought. Thought is, in other words, negative, it dissolves the hard and fast divisions of the world through reflection and in this way prepares the ground for conscious changes. Thus, Foucault clearly returns to a position where self-conscious subjects are the ground for political agency and positive change.

The same trajectory of growing antipathy towards and ultimate restoration of elements of subjecthood is followed by Lyotard.

Lyotard was perhaps the most trenchant critic of the notion of subjecthood. His later works abandon even the linguistic reduction of subjecthood to subject-position. Instead, as we have seen, he presents a nightmare vision of meaninglessly increasing social complexity that captures everyone and programs them to serve its needs. Alongside this omnivorous technological system, however, there is a simultaneous rehabilitation of certain inner capacities specific to human beings. These inner capacities serve as our only refuge from the inevitable dynamics of development. Before examining this ultimate return of a crucial aspect of subjecthood, however, it is essential to illustrate how this element is presupposed, even in his most stridently antihumanist work.

Lyotard's politics have always shown a concern for minority opinion and a defence of incommensurability. Right from the beginning of his pagan/postmodern period (which commenced circa 1977) he identified minorities as, in the words of *Just Gaming*, "territories of language." Minorities are therefore not first and foremost groups of people with different needs, hopes, and projects but units of discourse with human material as their content. Lyotard's concern, recall, is to defend these minorities, not simply to understand them. Thus there is a strong normative dimension to his social investigations. There is no point defending something that is inert. There must be something worthwhile inherent in minorities if one believes that maximizing minority positions is a worthwhile goal. When Lyotard offers examples of the minorities he thinks are important, he mentions groups such as women, gays and lesbians, and people of the Third World. These groups have, over the last thirty or so years, been the focus of most progressive thinking. They have been supported not just because they are minorities but, rather, because they are minorities who have suffered historical violence. A minority controls the resources of the world, but Lyotard does not believe that that minority is in need of defence. Lyotard clearly concurs with this assessment; if he did not, he would have given other examples. Moreover, he offers a political program – the invention of new games. However, if the groups who are to invent new games are identified first and foremost as territories of language, with nothing proper to themselves that would allow them to alter their own circumstances, then the injunction to invent new games is self-contradictory.

Invention presupposes a capacity to free oneself from mere determination by given circumstances and produce unforseen combinations. However, Lyotard is quite clear that "selves" do not have such a capacity; they are "posts through which various kinds of message pass"; they are able to alter the direction or content of messages only within the limits posited by the system. If that is the case, however, then the ground essential to critique is lost, because no self is deprived of something that it essentially has. However, because Lyotard also objects to the instrumentalism of the given world, one finds the notion of "invention" entering into his argument. This notion does supply a ground upon which a normative argument could be constructed (the forces of instrumental reason oppose our capacities for invention, and this is wrong since it denies us the exercise of an essential capacity), but that normative sense, as we can see, presupposes an underlying human capacity that his analysis denies.

If Lyotard were to obviate this criticism by positing language as the creative, inventive force, then his argument would merely be an anthropomorphization of language. There can be no injustice against a nonliving process, so if Lyotard believes that exclusion is wrong – and he clearly does – then either groups of humans have been discriminated against or language has. In either case the wrong stems from the exclusion of capacities that could otherwise be manifested. If this wrong is committed against language, then language must have capacities that humans violate when they try to control it. Regardless of whether or not this makes any sense, it would nevertheless anthropomorphize language, something that Lyotard explicitly attacks in the passage from *The Differend* cited in part 1. If it is the case that Lyotard's criticism rests upon such an anthropomorphization, then he has understood language according to a humanist metaphor and therefore extended humanism's reach, rather than ended its reign.

On the other hand, if Lyotard supports the struggles of women, gays and lesbians, and non-Western peoples because a difference specific to those groups is ruled out by liberal-capitalist society, then he must presuppose exactly the capacity and the right for self-determination that his analysis seeks to eliminate. If a minority group requires a struggle to exist or grow, then there must be a capacity that is not reducible to the empirically given context in which they are determined. That contextual determination is exactly what must be overcome. If self-determination were present in the dominated position as a discursive structure, then that structure would not be an oppressive one. Only if the determining structure impairs something real from being brought forth can it be considered oppressive. Lyotard insists that humans are just networks through which messages pass, their only activity being to alter the direction or modify the content of the message. Struggles over justice, however, concern not just the content but the form of messages. If justice, even Lyotard's justice of multiplicity, is to become actual, then this power to alter the form of society must be present within and claimed by the minorities themselves. To the extent that Lyotard makes normative claims regarding justice and ties these claims to the expansion of minority positions, he presupposes the capacity for self-determination that his social analysis reduces out of existence.

Without the presupposition of subjecthood Lyotard's critique of modernity would lack all political meaning and be but a metaphysical position of the highest abstraction. It would simply claim (as indeed his later work does) that difference is a basic ontological principle, not only of human society but of organic matter in general. There would be no need to struggle for differences; they would manifest themselves as part of an evolutionary process.

It is a curious feature of Lyotard's work, however, that as it becomes more reductionist, it returns to an understanding of humanity as endowed with a capacity that is not determined by external forces and dynamics. This capacity clarifies the manner in which humans can invent new games. While he has given up hope that the general direction of social evolution can be resisted, he nevertheless carves off an inner space that must be preserved if any value to existence is to be maintained. This inner space, which, as we have seen, Lyotard calls "the inhuman," is what grounds the basic civil rights characteristic of modern liberal society.

It is perhaps surprising to witness the reemergence of the notion of right in Lyotard's work. One would have expected that this characteristic liberal motif would have collapsed along with the metadiscourse that supported it. Lyotard's postmodern justice did not make any positive appeal to rights but relied solely upon a critique of the necessarily terroristic nature of efforts to create agreement and unity. Nevertheless, Lyotard ultimately rests his politics upon the defence of the rights of minorities, not as territories of language, but as real suffering groups. He writes that "militant practice, in our countries at least, has become defensive. It is necessary to constantly reaffirm the rights of minorities: women, children, homosexuals, the South, the Third World, the poor, the right to culture and to education."[29] The fact that Lyotard admits that militant practice today is defensive already proves that a capacity for self-determination on his part has been readmitted. If these rights are to be defended, they must exist. But how else could they have come into existence save through struggle?[30] And why would minorities struggle for rights if they were nothing more than territories of language or posts through which messages pass? It is senseless to suppose that they would. But the struggle for minority rights is no mere supposition on the part of philosophers; it is a matter of historical record, explicable only by reference to a self-determining capacity that Lyotard's social theory denies but his politics presupposes. The content of these minority rights may be particular (for example, spousal benefits for same-sex partners), but the struggle for one minority right is not essentially distinct from the struggle for another minority right. When struggling for a special right, the group in question is asserting the claim that this special right is necessary to remove an illegitimate social limitation standing in the way of free self-development. Ultimately, what one is defending when one defends minority rights, therefore, is not the particular right of this or that minority but rather the general capacity that oppressed groups have displayed to determine their own situation.

Lyotard never explicitly recognizes a universal capacity for self-determination. However, he does readmit as a ground for such rights as exist today a universal inner capacity that is distinctive of human beings. This space, "the inhuman," or a "no-man's land," is characterized by its freedom from determination by all external forces. As we have seen, it is an indeterminate inner space whose products cannot be predicted in advance. This indeterminacy explains why this aspect of human being alone is free. As the "inhuman" is beyond the control of external forces, it is the source of whatever creativity humans have. It must be defended against the encroachments of the forces of efficiency and control: "If man does not preserve the inhuman region ... which escapes from the ready-made exercise of rights, he does not deserve the rights that we recognize ... Why should we have the right to freedom of expression if we have nothing to say beyond what has already been said? And how can we have the chance to say that which we do not yet know how to say unless we listen to the silence of the other within? This silence is an exception to the reciprocity of rights, but in so being is its legitimation."[31] This "other within" legitimates rights because it is the source of whatever it is that rights are supposed to protect. It is an exception to the reciprocity of rights not because its exercise violates the rights of others but rather because it is essentially "the right to remain separate."[32] Separation is a condition for the fruitful exercise of rights. As such, it legitimates the rights that are currently recognized in the West.

In Lyotard's final work, written in 1997 but published posthumously three years later, his paradoxical rehabilitation of the essential freedom of inner life is even more pronounced. His last work is a dialogue with the *Confessions* of St Augustine. It is a moving interrogation of the human consciousness of time, its quality of always slipping away, a sympathetic engagement with the most intensely personal mode of soul bearing. Most interestingly from our perspective, however, it is also a vindication of the I, of the soul that brings itself to light through its introspection and confession. While Lyotard is careful to distinguish introspection and confession from philosophy, he nevertheless grants to the I the power to genuinely reflect and strive to know itself. Certainly, what it learns is traversed by tension and contradiction; the Augustinian I is never fully transparent to itself. Contrasting confession to philosophy, he writes that "the *Confessions* are ... neither a plea whose end would be mastered and fixed by a virile intellect ... nor a treatise of philosophy ... Confession does not decide: on the contrary, a fissure zigzags across all that lends itself to writing ... The here and now, the stretches of time, the places, the lives, the I presents themselves as fissured."[33] No, Augustine is not Hegel: the I can never perfectly know itself or master all to which it is opposed. Yet, despite the fact that the I is always conscious of the fissure, the divide that separates it from itself, from truth, it is nevertheless the I and not a territory of language or a phrase that is conscious of the fissure. What is most important, then, is that Lyotard gives positive significance to what he had formerly seen only as a blank space of indeterminacy (the inhuman).

If one compares this new-found inner space with Lyotard's postmodern reduction of the subject to subject-positions, one detects a trajectory similar to the one followed by Foucault. The problem Lyotard's early work faced was that it could not account for the value of the novel practices that it nevertheless posited as modes of resistance to the tyranny of efficiency. The "inhuman" solves this problem because it counts as a region that is qualitatively distinct from the oppressive forces of the external world. Its products are thus also distinct from the products created by the dominant social forces. The authentic products of this inner realm differ in that they are freely produced and do not in themselves serve purposes of increased efficiency. Hence their distinctive character and value.

While this inner region may not be identical to Marx's notion of labour or the Romantic ideal of expressive individuality, it is definitely analogous to these nineteenth century conceptions.[34] It is analogous, moreover, on the essential point at issue. That is, Lyotard reintroduces the distinction between external forces of determination and a defining subjective capacity that is in principle free from those forces, even if it is not always so in practice. Rather than being mere posts through which messages pass, humans are now understood to possess a capacity to be free within and on that basis to create new messages themselves. Freedom as the essence of human being has thus been readmitted by Lyotard. It now remains to be seen how subjecthood reenters the work of Derrida.

Derrida's work, original and diverse in content as it is, is bound together by two unifying threads. The first is that the future is always undetermined, and the second is that each person has an undeconstructable responsibility to remain open to the address of the other. Derrida plays Hamlet to Western philosophy's Horatio, always reminding it that there is more to the universe than is contained in the conceptual discriminations of Western metaphysics. What attracts Derrida's profound powers of textual criticism is the tendency within Western philosophy to attempt to foreclose on the future, to master it through teleological philosophies of history. The political upshot of the deconstruction of the arrogance of reason has always been a defence of the unbounded and open character of meanings and practices. Deconstruction has always sought to remind us that history is an open field of possibilities whose openness cannot be effaced but that attempts to do so can be made at frightening costs. Thus, in the early 1990s Derrida began to speak of a "promise of emancipation" that is always before us but that, if it is to remain critical, must forever be unfulfilled. Crucial to this strategy is the deconstruction of the foundation of teleological thinking, the rationally self-determining subject.

However, although this argument defines the basic orientation of deconstructive politics, Derrida also considers the evaluation of mundane political struggles important. It is just when deconstruction descends from heaven to earth, so to speak, that it finds itself embroiled in the ultimate self-contradiction of antihumanist, postmodern thinking. The reasons for this outcome will be most apparent in a reconsideration of Derrida's most passionate political engagement, the struggle against apartheid.

In the critique of apartheid the immediate goal of deconstruction (demonstrating how the binary thinking of Western metaphysics creates the context in which apartheid can grow) runs into the contradictions of its positive philosophical practice (to undo any and all fixed opposition). It is one thing to espouse a philosophical doctrine that is designed to maintain hope in a better future but that nevertheless refuses to advocate determinate plans. It is quite another to intervene in real political struggles. Unfortunately for deconstruction, its general strategy cannot usefully inform determinate political tactics unless it presupposes the very concept of subjecthood that it deconstructs. To the extent that deconstruction intervenes in struggles, it must take sides, and if it takes sides, it must admit that the side it takes has the capacity to define itself.

In his critique of apartheid, Derrida sought to demonstrate how Western thought had paved the way for South African state racism and to aid the struggle against it by deconstructing the discourse of legitimation espoused by the South African state. In so doing, deconstruction fulfils its mandate of being responsible to the other. That is, deconstruction does not impose a plan upon the other but opens a space where the other can speak for itself. Deconstruction supposedly opens a clearing for a practice that is not final or concerned with the "truth" of the other. The problem is, however, that the struggle of the other itself manifests the capacity for self-definition and a desire for the total overcoming of the oppressive structure that deconstruction defines as the foundation of oppression. There are only two ways in which deconstruction could escape from this self-contradiction. Either the oppressed Africans are not subjects, or they are subjects in Derrida's qualified sense, functions of language that display certain elements to which the essentialist notion of subjecthood refers.

The first possibility is ruled out once the meaning of "subject" in the Western tradition is recalled. "Subject" denotes the active side of the relationship subject/object. It understands human beings as an active force in nature and history. To the extent that one concerns oneself with the real struggle against apartheid, one is dealing with the self-assertion of a majority wrongly excluded by a minority. Derrida does support the struggle, so he cannot intend to reduce the African majority to the status of passive object. Perhaps, then, Derrida takes them to be subjects in the qualified sense in which he uses the term – functions of language that appear to speak in their own name but that are really spoken by the language of which they are functions.

This alternative, however, is ultimately no better than the first. Just as in the case of Foucault and Lyotard, if the real dynamics of struggle are beyond human control, then there is no reason to actively support the surface appearance of these struggles. If the true transformative power lies in language and if this power cannot be utilized by human beings, then those in struggle are in fact deluded about the nature of their struggle if they think that they are in fact asserting themselves. If humans really are functions of language, then language asserts us. We, at root, do not assert anything. However, if there had not been something in the Africans irreducible to their "nature" conceived of as a function of language, then their resistance to apartheid would have been groundless. What they asserted, their true identity, which was denied them by the South African state, would have been illusory, as would their goal of gaining control over the forces that determined their lives, the forces that made them "functions" of an oppressive regime. Clearly Derrida did not believe that the struggle against apartheid was groundless. If he had, his commitment to the actual people involved would have been inexplicable.

Perhaps the context of South Africa changes something fundamental in the nature of subjecthood. That is, perhaps the colonized space is one from which the colonised can assert what they are. Perhaps there is a special power of the margins that is essentially different from the power of the centre. In other words, it may be the case that the self-activity of the oppressed is fundamentally distinct from the core rationalism of Western thought, which Derrida finds problematic.

If that were so, then Derrida could support such struggles without contradicting his deconstruction of subjecthood. However, if the self-activity of the oppressed is fundamentally distinct, then such a fundamental difference must be identified. Try as one might to find it, there do not seem to be any apparent candidates for the role of this difference. The African opposition was mounted from various positions – the left-nationalism of the ANC, the separatist nationalism of the PAC, the Christianity of Bishop Tutu, the workerism of COSATU – but these positions all have their roots in European thinking and presuppose the capacity for self-determination that is characteristic of that thought.[35] Of course, the particular development of these positions is relative to the real context, but at a philosophical level there are no significant differences between the South African and the Western positions that oppose apartheid. Underlying both positions is the idea that apartheid is abominable precisely because it deprives the black majority of access to the wealth of the nation and equal legal standing with whites. In other words, both positions rest on the belief that self-determining human beings are deprived of the ability to manifest this capacity because of an unessential difference – their skin colour and cultural heritage. If Derrida deconstructs this capacity for self-determination, then he deconstructs the most important difference – the difference between those who believe that humans are essentially self-determining, a belief that impels those who hold it to struggle against oppressive conditions, and those who believe that only a privileged few should enjoy the benefits of freedom.

As one explores Derrida's position, the truth of this claim becomes apparent. Derrida does not posit any special capacity on the part of the marginalised party in a colonial context. On the contrary, he supports the South African struggle on well-established liberal-humanist grounds. While rightly identifying the Western roots of the system, Derrida nevertheless supports Mandela's left-liberal program for change. At his trial, Mandela argued that he was forced to terrorism because the state would not respect the spirit of the law. That is, the South African state claimed to be constitutional, based upon the rule of law, not arbitrary force, but was nevertheless structured in such a way that the majority were deprived of all legal standing and were instead ruled by armed might. Mandela claimed that his action was justified because the spirit of the law had been thus perverted in South Africa. Thus, he and his comrades were forced to wield the true spirit of the law, universal equality of all under the law, against its letter.

Derrida does not deconstruct but rather endorses this defence. He writes that "the exemplary witnesses are often those who distinguish between the law and laws, between respect for the law which speaks immediately to the conscience and submission to positive law (historical, national, institutional) ... The exemplary witnesses, those who make us think about the law they reflect, are those who, in certain situations, *do not respect* laws. They are sometimes torn between conscience and law."[36] Conscience, which counterposes the spirit of the law to the letter of the law, can thus force one to act in the name of the rule of law against positive laws that are arbitrary and contrary to the universality implied by the notion "the rule of law." Who would disagree? Certainly not the present author. Although Derrida argues that the extremity of the situation in South Africa gave the confrontation between law and conscience a rawness not found, "except briefly," in the West, he does not claim that it is essentially distinct.[37] Whatever the difference of degree, the struggles of Natives, of students, of workers, of abortion activists, or of gays and lesbians in the West that go beyond the letter of the law in the name of conscience are not different in essence from the struggle in South Africa.

So where in this analysis is the deconstruction that Derrida once said was too radical for traditional political idioms? The opposition between law and conscience pre-dates deconstruction by millennia (receiving classical expression in Sophocles' *Antigone*). Why is this opposition not deconstructed? Why is not the monstrous, open character of the future opposed to the quite determinate plans of the Africans for their liberation? The answer is obvious – to deconstruct the discourse and practice of liberation would be to undermine the struggle one supports.

To the extent that deconstruction is a useful political tool, therefore, it must presuppose the notion of subjecthood that its radical philosophical moment sought to deconstruct. One cannot remain endlessly open and still wage a focussed and efficacious struggle against the forces of oppression. One must plan, choose, and act. Doing so requires someone capable of planning, choosing, and acting. Indeed, it requires someone to plan and choose and act in response to a historical reality of oppression that cannot be deconstructed but only overthrown. In his more passionate moments, Derrida appeals to this very notion of historical reality, which one would have thought would be utterly incompatible with deconstruction. Derrida argues, in a response to two critics of his reading of apartheid, that "historical reality, dear comrades, is that in spite of all the lexicographical contortions you point out, those in power in South Africa have not managed to convince the world, and first of all because, still today, they have refused to change the real, effective, fundamental meaning of their watchword – apartheid."[38] This claim is simply incompatible with the critical thrust of deconstruction. As we saw in part 1, deconstruction held that signs had no "real, effective, fundamental" meaning. Instead, every sign pointed beyond itself, not to historical reality but to more signs, in an endless movement of differing and deferral.

Clearly Derrida cannot bring this strategy into play without deconstructing the "historical reality" of apartheid, which quite rightly sickened him. Indeed, he rejects interpretations of deconstruction that see in it "a modern form of immorality, of amorality, or of irresponsibility."[39] However, in order to arrest the frivolous employment of deconstruction, Derrida must restore a nonarbitrary ground to his critical practice.

Like Foucault and Lyotard, Derrida realizes (at least implicitly) the truth of this criticism. Once again one finds that an essential feature of subjecthood is readmitted into Derrida's work. This is evident once Derrida's understanding of responsibility is recalled. It is important to remember that Derrida maintains that responsibility is "undeconstructable." It thus serves as the foundation for deconstruction. To be undeconstructable was the essential nature of philosophical foundations from Parmenides forward. For Derrida, however, this foundation is not a philosophical principle but a certain relationship with regard to what is other than one's self. If I am to be responsible to the other, then the nature of this responsibility must be a possible object of consciousness. As *my* responsibility, however, this object is not a natural object or a mere component of my being as a "function" of language. This responsibility is the very heart of my relationship to others, the animating principle that compels me to work in whatever way towards a better world.

If this responsibility is to be the very soul of my life in relation to others, if I am to fulfil my responsibility towards the other, then not only must it be most intimately my own but I must also, and essentially, be able to express it through my actions. I must be able to say what I am – in other words, this person, here, with a real responsibility to listen others. This responsibility cannot be both undeconstructable and a vanishing moment in a chain of signification. Ethics requires openness and sensitivity to context to be sure, but it also requires, even for Derrida, as we have seen, that a decision be taken. Decisions bring closure to openness. The responsible person does not hide behind the variability of contexts and meanings but owns up to the consequences of the decision s/he has taken. If our decisions could be deconstructed like texts, then my responsibility would be endlessly dissolved, since my actions would not be under my control. But Derrida says that I must answer for myself, and I can answer for myself only if I am responsible for my decisions, and I can be responsible for my decisions only if they follow from a real action and a real capacity on my part. Therefore, the notion of responsibility presupposes the capacity for self-determination. If my decisions did not follow from what is in fact a real feature of my being, I could not be responsible for them, and responsibility, as a consequence, would not be the undeconstructable core of deconstruction.

Furthermore, this responsibility, as a political responsibility towards those external to myself, must be reciprocal. As each self is both self and other, each person must share in this defining responsibility. Thus, not only is responsibility a foundation from which our relations with one another flow, it is a universal foundation. In short, responsibility, undeconstructable responsibility, presupposes that humans are not functions of language but rather subjects – beings with an underlying solidity and capacity to determine the world. Derrida himself admits as much in the article "The Politics of Friendship." His sense of responsibility means that "one *answers for oneself*, for what one is, says, or does, and this beyond the simple present. The 'oneself' or 'myself' thus supposes the unity, in other words the memory, of the one responding. This is often called the unity of the subject, but one can conceive such a synthesis of memory without necessarily having recourse to the concept of subject. Since this unity is never secured in itself as an empirical synthesis, the recognition of this identity is entrusted to the instance of the name. 'I' am held responsible for 'myself,' which is to say, for everything that can be imputed to that which bears my name. Imputability supposes freedom, to be sure, but it also supposes that that which bears my name remains the 'same.'[40] What is remarkable here is that although Derrida claims that the unity necessary for responsibility "can be conceived of without necessarily having recourse to the subject," his explication repeats rather than deconstructs the essential motifs of the modern understanding of the subject, its freedom and self-identity. In his own formulation he marks a difference between the name and that which *bears* my name. The "that which bears my name" is that which is responsible. If, as he says, one is responsible only if one remains the same and the "that which bears my name" is that which remains the same, then this must be an underlying, stable, self-identical ground for responsibility. In "The Politics of Friendship" Derrida nowhere disagrees with the claim that responsibility requires the unity that he describes, nor does he provide any argument that would persuasively illuminate what this unity might be if it is not the unity of the subject. In fact, his own description cited above is rather more persuasive as an argument about why the subject is the best concept with which to explain the unity required of responsibility. I am a being defined by the capacity to say what I mean, and I act accordingly. I do not flee from this responsibility by deconstructing my words, I stand up for myself, I answer for myself, I am the underlying "that which bears my name." On Derrida's own terms, no mere function of language can be this stable basis, since the "principle" of language is *différance*, and if there is a third alternative, Derrida does not state it.

The return of the idea of subjecthood is even more pronounced in Derrida's latest reflections on the theme of responsibility. Not only does he continue to insist upon the undeconstructable nature of responsibility, he has integrated it into an explicitly ethical framework with universal scope. Struck by the horrific clash of differences in the former Yugoslavia and Rwanda, by a xenophobic immigration law passed in France in 1996, and by the ongoing "peace" process in Israel, which produces no peace, Derrida readmits into his discourse what he had formerly deconstructed – humanism as a framework for the harmonious reconciliation of differences. In his testimonial to Emmanuel Levinas, Derrida laments the lack of hospitality shown the other by the dominant political forces of the world. To be hospitable, Derrida argues, is to welcome the other into one's home, to be bound to the other through a fundamental tie of belonging. Hospitality is the activity of responsibility. But hospitality does not play, does not differ and defer, and it does not deconstruct the idea of humanity but rather opens us up to our universal connection to one another. As he argues, hospitality "opens the way to the humanity of the human in general. There is here, then, a daunting logic of election and exemplarity operating between the assignation of a singular responsibility and human universality – today one might even say humanitarian universality, in so far as it would at least try, despite all the difficulties and ambiguities, to remain, in the form, for example, of a non-governmental organization, beyond Nation-States and their politics."[41] Thus, our responsibility to the other is what opens up for us the *humanity* of the other, not its difference. We welcome the other, the Kosovar, the Palestinian, the Tutsi, because, just as Hegel taught long ago, the other is really the same in otherness, *human* being in a specific form.

Thus, Derrida's politics of difference, like the politics of Foucault and of Lyotard, ultimately makes sense only if it is set upon the ground of self-determining subjecthood. Above, he described responsibility in terms of the subject. Even before he began to deal seriously with the question of responsibility, he was concerned with the consequences of a one-sided embrace of particularity. Derrida himself admits that the ungrounded affirmation of diversity is self-defeating. He argues that "one cannot, for all that, plead *simply* for plurality, dispersion, or fractioning, for the mobility of screening places [in the public sphere] or of the subjects who occupy them. For certain socioeconomic forces might still take advantage of ... this absence of a general forum."[42] Unfortunately, Derrida has not yet developed a critique of those socioeconomic forces that he says will always "abuse the absence of a general forum," nor has he explicated just what such a general forum would look like. My suggestion is that this general forum is and must be the idea of the human essence as the capacity for self-determination. It and it alone provides grounds for the reconciliation of differences, because it and it alone explains how differences come to be as the result of the differential expression of the self-same human activity and because it and it alone highlights the source of oppression in socioeconomic dynamics governed by the imperative of increasing monetary value at the expense of human value.

The return of the repressed in the work of these defining postmodern thinkers is not surprising if one takes their politics seriously. As chapters 6 and 7 argued, there are deep contradictions within a politics that both values human diversity and dissolves human beings into posits of nonhuman forces. Without a ground in subjecthood, such politics wander between the poles of their immanent contradictions. Just as repressed desires manifest themselves in neurotic behaviour, so too does subjecthood return in postmodern thought. The repressed material returns in disguised or altered form, but underlying this form is the material that has been repressed. The concept of subjecthood that makes its force felt in the later works of Lyotard, Foucault, and Derrida is not identical in every detail to the subjecthood that they criticized, but the function that it serves is the same. In each case a defining feature of human being is posited as the normative ground of political practice, which is exactly what each claimed could not and should not be.

Conclusion

This text has explained the core philosophical concepts upon which the radical politics of difference is based and has traced the self-confuting logic of that politics back to its deconstruction of the idea that human beings are defined by an essential capacity for self-determination. This self-confuting logic is confirmed by the fact that the only way the politics of difference can be understood as a criticism of the relationship between the dominant powers of the globe and oppressed minorities is if it is read as actually presupposing this conception of subjecthood. In fact, we have seen that this concept is both presupposed and rehabilitated by the major theorists of postmodern criticism. But what of this notion of subjecthood as a tool in the practical criticism of the decisive conflicts between different minorities that continue to rack the globe? Can it be anything more than a platitude?

I believe that it can be, provided that the practical nature of philosophy is understood properly. Philosophy is not a *deus ex machina*; it cannot automatically resolve conflicts of long standing. What it can do, as I have tried to show here, is to bring to light what is often hidden in the complexities of actual political conflicts. By standing apart from the fray, critical philosophy is able to bring to light the shared ground of human differences that is necessary to any just resolution of the claims of the oppressed. By freeing the idea of self-creation or self-determination from its attachment to particular cultural, social, ethnic, and sexual differences, it brings to light the equality of the normative claims advanced by conflicting struggles. In bringing to light the shared normative basis of different struggles, it establishes a framework for negotiation and solidarity. Actual solidarity, however, can only be the result of dialogue between differences as to the best way forward. To use the case of the Québécois and Canada's First Nations once again, critical humanism brings to light a shared history of oppression in which each were denied the material and institutional resources needed to freely produce its cultural differences. It illuminates the shared grounds of cultural difference and thus makes it possible to see beyond the hard and fast lines of distinction. It reveals, therefore, that the enemy is not the other but forces that do think of cultures not as the objective expressions of human value but as exploitable resources that must adapt to the realities of the ruling interests, both political and economic, or perish.

The same holds true for other struggles not explicitly rooted in claims to cultural or ethnic difference. The struggles of working class people here and abroad to maintain wage levels and the evolved public infrastructure that provides them with a modicum of social safety and freedom, the struggles of women for gender-specific legislation and support services, the struggles of gays and lesbians for the space to express themselves without danger of bigoted attacks, and the struggles of disabled people for accessible public spaces are not private and unique struggles. They are all the same struggle, but with different content. They are all struggles for the freedom to realize the self-creative, self-determining capacity of human being in specific ways. If we can understand this metaphysical common ground, a framework – but only a framework – emerges for the construction of a political common ground, an alliance of the marginalised, the oppressed, the exploited, and the brutalised against the homogenizing, life-denying dynamics of the global corporate agenda and its political servants.

The coalition of the oppressed that Laclau and Mouffe called for is therefore just what is required today. But the solidarity envisaged by critical humanism is distinct from the postmodern kaleidoscope of differences. Solidarity presupposes common interests, and common interests are not merely accidental but must be rooted in a common human nature. Lacking objective grounds, merely convergent interests all too easily give way to factionalization when the hard business of politics begins. Of course, solidarity can come to be only through political negotiations, but negotiations must be anchored in the recognition of a shared nature. I have argued that our essential capacity for self-determination, which defines us as humans, is the shared nature from which the struggle for freedom in all its diversity grows. The reality of this shared essence has been recorded whenever one group of humans has tried to suppress another. In every case the group subjugated to the violence of ignorance, exploitation, and hatred has said, "No, we are not what you say we are, and we will prove it to you, by force if necessary." Today, while oppression exists still, it can no longer look to philosophy for cover. The natural inferiority of races, the natural place of women, and the natural ignorance of the poor have been objectively refuted by the "inferiors." As Marx said, the essence of human being is no abstraction inherent in each individual. It is, we conclude, the freedom of human beings to resist, to transform, and to create anew.

Notes

INTRODUCTION

1 Gilbert, "Political Correctness Has Failed," 9.
2 Aristotle, *Politics* 1254a16–1255a, 512–14.
3 Mill, *On Liberty*, 11.

CHAPTER ONE

1 Derrida, *Of Grammatology*, 11.
2 Derrida, *Positions*, 6–7.
3 Kearny, *Dialogues*, 117.
4 Derrida, "Structure, Sign, and Play," 278–9.
5 Kearny, *Dialogues*, 118.
6 Derrida in fact distinguishes his work from Foucault's early work in published criticism. Derrida, "Cogito and the History of Madness," 31–63. Further discussion of their opposition can be found in Megill, *Prophets of Extremity*, 269–70.
7 Foucault, "What is Enlightenment?" 28.
8 Foucault, *Language, Counter-memory, Practice*, 216.
9 Foucault, "Two Lectures," 80–1.
10 Foucault, "Nietzsche, Genealogy, History," 85.
11 Foucault, *The Archaeology of Knowledge*, 12.
12 Ibid., 67.
13 Foucault, "Truth and Power," 113.
14 See Cook, *The Subject Finds a Voice*, 130.

15 See Kellner and Best, *Postmodern Theory*, 1–34, 274–83.
16 Lyotard, *The Postmodern Condition*, xxiv.
17 Lyotard, *Rudiments paiens*, 164–5, my translation: Une histoire libidinal se refuse à cette finalité qui est celle du savoir et du pouvoir princiers. Il faut au moins appliquer a son "corpus" ... le principe de relativité généralisée que les physiciennes de la univers du noyau connaissent, et qui implique qu'il n'y a pas de poste privilégiée pour le déchiffrage des organisations d'énergie.
18 Lyotard, *The Postmodern Condition*, 41.
19 Ibid., xxiv.
20 Lyotard, *Just Gaming*, 61.

CHAPTER TWO

1 The modern origin of this mode of analysis may be found in Montesquieu, *The Spirit of the Laws*. Adam Ferguson continued this attempt to account for cultural difference in terms of a constant human nature responding to different environments in *An Essay on the History of Civil Society*. More or less the same approach is adopted by Marx in *The German Ideology*.
2 Lyotard, *The Postmodern Condition*, 15.
3 Lyotard, *Peregrinations*, 5–6.
4 Lyotard, *The Postmodern Condition*, 15.
5 John Keane, "The Modern Democratic Revolution," 86.
6 Lyotard, *The Postmodern Condition*, 65.
7 Van Den Abbeele, "Interview with Jean Francois Lyotard," 17.
8 Lyotard, *The Differend*, xi.
9 Foucault, *Language, Counter-memory, Practice*, 199.
10 Foucault, *The Order of Things*, xi.
11 Wilkins, "Chomsky and Foucault," 183.
12 Foucault, *The History of Sexuality*, 94.
13 Ibid.
14 Foucault, "Truth and Power," 119.
15 Ibid., 118.
16 Foucault, "Nietzsche, Genealogy, History," 56–7.
17 Hanssen, *Critique of Violence*, 47.
18 Foucault, *Discipline and Punish*, 255.
19 Foucault, quoted in Callinicos, *Against Postmodernism*, 87.
20 Foucault, *Discipline and Punish*, 303.
21 Dews, "Foucault and the *Nouvelle Philosophie*," 152.
22 Habermas, *The Philosophical Discourse of Modernity*, 284.
23 Caputo, *Deconstruction in a Nutshell*, 31.
24 Derrida, *Of Grammatology*, 33.

25 Derrida, *Speech and Phenomena*, 50.
26 Kearny, "Deconstruction and the Other," 125.
27 Derrida, *Of Grammatology*, 50
28 Kearny, "Deconstruction and the Other," 117.
29 Ibid., 11.
30 Ibid., 9.
31 Derrida, *Of Grammatology*, 158.
32 Derrida can be vicious when this statement is misinterpreted. See Derrida, "But, beyond," 168–70.
33 Derrida, "Signature, Event, Context," 310.
34 Derrida, *Specters of Marx*, 170.
35 Derrida, "But, beyond," 169.

CHAPTER THREE

1 Lyotard, "Universal History and Cultural Difference," 315.
2 Ibid., 316.
3 Ibid., 318.
4 Ibid., 315–16.
5 Lyotard, *The Differend*, xiii.
6 Ibid.,129.
7 Cook is perhaps the strongest proponent of this reading. Cook, *The Subject Finds a Voice*, 130. I shall have occasion to comment on her argument in more detail in the final chapter.
8 For a very thorough exegesis of Foucault's evolution from archaeologist to genealogist to ethicist, see Hanssen, *Critique of Violence*, 30–96.
9 Foucault, *Remarks on Marx*, 46.
10 Ibid., 31.
11 Foucault, *The Order of Things*, 308.
12 Foucault, *The Archaeology of Knowledge*, 117.
13 Foucault, "Birth of a World," 61.
14 Sprinker, "The Use and Abuse of Foucault," 3.
15 Foucault, *The Order of Things*, 369.
16 Foucault, "Nietzsche, Genealogy, History," 56. Despite his important criticisms of Foucault's analysis of power, Habermas makes analogous criticisms against the tradition of subject-centred philosophy. Habermas, *The Philosophical Discourse of Modernity*, 79.
17 Foucault, "Truth and Power," 117.
18 Foucault, *The History of Sexuality*, 60.
19 Foucault, "The Subject and Power," 212.
20 Ingram, "Foucault and Habermas on the Subject of Reason," 221.
21 Foucault, "What is Enlightenment," 46.
22 Foucault, "La grand colère des faits," 85, my translation: Avec la

Goulag, on voyait non pas les conséquences d'une malheureuse erreur mais les effets des théories le plus "vraie" dans l'ordre politique.

23 Foucault, "What is Enlightenment?" 47. The problem with this argument is that it presupposes a law-like structure of history, even as it claims that the belief in a law-like structure inevitably results in totalitarianism. While the totalitarian outcome is a contingent historical product that is dependent upon the adoption of the universalist perspective, it is nevertheless an inevitable outcome once that perspective has been adopted. History is not, therefore, contingent but determined by a law-like structure. The difference is that the critique of universalism complicates the laws, but it does not abandon them. One need only look at the howls that are produced by the neoconservative inheritors of these ideas whenever someone interferes with the "laws of the market" to see the truth of this claim. The dispute boils down to a dispute about which laws one believes in.

There is a second problem here that follows from the first. In the rush to deduce "totalitarianism" in general from a philosophical position, only one side of the revolution is examined – the role of the Bolshevik Party. In the case of Russia certain salient features of the history of the revolution are effaced, so as to validate the claim that Leninism is Stalinism. However, it cannot be denied that the Bolsheviks waited until they had a majority in the soviets until calling for the overthrow of the provisional government; that that government, regardless of the openly expressed views of hundreds of thousands of people, continued the war and refused to meet the peasantry's land claims; that the October Revolution was the culminating point of struggles in which hundreds of thousands of people participated; that Stalin exiled or killed the vast majority of the members of the Central Committee of the party after taking power; and that there was a left-opposition to Stalin that was systematically destroyed, a process that culminated half a world away when Trotsky was executed in Mexico. This is not to say that the internal structure of the party was not partly responsible for the degeneration of the revolution, as, for example, Rosa Luxembourg maintained. It is to insist, however, that if Stalinism was both inevitable and consistent with the program of the Bolshevik Party, then the left-wing struggle against it is inexplicable. Taking into account the events of the period, one can see that Stalinism was not inevitable, much less a necessary logical function of Marxist humanism, but was the result of the isolation of the revolution. This isolation and the misery it produced necessitated the authoritarian degeneration, which then created the context in which Stalin could come to power. An excellent critical evaluation of the various attempts to link the totalitarian outcome of the revolution with

the process of revolution itself may be found in Rees, "In Defence of October," 1–52.
24 Derrida, "Différance," 15.
25 Martin, *Matrix and Line*, 52.
26 Kearny, *Dialogues with Contemporary Continental Thinkers*, 125.
27 Hobson, *Jacques Derrida*, 79.
28 Kearny, *Dialogues with Contemporary Continental Thinkers*, 117.
29 Derrida, *Specters of Marx*, 91.
30 Ibid., 105.
31 Ibid., 98.
32 Ibid., 74–5.

CHAPTER FOUR

1 Pheby, *Interventions*, 2. Pheby uses the term "deconstruction" to denote a general politics premised upon the repudiation of the concept of subjecthood. He thus includes Foucault and Lyotard, as well as Heidegger and Nietzsche, in this camp.
2 Lyotard, *Just Gaming*, 73–4. See also in this regard Lyotard, *Rudiments paiens*, 146.
3 Ibid.
4 Ibid., my translation: Ces luttes sont des minoritaires visant à rester minoritaire et à être reconnue comme tels ... En interdirant leur cultures, leur patois, on veut détuire leur force affirmatrice, la "perspective" en sens nietzschéen, que trace chacun des luttes dans une temps qui n'est pas cumulatif.
5 Ibid., 77, my translation: Une autre espace, une autre logique, une autre histoire que ce dans lesquelles le platonisme et le judaïsme conjugués ont cherche et cherchant encore, sous l'autorité des jacobinisme, léninisme, trotskysme, libéralisme, a consigné ces spasmes et les neutralises.
6 Lyotard, *Just Gaming*, 95.
7 Williams, *Lyotard*, 70. Supportive commentators have failed to note the very serious problems that attend a politics that affirms resistance to a defined set of social problems with an unlimited number of possibilities. See Brodsky, "Postmodernity and Politics," 298, and Benjamin, *Judging Lyotard*.
8 Lyotard, *Just Gaming*, 100.
9 Kellner and Best, *Postmodern Theory*, 247–8.
10 Lyotard, "Oikos," 101.
11 Lyotard, *The Inhuman*, 62.
12 Ibid., 6.
13 Browning, *Lyotard and the End of Grand Narratives*, 74.
14 Lyotard, *The Inhuman*, 4.

15 Browning, *Lyotard and the End of Grand Narratives,* 89. See also Sim, "Lyotard and the Politics of Anti-Foundationalism," 8–13, and Kellner and Best, *Postmodern Theory,* 171–81.
16 Habermas, *The Philosophical Discourse of Modernity;* Ingram, "Foucault and Habermas on the Subject of Reason."
17 Druron, "Deconstructing the Subject"; Cook, *The Subject Finds a Voice.*
18 Laclau and Mouffe, *Hegemony and Socialist Strategy;* Clifford, "Crossing Out the Boundary," 223–33; and Ross, "Foucault's Radical Politics."
19 Keikel, "La fin de l'homme"; Poster, *Critical Theory after Poststructuralism.*
20 Bevire, "Foucault and Critique."
21 Foucault, "Polemics, Politics, and Problematisations," 383–4.
22 Foucault, "The Subject and Power," 208.
23 Foucault, "The Ethic of the Care for the Self," 2.
24 Foucault, *Language, Counter-memory, Practice,* 35–6.
25 Foucault, *The Order of Things,* 342.
26 Foucault, "Two Lectures," 81–2.
27 Foucault, "What Is Enlightenment?" 44.
28 Ibid., 45.
29 Ibid., 46.
30 Ibid., 47.
31 Foucault, "The Ethic of the Care for the Self as a Practice of Freedom," 12.
32 Ibid., 4.
33 Ibid., 10.
34 For "normative confusion," see Fraser, "Foucault on Modern Power."
35 For a solid criticism of efforts to domesticate Derrida as a liberal, see Roderick, "Reading Derrida Politically," 87–102.
36 Derrida, "The Ends of Man," 150.
37 Derrida, *The Other Heading,* 24.
38 Kearny, "Deconstruction and the Other," 121.
39 See Perpich, "A Singular Justice." A more sustained explication of the ethical significance of the difference between the feminine and the masculine can be found in Irigaray, *An Ethics of Sexual Difference.*
40 Derrida, "Racism's Last Word," 294–5.
41 See Derrida, "The Law of Reflection" 34. Affirming Mandela's strategy of turning the spirit of the law against the letter of the law, Derrida writes, "As a 'lawyer worthy of the name,' he sets himself against the code in the code, reflects the code, but making visible thereby just what the code in action rendered unreadable ... This production of light is justice – moral or political ... It translates here the political violence of the whites, it holds to their interpretation of the laws ... whose letter is destined to contradict the spirit of the law."
42 Derrida, *Du droit à la philosophie,* 35–6, my translation: la détermination

philosophique de cette responsabilité, les concepts de son axiomatique (par exemple, la volonté, la propriété, le sujet, l'identité d'une "moi" libre et individuelle, la "personne" conscient, la présence à soi d'intention, etc.), peut toujours discutée, questionnée, déplacée, critiquée – et, plus radicalement, déconstruitées – ce sera toujours au nom de responsabilité plus exigeante, plus fidèle à la memoire et la promesse, toujours au-dela de la présent.

43 Bennington, *Interrupting Derrida*, 25.
44 Derrida, *Adieu: To Emmanuel Levinas*, 117.
45 Hobson, *Jacques Derrida: Opening Lines*, 141.
46 Martin, *Matrix and Line*, 146.
47 Kearny, "Deconstruction and the Other," 119.
48 Ibid., 118.
49 Derrida, *Specters of Marx*, 60.
50 Ibid., 59.
51 Ibid., 35.

CHAPTER FIVE

1 Aronowitz, *The Politics of Identity*, ix.
2 A history of post-Marxism from 1985 to the present would constitute too much of a digression. Thus, I will focus only on the basic premises of Laclau and Mouffe as spelled out in their first text. The subsequent career of post-Marxism can be traced in the following texts. Laclau, *New Reflections*; Mouffe, *The Return of the Political*; Mouffe, *The Democratic Paradox*; Callari, Cullenberg and Biewener, *Marxism in the Postmodern Age*; Aronson, *After Marxism*; Aronowitz, *The Death and Rebirth of American Radicalism*; Magnus, *Whither Marxism*; Rockmore, *Marx after Marxism*.
3 Bennington suggests that the "work of Ernesto Laclau and Chantal Mouffe ... is arguably the only political theory as such to have engaged seriously with Derrida's work." Bennington, *Interrupting Derrida*, 198n.
4 Space prevents me from providing an adequate history of the emergence of the practical politics of difference from the failures of the New Left. A good overview is Gitlin, *Twilight of Common Dreams*.
5 A defence of Marxism from the criticisms of Laclau and Mouffe also falls outside the parameters of my argument. The most trenchant and concise response is Geras, "Post-Marxism?"
6 Derrida, "The Principle of Reason," 9–10.
7 Laclau and Mouffe, *Hegemony and Socialist Strategy*, 176.
8 Ibid., 115.
9 Mouffe, *The Democratic Paradox*, 19–20.
10 Young, "The Ideal of Community," 3.

11 Ibid., 4.
12 Young, *Justice and the Politics of Difference*, 116.
13 In the context of contemporary American political philosophy Young's primary target is the work of John Rawls. Rawls argues that justice is the result of a hypothetical social contract entered into by abstractly rational agents choosing a social and political structure from behind a veil of ignorance. By "veil of ignorance" Rawls means that prospective citizens of this society would not know what their identity would be (whether they would be women or men, black or white, poor or rich) and thus they would choose a structure in which the worst off were as well provided for as possible. For the most current versions of Rawls' argument see Rawls, *Political Liberalism*, and Rawls, *Justice as Fairness: A Restatement*.
14 Young, "Polity and Group Difference," 251.
15 Young, "Together in Difference," 158.
16 Young, "Deferring Group Representation," 357.
17 Ibid., 369.
18 Sarra-Bournet, "Nationalisme," 369, my translation: n'oubliez jamais: les trois cinquantièmes de ce que nous sommes ont voté oui.
19 Young, "Together in Difference," 161.

CHAPTER SIX

1 Haber, *Beyond Postmodern Politics*, 119. Haber's project bears a superficial resemblance to my own insofar as she questions the viability of a radical postmodern politics. However, there are some key differences.

First, she conflates the meaning of the term "subject" with that of "bourgeois individual." On the basis of this conflation, she undertakes a rethinking of the history of the term. This rethinking defends the thesis that individuality and community are necessarily counterposed in modern thought. She then proposes to resolve this contradiction through her notion of "subject-in-community." The problem with this position is that it is a one-sided reading of modern political thought. Individual and community are counterposed in classical liberalism but not essentially counterposed in the whole of modern thought. Classically, Mill understands that robust individuality has social presuppositions, while contemporary liberals like Kymlicka and Rawls offer very complex liberal defences of the social grounds of individuality. Haber also ignores the quite different meaning of the term "subject" in the Hegelian and Marxist traditions. The whole of *The Phenomenology of Spirit* argues that historical progress must be measured by the extent to which the essential reciprocity between individual and community is consciously affirmed by individuals and expressed by civil society.

Hegel's notion of Spirit – "I" that is "We" and "We" that is "I" – is the metaphysical foundation for the resolution of the empirical contradiction between individual and community. Marx most obviously rejects the essential contradiction between individual and community, arguing bluntly that "The individual is the social being." (Marx, *Economic and Philosophical Manuscripts of 1844*, 138.) Haber's argument is thus based on a seriously flawed understanding of the history of nineteenth-century philosophy, and her notion of subject-in-community is not essentially distinct from positions characteristic of modernity if the full range of modern thinking is admitted into the argument.

A more serious problem, however, is that she follows postmodern thinking in conflating subjecthood with subject-position. Subject-in-community amounts to a recognition of the different contexts in which empirical identities are formed. But, as shall become clear in the following chapters, subjecthood is not identical to one's empirical identities. Subjecthood is the underlying, essential capacity from which different empirical identities are formed. By equating subject-in-community with different empirical identities, Haber undermines the grounds for solidarity that her politics nevertheless posits as its goal. One can argue that differences have social presuppositions, but this does not entail that the various differences will live together harmoniously unless it can be shown that the freedom of one position rests upon the freedom of all positions. By accepting difference as fundamental, Haber's politics lacks strong grounds for solidarity between the different subjects-in-community. Furthermore, such a politics risks exacerbating the struggles between marginalized communities, because it claims that politics must begin from the dispersed cultural positions extant at a given time. But there is nothing in the notion of subject-in-community, resolvable as it is into different subjects-in-communities, that rules out separate, dispersed struggles. In a competitive framework where different groups are competing for scarce resources, it is no more likely that such groups, even if they are all marginalized, will co-operate rather than compete, especially if the political project which hopes to reconcile them accepts differences as basic.

2 Canadian multicultural policy has been criticised on this ground. Mackey, *The House of Difference*.
3 Derrida, *Spectres de Marx*, 60.
4 Derrida, *Of Grammatology*, 115.
5 Foucault, *Language, Counter-memory, Practice*, 34–5.
6 Foucault, "What is Enlightenment?" 46.
7 Lyotard, *The Postmodern Condition*, 81.
8 Derrida, *On the Name*, 25.
9 Derrida, quoted in Bernstein, "Serious Play," 94.

10 Foucault, "Nietzsche, Genealogy, History," 85.
11 Lyotard, *The Inhuman*, 4.
12 Derrida, "Choreographies," 108.
13 Foucault, *Language, Counter-memory, Practice*, 233.
14 Foucault, *Remarks on Marx*, 46.
15 Lyotard, *The Postmodern Condition*, 65–6.
16 Ibid., 67.
17 Let me be clear that the analysis and discussion of Quebec nationalism in this and the following chapter makes no claim to be a complete historical analysis of the relationship between English Canada and the Québécois. Nor is it concerned with a precise political analysis of the current state of the nationalist movement in Quebec. It is focussed on the underlying metaphysical and normative grounds of nationalisms of historically oppressed minorities. For the record, I believe that the Québécois are a historically oppressed nation in Canada, but this position should not be construed as an affirmation of any particular political movement against that oppression, much less an endorsement of the Parti Québécois, the Bloc Québécois, or any other concrete political movement in Quebec. As we will see, the struggle of national minorities points beyond itself to a human struggle for the conditions in which cultural differences are secure and, in being secure, promote the grounds for the creation of new forms of human culture. The same holds true for the subsequent analysis of the struggles of Canada's First Nations.
18 Valliers, *White Niggers of America*, 48–50; Bourque and Legue, *Le Québec*, 167–215; Drache, *Quebec*, 3–36.
19 Monière, *Ideologies in Quebec*, 113.
20 Ibid., 114.
21 Lévesque, *Quebec-Canada: A New Deal*, 101.
22 Quoted in Nemni, "Organicisme, Historicisme, et Culturalisme," 193, my translation: inspirés par une conception culturelle de la nation, se donneront une organisation politique en conséquence. To be sure, there are alternative grounds for the nationalist movement in Quebec today. In fact, the discourse of ethnic nationalism has been increasingly supplanted by the liberal discourse of civic nationalism. To sort out the differences between the two would take me beyond the purview of the present study. For my purposes ethnic nationalism is the more important test case. If, as I will attempt in the next chapter, we can find a universal human capacity that is implicit in the claim to difference then my argument that a proper understanding of cultural differences depends upon grasping it as an expression of an underlying human essence will be all the stronger. The pernicious effects of ethnic nationalism can be checked only by discovering this universal ground underlying the

differences. For the development of an inclusive liberal nationalist theory and practice in Quebec see Bouchard, "Ouvrir la Cercle de la Nation," 307–28.

23 The rebellions of 1837 occurred at a moment of European-wide nationalist struggle. Although we cannot fully substantiate the point here, it is the case that Québécois nationalism has been cosmopolitan in its outlook at those moments (the mid–nineteenth century, the 1960s) when it was part of a global, multinational struggle for national self-determination. It has been most xenophobic and withdrawn (the Ultramontanist period of 1867–96, the period of *survivance* and Dupleissis (1896–1945)) when global struggles were on the wane. I will return to the importance of internationalism in the next chapter. The historical variations in nationalist ideology are superbly traced in Moniere, *Ideologies in Quebec*.

24 Côté, *La marche d'un peuple*, 15–6, my translation: Par ses origines, son histoire, sa langue maternelle ... son vouloir-vivre collectif, le Québec forme une authentique nation ... En 1945 le droit des peuples a disposer d'eux mêmes a été reconnue par les articles 1 et 51 de la Chartre des Nations Unis.

25 Kymlicka, *Finding Our Way*, 132. Kymlicka is one of the most sensitive philosophical commentators on the problem of ethnic and national relations in Canada today. Space prevents me from entering into a detailed evaluation of his analysis and prescriptions.

CHAPTER SEVEN

1 It also puts itself at odds with arguably the most sophisticated criticism of postmodern philosophy, that of Jürgen Habermas. While Habermas rejects the way in which subjecthood is deconstructed by postmodernism, he too rejects essentialist interpretations of it. See Habermas, *The Philosophical Discourse of Modernity*, 294–326.
2 Emberly, *Thresholds of Difference*, 15.
3 For a discussion of the splits in the Mohawk community see Ciaccia, *The Oka Crisis*, 161–6. Ciaccia was the Quebec minister responsible for Aboriginal affairs during the crisis, and much of his presentation is self-serving. Nonetheless, it is in many respects an importantly insightful look into the political complexities of the crisis.
4 MacLaine and Baxendale, *This Land is Our Land*, 1.
5 Ibid., 76.
6 Johnston, "Native Rights as Collective Rights," 194.
7 Ciaccia, *The Oka Crisis*, 71.
8 Ibid., 106. Of course, politicians often find it easier to see through to unifying grounds when they are not running the show. One wonders

how Landry would respond if tensions should flair on his watch. Again, the point here is not to dissect the honesty of politicians but to draw out the universal grounds underlying nationalist struggles, grounds that Landry nicely expresses here, regardless of whether he was merely trying to score political points. The official policy of the PQ regarding Aboriginal self-government as spelled out in the 1994 Referendum Act is weaker than the implications of Landry's claim, but it puts paid to the myth that federalists were only too happy to float that the nationalist movement in Quebec is inherently racist. The relevant section of the act maintains that "The constitution shall include a charter of human rights and freedoms ... It shall also recognize the right of Aboriginal nations to self-government on lands over which they have full ownership. Such guarantee and such recognition shall be exercised in a manner consistent with the territorial integrity of Quebec." Quoted in Whittaker, "Quebec's Self-determination and Aboriginal Self-government," 211.

9 Editorial Collective Autonomedia, "Declaration of War," 49–50.
10 Ibid., 50. In particular, the struggle is legitimated by appeal to article 39, which reads: "National Sovereignty essentially and originally resides in the people ... the people have, at all times, the inalienable right to alter or modify their form of government."
11 Lyotard, *Rudiments paiens*, 146, my translation: des luttes minoritaires visant rester minoritaire.
12 "Interview with Luis Hernandez," 4–5.
13 Editorial Collective of *Canadian Dimension*, "Zapatista Leader Makes the Links." I am greatful to John McMurtry for bringing this passage to my attention.
14 Fernandez, "Globalization Doesn't Break Down Borders, It Creates Them: Interview with Commander Marcos," 2. Originally in Spanish. This translation downloaded from http://blackened.net/revolt/mexico/ezln/2001/marcos_inter_jan28.html
15 Kymlicka, *Finding Our Way*, 6.
16 Maracle, *I Am Woman*, 17–18.
17 Ibid., 80.
18 Ibid., 110.
19 Ibid., 95, 124.
20 Adams, *Prisons of Grass*, 169.
21 Laforest, "Souveraineté et Humanisme," 8.
22 Taylor, "The Politics of Recognition," 38.
23 Young, "Together in Difference," 126.
24 Hegel, *The Phenomenology of Spirit*, 113.
25 Ibid., 113–14.
26 Fanon, *The Wretched of the Earth*, 43.

27 Ibid., 314.
28 Gordon, *Fanon and the Crisis of European Man*, 103.
29 West, "The New Cultural Politics of Difference," 29.
30 Soper, "Postmodernism, Subjectivity, and the Question of Value," 21.
31 Foucault, "What Is Enlightenment?" 47.
32 Hartsock, quoted in Sawicki, "Foucault, Feminism, and Questions of Identity," 312.
33 McClure, "On the Subject of Rights," 108

CHAPTER EIGHT

1 Spivak, *In Other Worlds*, 202.
2 Soper, *Humanism and Anti-humanism*, 106.
3 Sawicki, "Foucault and Feminism," 294.
4 Ornstein, *Ethno-Racial Inequality in Toronto*.
5 This generalisation applies even to the case where successful resistance is hopeless. The key to understanding resistance is not in the end but in the fact of resistance itself. The martyrs of the Warsaw ghetto, for example, knew they could not win. They also knew that they were not inert matter to be trampled upon – they were living agents capable of fighting back; their ultimate defeat is irrelevant to the dignity of the struggle.
6 For Aristotle's criticisms of the theory of Forms and his account of essence see *Metaphysics* 307–8, 311–13, 1039a23–1039b20; 1041a7–1042a.
7 Marcuse, "The Concept of Essence," 69.
8 Ibid., 73.
9 Eagleton, *The Illusions of Postmodernism*, 101.
10 Marx, quoted in Suchting, "Marx's *Theses on Feuerbach*," 18.
11 Althusser, *For Marx*, 227.
12 Marx, quoted in Suchting, "Marx's *Theses on Feurbach*," 12.
13 Marx, *The Communist Manifesto*, 54.
14 Dews, "The Return of the Subject," 37.
15 Cook, *The Subject Finds a Voice*, 121.
16 Taylor, "Foucault on Freedom and Truth," 69–102; Walzer, "The Politics of Michel Foucault," 51–68.
17 Cook, *The Subject Finds a Voice*, 130.
18 Ibid., 129.
19 Ibid., 137.
20 Ibid.
21 Foucault, "On the Genealogy of Ethics," 237.
22 Cook, *The Subject Finds a Voice*, 132.
23 Foucault, *Madness and Civilization*, 279.
24 Foucault, *Discipline and Punish*, 308.

25 Foucault, *The Final Foucault*, 2.
26 Foucault, "Polemics, Politics, and Problematisations," 388.
27 Foucault, "La grand colère des faits," 84.
28 G.W.F. Hegel, *Logic*, 42.
29 Lyotard, *Moralités postmodernes*, 66, my translation: La practique militante, dans nos pays du moins, est devenue défensive. Il nous faut constamment réaffirmer les droits des minorités; femmes, enfants, homosexuels, le Sud, le tiers monde, les pauvres, le droit à culture et à l'éducation.
30 A concise history of the struggle over the expansion of rights may be found in Wood, *Democracy against Capitalism*, 204–38.
31 Lyotard, *Moralités postmodernes*, 110, my translation: si l'homme ne préserve pas la région inhumaine ... qui échappe toute a faite à l'exercice des droits, il ne mérite pas les droits qu'on lui reconnaît ... Pourquoi aurions-nous droit à la liberté d'expression si nous n'avions rien à dire que la déjà dit? Et comment avoir chance de trouver à dire ce que nous ne savons pas dire si nous n'écoutons pas du tout le silence de l'autre au dedans. Ce silence est un exception à la réciprocité des droits, mais il en est la légitimation.
32 Ibid., 106, my translation: La droit de rester séparé.
33 Lyotard, *The Confession of Augustine*, 48–9.
34 This ideal of expressive individuality is perhaps best expressed in Schiller, *Letters on the Aesthetic Education of Man*.
35 For a useful historical survey of the antiapartheid movement in South Africa, see Callinicos, "Working Class Politics in South Africa," 59–127.
36 Derrida, "The Law of Reflection," 38.
37 Ibid.
38 Derrida, "But, beyond," 159.
39 Derrida, *On the Name*, 15.
40 Derrida, "The Politics of Friendship," 638.
41 Derrida, *Adieu: To Emmanuel Levinas*, 72–3.
42 Derrida, "The Other Heading," 99–100.

Bibliography

Adams, Howard. *Prisons of Grass*. Saskatoon, SK: Fifth House Publishers 1989.
Althusser, Louis. *For Marx*. London: New Left Books 1969.
Aristotle. *Metaphysics: A New Aristotle Reader*. J.L. Ackrill, ed. Princeton: Princeton University Press 1989.
– *Politics: A New Aristotle Reader*. J.L. Ackrill, ed. Princeton: Princeton University Press 1989.
Aronowitz, Stanley. *The Politics of Identity*. New York: Routledge 1992.
– *The Death and Rebirth of American Radicalism*. New York: Routledge 1996.
Aronson, Ronald. *After Marxism*. New York: Guilford 1995.
Benjamin, Andrew, ed. *Judging Lyotard*. London: Routledge and Kegan Paul 1992.
Bennington, Geoffrey. *Interrupting Derrida*. London: Routledge 2000.
Bernstein, Richard. "Serious Play: The Ethical-Political Horizon of Jacques Derrida." *The Journal of Speculative Philosophy* 1, no. 2 (1987): 93–113.
Bevire, Mark. "Foucault and Critique: Deploying Agency against Autonomy." *Political Theory* 27, no. 1 (February 1999): 65–84.
Bouchard, Michel. "Ouvrir la cercle de la nation, activer la cohésion sociale: Réflection sur le Québec et la diversité." In *Les nationalismes au Québec du XIXe au XXie siècles*, edited by Michel Sarra-Bournet. Quebec: Presses de l'Université Laval 2001.
Bourque, Gilles, and Anne Legue. *Le Québec: La question nationale*. Paris: Editions François Maspero 1979.
Brodsky, Gary. "Postmodernity and Politics." *Philosophy Today*, no. 31 (winter 1987): 291–305.
Browning, Gary. *Lyotard and the End of Grand Narratives*. Cardiff: University of Wales Press 2000.

Calari, Andrew, Stephen Cullenburg, and Carol Biewiner, eds. *Marxism in the Postmodern Age.* New York: Guilford 1995.

Callinicos, Alex. "Working Class Politics in South Africa." In *South Africa: Between Reform and Revolution.* London: Bookmarks 1988.

– *Against Postmodernism.* London: Polity Press, 1989.

Caputo, John D. *Deconstruction in a Nutshell.* New York: Fordham University Press 1997.

Ciaccia, John. *The Oka Crisis.* Dorval, PQ: Maren Publications 2000.

Clifford, Michael. "Crossing Out the Boundary: Foucault and Derrida on Transgressing Transgression." *Philosophy Today* 31, nos. 3–4 (fall 1987): 223–35.

Cook, Deborah. *The Subject Finds a Voice.* New York: Peter Lang 1993.

Côté, Jean. *La marche d'un peuple vers la souveraineté.* Montreal: Editions Ordine 1999.

Derrida, Jacques. *Speech and Phenomena.* Evanston, IL: Northwestern University Press 1973.

– *Of Grammatology.* Baltimore, MD: Johns Hopkins University Press 1974.

– "Cogito and the History of Madness." In *Writing and Difference.* Chicago: University of Chicago Press 1978.

– "Structure, Sign, and Play in the Discourse of the Human Sciences." *Writing and Difference.* Chicago: University of Chicago Press, 1978.

– *Positions.* Chicago: University of Chicago Press 1981.

– "Différance." In *Margins of Philosophy.* Chicago: University of Chicago Press 1982.

– "Signature, Event, Context." In *Margins of Philosophy.* Chicago: University of Chicago Press 1982.

– "The Principle of Reason: The University in the Eyes of its Pupils." *Diacritics* 13 (fall 1983): 1–20.

– "Racism's Last Word. *Critical Inquiry* 12 (autumn 1985): 108–19.

– "But, beyond: An Open Letter to Anne McClintock and Rob Nixon." *Critical Inquiry* 13, no. 2 (autumn 1986): 155–70.

– "The Law of Reflection." In *For Nelson Mandela*, edited by Jacques Derrida and M. Tlili. New York: Henry Holt 1987.

– "The Ends of Man." In *After Philosophy: End or Transformation?* Edited by Kenneth Baynes, James Bohman, and Thomas McCarthy. Cambridge, MA: MIT Press, 1987.

– "The Politics of Friendship." *The Journal of Philosophy* 85, no. 11 (November 1988): 632–44.

– *Du droit à la philosophie.* Paris: Editions Galilée 1990.

– *The Other Heading.* Bloomington, IL: Indiana University Press 1992.

– *Specters of Marx.* New York: Routledge, 1994.

– *On the Name.* Stanford, CA: Stanford University Press 1995.

– "Choreographies." In *Points ... Interviews, 1974–1994.* Stanford, CA: Stanford University Press 1995.

- *Adieu: To Emmanuel Levinas.* Stanford, CA: Stanford University Press 1999.
Dews, Peter. "Foucault and the *Nouvelle Philosophie.*" *Economy and Society* 8, no. 2 (1979): 127–71.
- "The Return of the Subject in Late Foucault." *Radical Philosophy*, no. 51 (spring 1989): 37–47.
Drache, Daniel, ed. *Quebec: Only the Beginning.* Toronto: New Press 1972.
Druon, Michel. "Deconstructing the Subject." *Inquiries into Values.* Lewiston, NY: Mellon Press 1990.
Eagleton, Terry. *The Illusions of Postmodernism.* Oxford: Blackwell Publishers 1997.
Editorial Collective of Autonomedia. "Declaration of War." *Zapatistas! Documents of the New Mexican Revolution.* New York: Autonomedia 1994.
Editorial Collective of *Canadian Dimension.* "Zapatista Leader Makes the Links." *Canadian Dimension* 28, no. 5 (October-November 1994): 1.
Emberly, Julie. *Thresholds of Difference: Feminist Critique, Native Women's Writings, Postcolonial Theory.* Toronto: University of Toronto Press 1993.
Fanon, Franz. *The Wretched of the Earth.* New York: Grove Press 1982.
Ferguson, Adam. *An Essay on the History of Civil Society.* Cambridge: Cambridge University Press 1999.
Fernandez, Aurelio. "Globalization Doesn't Break Down Borders, It Creates Them: Interview with Commander Marcos." *La Jornada*, 2 February 2001 Http://blackened.net/revolt/mexico/ezln/2001/marcos_inter_jan28.html
Foucault, Michel. *The Order of Things.* New York: Random House 1971.
- *The Archaeology of Knowledge.* London: Tavistock Publications 1972.
- *Discipline and Punish.* New York: Vintage Books 1977.
- "La grand colère des faits." *La Nouvelle Observateur*, 9 May 1977, 84–7.
- *Language, Counter-memory, Practice.* Ithaca, NY: Cornell University Press 1977.
- *The History of Sexuality.* Vol. 1. New York: Random House 1978.
- "Truth and Power." In *Power/Knowledge*, edited by Colin Gordon. New York: Pantheon 1980.
- "Two Lectures." In *Power/Knowledge*, edited by Colin Gordon. New York: Pantheon 1980.
- "On the Genealogy of Ethics," appendix to *Michel Foucault: Beyond Structuralism and Hermeneutics*, by Paul Robinson and Hugh Dreyfus. Evanston, IL: Northwestern University Press 1983.
- "The Subject and Power." *Michel Foucault: Beyond Structuralism and Hermeneutics.* Evanston, IL: Northwestern University Press 1983.
- "Nietzsche, Genealogy, History." In *The Foucault Reader*, edited by Paul Rabinow. New York: Pantheon 1984.
- "Polemics, Politics, and Problematisations." In *The Foucault Reader*, edited by Paul Rabinow. New York: Pantheon 1984.
- "What Is Enlightenment? In *The Foucault Reader*, edited by Paul Rabinow. New York: Pantheon 1984.

- "The Ethic of the Care for the Self as a Practice of Freedom." In *The Final Foucault*, edited by James Bernauer, and David Rasmussen. Cambridge, MA: MIT Press 1987.
- *Madness and Civilization*. New York: Vintage Books 1988.
- "Birth of a World." In *Foucault Live*. New York: Semiotext(e) 1989.
- *Remarks on Marx*. New York: Semiotext(e) 1991.

Fraser, Nancy. "Foucault on Modern Power: Empirical Insights and Modern Confusions." In *Unruly Practices*. Minneapolis, MN: University of Minnesota Press 1989.

Geras, Norman. "Post-Marxism." *New Left Review* 163 (June 1987): 40–82.

Gilbert, Sky. "Political Correctness Has Failed." *eye*, 9 October 2000, 9.

Gitlin, Todd. *The Twilight of Common Dreams*. New York: Henry Holt 1995.

Gordon, Lewis R. *Fanon and the Crisis of European Man*. New York: Routledge 1995.

Haber, Honi Fern. *Beyond Postmodern Politics*. New York: Routledge 1994.

Habermas, Jürgen. *The Philosophical Discourse of Modernity*. Cambridge, MA: MIT Press 1987.

Hanssen, Beatrice. *Critique of Violence: Between Poststructuralism and Critical Theory*. New York: Routledge 2000.

Hegel, G.W.F. *Logic*. Oxford: Oxford University Press 1972.
- *The Phenomenology of Spirit*. Oxford: Oxford University Press 1977.

Hobson, Marian. *Jacques Derrida: Opening Lines*. New York: Routledge 1998.

Ingram, David. "Foucault and Habermas on the Subject of Reason." In *The Cambridge Companion to Foucault*, edited by Gary Gutting. Cambridge: Cambridge University Press 1994.

"Interview with Luis Hernandez." *America's Update* 15, no. 2 (1994): 4–5.

Irigaray, Luce. *An Ethics of Sexual Difference*. Ithaca, NY: Cornell University Press 1993.

Johnston, Darlene M. "Native Rights as Collective Rights: A Question of Group Self-Preservation." In *The Rights of Minority Cultures*, edited by Will Kymlicka. Oxford: Oxford University Press 1995.

Keane, John. "The Modern Democratic Revolution." In *Judging Lyotard*, edited by Andrew Benjamin. London: Routledge and Kegan Paul 1992.

Kearny, Richard. "Deconstruction and the Other: An Interview with Jacques Derrida." *Dialogues with Contemporary Continental Thinkers*. Manchester: University of Manchester Press 1984.

Keikel, Aron. "La fin de l'homme et le destin de la pensée." *Man and World* 18, no. 3 (1985): 1–34.

Kellner, Douglas, and Steven Best. *Postmodern Theory*. New York: Guilford Publications 1991.

Kymlicka, Will. *Finding Our Way: Rethinking Ethnocultural Relations in Canada*. Oxford: Oxford University Press 1998.

Laclau, Ernesto. *New Reflections on the Revolution of Our Time*. London: Verso 1990.

Laclau, Ernesto, and Chantal Mouffe. *Hegemony and Socialist Strategy.* London: Verso 1985.
Laforest, Guy. "Souveraineté et humanisme." *Le Devoir*, 12 Mai 1995, 8.
Lévesque, René. *Québec-Canada: A New Deal.* Quebec: Government of Québec 1979.
Lyotard, Jean François. *Rudiments paiennes.* Paris: Union générale d'Editions 1977.
- *The Postmodern Condition.* Minneapolis, MN: University of Minnesota Press 1984.
- *Just Gaming.* Minneapolis, MN: University of Minnesota Press 1985.
- *The Differend: Phrases in Dispute.* Minneapolis, MN: University of Minnesota Press 1988.
- *Peregrinations: Law, Form, Event.* New York: Columbia University Press 1988.
- "Oikios." In *Political Writings.* Oxford: Oxford University Press 1989.
- "Universal History and Cultural Difference." In *The Lyotard Reader*, edited by Andrew Benjamin. Oxford: Oxford University Press 1989.
- *The Inhuman.* Stanford, CA: Stanford University Press 1991.
- *The Confession of Augustine.* Stanford, CA; Stanford University Press 2000.
Mackey, Eva. *The House of Difference: Cultural Politics and National Identity in Canada.* New York: Routledge 1999.
MacLaine, Craig, and Michael Baxendale. *This Land Is Our Land.* Montreal: Optimum Publishing 1990.
Magnus, Bernd, ed. *Whither Marxism?* New York: Routledge 1995.
Maracle, Lee. *I Am Woman.* Vancouver, BC: Press Gang Publishers 1996.
Marcuse, Herbert. "The Concept of Essence." In *Negations: Essays in Critical Theory.* Boston: Beacon Press 1968.
Martin, Bill. *Matrix and Line.* Albany, NY: State University of New York Press 1992.
Marx, Karl. *Economic and Philosophical Manuscripts of 1844.* New York: International Publishers 1964.
- *The German Ideology.* Moscow: Progress Publishers 1975.
- *The Communist Manifesto.* Moscow: Progress Publishers 1986.
McClure, Kirstie. "On the Subject of Rights: Pluralism, Plurality, and Political Identity." In *Dimensions of Radical Democracy*, edited by Chantal Mouffe. London: Verso 1992.
Megill, Alan. *Prophets of Extremity.* Berkeley, CA: University of California Press 1985.
Mill, John Stuart. *On Liberty.* New York: Norton 1974.
Monière, Denis. *Ideologies in Quebec: The Historical Development.* Toronto: University of Toronto Press 1981.
Montesquieu. *The Spirit of the Laws.* Cambridge: Cambridge University Press 1994.
Mouffe, Chantal. *The Return of the Political.* London: Verso 1993.

- *The Democratic Paradox.* London: Verso, 2000.
Nemni, Max. "Organicisme, historicisme, et culturalisme dans la nationalisme Québécois d'aujourd'hui." In *Les nationalismes au Québec du XIXe au XXIe siècle.* Quebec: Les Presses de l'Université Laval 2001.
Ornstein, Michael. *Ethno-Racial Inequality in the City of Toronto: An Analysis of the 1996 Census.* Toronto: City of Toronto 2000.
Perpitch, Diane. "A Singular Justice: Ethics and Politics between Levinas and Derrida." *Philosophy Today,* SPEP Supplement (1999): 57–69.
Pheby, Keith. *Interventions: Displacing the Metaphysical Subject.* Washington, DC: Maissoneuve Press 1988.
Poster, Mark. *Critical Theory after Poststructuralism.* Ithaca, NY: Cornell University Press 1990.
- *The Mode of Information.* Chicago: University of Chicago Press 1990.
Rawls, John. *Political Liberalism.* New York: Columbia University Press 1993.
- *Justice as Fairness: A Restatement.* Cambridge, MA: Harvard University Press 2001.
Rees, John. "In Defence of October." *International Socialism,* no. 52 (October 1991): 1–52.
Rockmore, Tom. *Marx after Marxism: The Philosophy of Karl Marx.* Oxford: Blackwell 2002.
Roderick, Rick. "Reading Derrida Politically (contra Rorty)." *Praxis International* 4 (January): 1987.
Ross, Steven David. "Foucault's Radical Politics." *Praxis International* 5, no. 2 (July 1985): 131–43.
Sarra-Bournet, Michel. "Nationalisme et Question Nationale au Québec." In *Les nationalismes au Québec du XIXe au XXIe siècle,* edited by Michel Sarra-Bournet. Quebec: Les Presses de l'Université Laval 2001.
Sawicki, Jana. "Foucault, Feminism, and Questions of Identity." In *The Cambridge Companion to Foucault,* edited by Gary Gutting. Cambridge: Cambridge University Press 1994.
Schiller, Friedrich. *Letters on the Aesthetic Education of Man.* Oxford: Oxford University Press 1989.
Sim, Stuart. "Lyotard and the Politics of Anti-foundationalism." *Radical Philosophy,* no. 44 (autumn 1986): 8–13.
Soper, Kate. *Humanism and Anti-humanism.* London: Hutchinson 1986.
- "Postmodernism, Subjectivity, and the Question of Value." *Principled Positions.* London: Verso 1990.
Spivak, Gayatri Chakravorty. *In Other Worlds.* New York: Routledge 1988.
Sprinker, Michael. "The Use and Abuse of Foucault." *Humanities in Society* 3, no. 1 (1980): 1–21.
Suchting, Wal. "Marx's *Theses on Feuerbach:* Notes towards a Commentary and a New Translation." In *Issues in Marxist Philosophy.* Vol. 2 of *Materialism,* edited by John Mepham and David-Hillel Ruben. Atlantic Highlands, NJ: Humanities Press 1979.

Taylor, Charles. "Foucault on Freedom and Truth." In *Foucault: A Critical Reader*, edited by David Hoy Couzens. Oxford: Basil Blackwell 1986.
- "The Politics of Recognition." In *Multiculturalism*, edited by Amy Guttman. Princeton: Princeton University Press 1994.

Valliers, Pierre. *White Niggers of America*. Toronto: McClelland and Stewart 1971.

Van Den Abbeele, George. "An Interview with Jean Francois Lyotard." *Diacritics* 14, no. 3 (fall 1984): 16–24.

Walzer, Michael. "The Politics of Michel Foucault." In *Foucault: A Critical Reader*, edited by David Couzens Hoy. Oxford: Basil Blackwell 1986.

West, Cornell. "The New Cultural Politics of Difference." In *Keeping the Faith: Philosophy and Race in America*. New York: Routledge 1993.

Whitaker, Reg. "Quebec's Self-determination and Aboriginal Self-government." In *Is Quebec Nationalism Just?* edited by Joseph H. Corens. Montreal: McGill-Queen's University Press 1995.

Wilkins, Peter. "Chomsky and Foucault on Human Nature: An Essential Difference?" *Social Theory and Practice* 25, no. 2 (summer 1999): 177–210.

Williams, James. *Lyotard: Towards a Postmodern Philosophy*. Cambridge: Polity Press 1998.

Wood, Ellen Meiksins. *Democracy against Capitalism*. Cambridge: Cambridge University Press 1995.

Young, Iris Marion. "The Ideal of Community and the Politics of Difference." *Social Theory and Criticism* 12, no. 1 (spring 1986): 1–26.
- "Polity and Group Difference: A Critique of the Ideal of University Citizenship." *Ethics* 99 (January 1989): 247–73.
- *Justice and the Politics of Difference*. Princeton, NJ: Princeton University Press 1990.
- "Together in Difference: Transforming the Logic of Group Political Conflict." In *The Rights of Minority Cultures*, edited by Will Kymlicka. Oxford: Oxford University Press 1995.
- "Deferring Group Representation." In *Ethnicity and Group Rights*, edited by Will Kymlicka and Ian Shapiro. New York: New York University Press 1997.

Index

Adams, Howard, 115
Althusser, Louis, 135
ANC (African National Congress), 152
apartheid, 73, 150–5
archaeology, 18–19, 28–9, 46–7, 63, 141
Aristotle, 4, 12, 131–2
Augustine, 148–9

Balkans, 108
Bataille, Georges, 46, 64
Bennington, Geoffrey, 74
Berlin, Isaah, 51
Best, Steven, 60
Bevire, Mark, 63
Blanchot, Maurice, 46, 64, 65
Bouchard, Lucien, 103
Bourassa, Robert, 110
Browning, Gary, 61, 62

Canada, 15, 81, 105, 108
Caputo, John, 33
Charlottetown Accord, 103
Clifford, Michael, 63
concepts, 12–13, 29, 34, 36
conceptuality, 37
Cook, Deborah, 63, 141–3
COSATU (Congress of South African Trade Unions), 152
Côté, Jean, 103
Cree, Johnny, 109

decentring: of the subject, 32, 47–8, 50, 51, 63, 70, 119, 141, 143
deconstruction, 5, 14, 23, 33, 82, 140; Derrida on, 14, 34, 53, 74–5, 154; political implications of, 14–16, 38–9, 53–5, 57, 71, 74–7, 84–5, 94, 104, 150–2, 154; of subjecthood, 7, 22, 23, 26, 42–5, 52, 77, 84, 115, 121, 122, 123, 125, 128, 140, 142
DeGaulle, Charles, 118
democracy: deliberative, 89; liberal, 81, 86, 87–8, 121; radical, 84–6
Derrida, Jacques, 6, 7, 17–18, 28, 58, 82, 89, 90, 91, 127, 139; on conceptuality, 34, 36–7, 52; contradictions of, 73–4, 76, 150–8; on deconstruction, 14, 34, 53, 74–5, 154; on différance, 34–9, 52, 71, 156; on the feminine, 72, 98; on hospitality, 156–7; on identity thinking, 11–16, 52–4; on postmodernity, 20; on responsibility, 74–6, 150, 154–7; return of subjecthood in, 150–8; on South Africa, 73, 150–5; on struggles against oppression, 72, 94, 98, 152; on textuality, 37–8, 74; on writing, 33, 96
Descartes, René, 52
Dews, Peter, 32, 50
différance, 34–7, 52–3, 154, 156
difference, 3, 6, 12, 24; and freedom, 5–6; as function of cultural dynamics, 7,

28, 32, 115, 138–9; metaphysical understanding of, 34, 87; politics of, 3, 7, 8, 11, 14, 24, 59, 64, 78, 81–2, 83, 85, 89–91, 92, 97, 102, 104, 106–7, 108, 115–19, 122, 124–6, 127, 157, 159; as product of self-determining capacity, 17, 25, 28, 90, 114–15, 126, 137; relational understanding of, 90, 108
differend, 27, 44–5, 60
discourse, 19, 26, 47, 49, 65, 73
discursive formations, 18–19
discursive practice, 29–30, 32, 47
Druron, Michel, 63
Dumont, Fernand, 102
Durham, Lord, 100

Eagleton, Terry, 137
Emberly, Julia, 107
Enlightenment, 61, 66
essence, 12, 13, 35–6, 55, 94; and appearance, 13, 132; critical humanist understanding of, 131–8; deconstruction of, 36, 97, 116; human, 3–4, 5, 7, 47, 59, 63, 69, 70, 83, 89–90, 91, 93, 106, 107, 112, 113, 119, 121, 122, 126, 132, 133, 157, 161; as universal ground of cultural difference, 134–8. *See also* human nature
essentialism, 7, 41–2, 52, 54, 55, 59, 64, 71, 83, 112, 121, 135, 138, 140
episteme, 29–30, 49
ethnocentric fallacy, 28

Fanon, Frantz, 118–19, 130, 136
First Nations, 4, 8, 98, 99, 105, 107, 108, 128, 160; underlying unity with Québécois, 113–14, 160
Foucault, Michel, 6, 7, 16, 28, 39, 52, 54, 82, 90, 91, 127, 151, 157; on autonomy, 67–9; on the constitution of individuals, 31–2, 63, 66–8, 142–3; contradictions of, 64, 68–71, 140, 142; and Derrida, 16–18, 65; on ethics, 69–70; on identity thinking, 16–17; on philosophy of history, 17–18, 49, 51; on postmodernity, 20; on power, 17–19, 28, 30–3, 39, 49–52, 65, 66, 69, 141, 144; return of subjecthood in, 140–4; on struggles of the oppressed, 17, 94, 96, 98; on subjecthood, 46–52, 64, 69; on subjectification, 32, 50, 63
Fraser, Nancy, 141

freedom, 5, 43, 111, 126–7, 132, 144; content of, 132–3, 138; grounds of understanding of, 6–7, 118, 123; positive, 48, 53, 54, 90, 133, 138; postmodern understanding of, 44–5; and reason, 21; as self-determination, 5, 48, 114, 123, 131, 137–8, 160. *See also* self-determination

genealogy, 28, 30–1, 33, 49–52, 63, 65–6, 96, 98–9, 141, 142
Gilbert, Sky, 3, 93
globalization, 112
Glucksman, André, 51
Gordon, Lewis, 119

Haber, Honi Fern, 92, 170n1
Habermas, Jürgen, 33, 62, 99, 141, 173n1
Hansen, Beatrice, 31
Hartsock, Nancy, 122
Hayek, Friedrich, 51
Hegel, Georg Wilhelm Friedrich, 17, 18, 47, 52, 53, 117–18, 143, 144, 149, 157, 170n1
Hegelian, 65, 118, 144
Heiddeger, Martin, 63
Hernandez, Luis, 112
history: and identity thinking, 14, 17, 37, 127–8, 150; philosophy of, 17–18, 42, 55, 58, 150; as product of power, 31
Hobson, Marian, 53
humanism, 21–2, 44, 62, 65–7, 107, 115, 125, 146, 156; critical, 7, 8, 91, 107, 119, 121, 126, 137–9, 141, 160; and exclusion of difference, 58, 60, 96, 107
human nature, 4, 25, 26, 28, 29, 33, 133, 139, 144, 160; as product of power, 32, 39–40, 47, 51, 84. *See also*, essence, human

identity, 4–5, 13, 14, 92, 97; as function of exclusion, 15, 17, 23, 30, 53, 97
identity thinking, 7, 11–16, 18, 20, 22, 24, 37, 53, 101, 125; deconstruction of, 14, 16, 34–8, 39, 53, 93, 117
Ingram, David, 51, 62

Joyce, James, 72

Kahnawake, 109
Kanesatake, 109, 110
Kant, Immanuel, 42, 47, 52

Keikel, Aron, 63
Kellner, Douglas, 60
Kymlicka, Will, 104, 113, 173n25

Laclau, Ernesto, 63, 82, 86, 91; contradictions of, 85–6; as critic of Marxism, 82–3, 84–5; on pluralism, 83–4; on politics of difference, 82–3, 85
Laforest, Guy, 115
Landry, Bernard, 110
language: as basis of social relations, 25, 28, 65, 104–5, 138–9; and exclusion of cultural difference, 138–40; and metaphysics, 34–5, 44, 52
language games, 26–7, 39, 44, 99
Lévesque, René, 101
Levinas, Emmanuel, 75, 156
logocentrism, 15, 38, 53, 72. See also identity thinking
Lyotard, François, 6, 7, 16, 20, 33, 34, 39, 51, 52, 54, 70, 82, 90, 91, 127, 151, 157; contradictions of, 61–2, 70, 145–6, 149–50; on freedom, 44–5; on the inhuman, 61–2, 147–9; on justice, 59–60, 147; on language games, 26–7, 44, 98; on minority struggles, 58–60, 99, 109, 112, 145, 147; on modernity, 41–2, 96; on the nature of the social, 25–8, 44; on phrases, 27, 44; on postmodernity, 20–3, 43, 94–5; return of subjecthood in, 145–50; on the self, 26, 42–5, 146; on terroristic practices, 27, 44, 58, 60, 61, 147

Mandela, Nelson, 73, 153
Maracle, Lee, 114–15, 120
Marcos, Commander, 112
Marcuse, Herbert, 75; on the concept of essence, 132–3, 135
marginalization, 128–9
Martin, Bill, 53, 75
Marx, Karl, 38, 47, 53, 143; understanding of human essence, 134–5, 170n1
Marxism, 22, 38, 42, 48, 51, 54, 57, 76, 82, 85, 98, 121, 130; and other social movements, 83, 86–7; post-Marxism, 82
Mauriac, François, 118
McClure, Kirstie, 122
Meech Lake Accord, 103
metaphysics, 11–16; as practice of exclusion, 13–14, 38, 53–4, 71, 87, 89; of presence, 35–6, 87

metaphysical ground: of freedom, 104, 118, 123, 160; of conceptualizing oppression, 86, 101, 103
metaphysical tradition, 11–13
Michaud, Yves, 103
Mill, John Stuart, 4, 143
minorities, 58–60, 70, 89, 97, 107, 110, 112, 140, 145
Mohawks, 108, 109, 110, 113, 116, 137
modern philosophy, 21–2, 29, 39, 41–3, 46–8, 55, 57, 93, 97, 123, 143
Mouffe, Chantal, 63, 82, 86, 91, 160; contradictions of, 85–6; as critic of Marxism, 82–5; on pluralism, 83–4; on the politics of difference, 82–5

NAFTA, 111, 112
narrative, 22, 42; grand, 27; metanarrative, 20–3, 41, 58–9, 93, 118; small, 58–60, 66
Nazism, 51–2
needs, human, 25, 30, 39, 77, 85, 113
Nietzsche, Friedrich, 36, 46, 64, 72, 142
Nietzschean, 31, 58, 142

object: relation to subject, 12, 22, 36, 48–9, 83, 119, 122; of scientific theory, 18–19, 29, 32, 49
Oka, 108, 110, 134, 137
Onasakenarat, Joseph, 109
oppressed, the: basis of unity between, 84, 85, 104, 115–16, 121, 159–60; postmodern understanding of struggles of, 17, 59, 70, 87, 99–100, 102, 107, 117, 121, 123, 126; self-understanding of, 101–4; universal basis of struggles of, 70, 89, 90, 101, 102–3, 107, 109, 111–12, 115–16, 117–20, 126, 130–1, 133
ontology, 38, 132
oppression, 3, 6, 77, 78, 86, 116; grounds of coherent understanding of, 6, 28, 39–40, 63, 70, 77–8, 85–6, 88, 97–8, 122–4, 127–31; material grounds of, 92, 102–4, 113–14, 133, 157, 160; postmodern understanding of, 41, 55, 84, 86–7; structure of, 3, 114
other, the, 4, 14–16, 18, 22–3, 24, 46, 71, 74–7, 98, 99, 121–2, 150, 151, 156; of metaphysics, 33, 53, 154; radical openness towards, 95–6; in relation to self, 117–21, 122, universal voice of, 108. See also, oppressed, the

otherness, 58, 72, 75, 83, 88, 94, 120, 157; and writing, 96

PAC (Pan Africanist Congress), 152
Parent, Madeleine, 110
Parizeau, Jacques, 89
Parmenides, 154
Parti Québécois, 104, 110
particularity, 27, 42, 87–8, 90, 137, 157; universal grounds of, 8, 102–3, 104, 106–7, 109–10, 118, 120, 126, 131, 133
phallogocentrism, 72
Pheby, Keith, 57
philosophy, political function of, 5–6, 108, 159–60
Plato, 13, 14, 15, 131
pluralism, 6, 83–4, 86, 91, 108, 113, 121, 137, 157; postmodern understanding of, 60, 83–4; radical, 8, 85, 92, 94–5, 97, 99–100, 104–6, 123; total, 86
Popper, Karl, 51
Poster, Mark, 63
postmodernism, 5, 8, 12, 48; contradictions of, 73–4, 77–8, 90, 117, 121–3, 127, 133–4; Lyotard on, 20–3; philosophy of, 5, 39; political implications of, 4, 22–3, 24, 55–6, 57, 78, 82–90, 93, 117, 125; radicalism, 4, 5, 6, 40, 41, 57, 62, 90, 121, 128, 137. *See also* politics of difference
postmodernity, 20
poststructuralism, 92
power, 17, 28, 48, 92; as constitutive of human subjects, 28, 30, 67, 141; Foucault on, 17–19, 28, 30–3, 39, 49–52, 63, 65, 67, 69, 141, 144

Quebec, 81, 89, 107, 130
Québécois, 8, 89, 92, 98–100, 104, 106, 107, 110, 111, 113, 116, 128; historical struggles of, 100–3, 172n17; and the politics of difference, 100, 102, 116, 137; underlying unity with First Nations, 113–14, 160

reason, 12–13, 19, 65, 83; and freedom, 21, 61, 66, 71, 83
recognition, 120; struggle for, 47, 117–18
resistance: criterion of legitimacy, 136–7
responsibility, 74–6, 150, 154–7; and subjecthood, 155–6

Ross, Steven David, 63

Sawicki, Jana, 129
self, 6, 15, 75, 141, 155. *See also* subject
self-creation, 45, 48, 53, 57, 63, 126, 130, 142, 160
self-determination, 5, 8, 28, 32, 40, 43, 46–7, 57, 86, 104, 113, 131, 134, 139, 157; as basis for understanding oppression, 6, 33, 61, 63, 68–9, 74, 76–7, 78, 86, 90, 103, 104, 107, 114–17, 120, 122, 123, 130–1, 148, 152; as essence of human being, 5, 7, 47, 63, 69, 83, 89–90, 91, 93, 103, 112, 113, 125–6, 133, 136; as normative concept, 138. *See also* essence, human; freedom
self-identity, 15–16, 156
self-making capacity, 6
signs, 52–3
Soper, Kate, 121, 127
Sophocles, 153
Spivak, Gayatri Chakravorty, 125
Stalinism, 51, 54, 166n23
structure, 15, 35
subject, 5, 18, 20, 21, 22, 50, 60, 70, 86, 120, 122, 139, 151; as function of cultural dynamics, 6, 44, 46, 50, 63–4
subjecthood, 5, 140, 171n1; as basis of human freedom, 6, 33, 63, 68, 70, 86; deconstruction of, 3, 7, 22, 23, 42–5, 48–9, 55, 77, 84, 122, 128, 139; as essence of human being, 5, 40, 41, 69, 70, 86, 89, 103, 120, 123, 125, 129, 145, 149; as ground of cultural difference, 89, 103–4, 114, 119, 124. *See also* essence, human; self-determination
subject position, 47–8, 53, 83, 84, 86, 122, 123, 126

Taylor, Charles, 115, 141
text, the: in Derrida, 37–8
thinking, binary, 33–4, 100–2
totalitarianism, 17, 41, 51–2, 54, 55, 57, 62, 75, 77, 140, 166n23
totality, 17–18, 27, 36, 39, 68, 71, 83
totalization, 72, 99
transcendental signified, 12–13, 36, 37
transgression, 46, 52, 64–7, 94, 96, 102, 142, 144
truth, 11–12, 30, 35
truth effects, 30–1, 47

Tutu, Desmond, 152

universal, abstract and concrete, 119
universality, 34, 83; as ground of particularity, 8, 106–7, 109–10, 118, 120, 126, 131, 133; as product of exclusion of particularity, 4, 21, 83, 125

Walzer, Michael, 141
West, the, 14, 34, 35, 71–2, 73, 153
West, Cornell, 120

Western culture, 14–15, 121, 152
Williams, James, 60
writing, Derrida on, 33–4, 71, 96

Young, Iris Marion, 82, 86, 91, 97, 108, 117; on citizenship, 87–8; contradictions of, 88–90; on grounds of group difference, 87–90

Zapatistas, 111–12, 116